THE
YEARBOOK OF
LANDSCAPE ARCHITECTURE

THE
YEARBOOK OF
LANDSCAPE ARCHITECTURE

Historic Preservation

Edited by

RICHARD L. AUSTIN, ASLA
Associate Professor/University of Nebraska-Lincoln
Coordinating Editor

THOMAS KANE, FASLA
Pleasantville, New York
Contributing Editor

ROBERT Z. MELNICK, ASLA
Associate Professor/University of Oregon
Contributing Editor

SUZANNE TURNER, ASLA
Assistant Professor/Louisiana State University
Contributing Editor

VNR VAN NOSTRAND REINHOLD COMPANY
NEW YORK CINCINNATI TORONTO LONDON MELBOURNE

Published by Van Nostrand Reinhold Company Inc.
135 West 50th Street, New York, N.Y. 10020

Van Nostrand Reinhold
480 Latrobe Street
Melbourne, Victoria 3000, Australia

Van Nostrand Reinhold Company Limited
Molly Millars Lane
Wokingham, Berkshire, England

15 14 13 12 11 10 9 8 7 6 5 4 3 2 1

Library of Congress Cataloging in Publication Data

Main entry under title:

Yearbook of landscape architecture.

   Includes index.
   1. Historic sites—Conservation and restoration.
2. Landscape architecture—Conservation and restoration.
3. Historic sites—United States—Conservation and
restoration.   4. Landscape architecture—United States—
Conservation and restoration.   I. Austin, Richard L.
SB472.8.Y43   1983   363.69   82-17431
ISBN 0-442-20885-5

Contributing Authors

Catherine M. Howett, Assistant Professor
The School of Environmental Design
University of Georgia

Ann L. Marston, Assistant Professor
Department of Landscape Architecture and Regional Planning
University of Massachusetts

Suzanne Turner, Assistant Professor
School of Landscape Architecture
Louisiana State University

Ann Leighton
Historic Garden Consultant
Ipswich, Massachusetts

Darrell Morrison
Professor of Landscape Architecture
University of Wisconsin

Richard Macias
Resource Design Group, Inc.
Ann Arbor, Michigan

Patricia M. O'Donnell, Landscape Architect/Urban Planner
Westport, Connecticut

Steve McNiel, Assistant Professor
Department of Landscape Architecture
University of Wisconsin

Rueben M. Rainey, Assistant Professor
Division of Landscape Architecture
University of Virginia

Thomas Paine
Landscape Architect
Lincoln, Massachusetts

Kenneth I. Helphand, Associate Professor
Department of Landscape Architecture
University of Oregon

Project Contributors

Kerry J. Dawson, Assistant Professor
University of California—Davis

Johnson, Johnson and Roy, Inc.
Ann Arbor, Michigan

Land and Community Associates
Charlottesville, Virginia

Unicorn Studios
Baton Rouge, Louisiana

LeRoy Troyer Associates
Mishawaka, Indiana

Joseph S.R. Volpe, Associate Professor
University of Massachusetts

Carol R. Johnson and Associates, Inc.
Cambridge, Massachusetts

Kane and Carruth, P.C.
Pleasantville, New York

Entourage, Inc.
Austin, Texas

Preface

Thomas J. Kane, FASLA

In recent years an accelerating confluence of social, economic, and spiritual forces has illuminated and rekindled an awareness of, and indeed, a critical concern for our natural and cultural environment, both of which are embraced in "landscape," the term used to describe our perception of the outdoor environment. Certainly part of this renewed interest has to do with time and cycle. The period of reaction to the Victorian era has passed and predictably has been followed by a resurgence of interest in that time of history. This has suddenly released and revealed a huge backlog of cultural fabric, overlooked for decades, that gazed back to the seventeenth and eighteenth centuries. This phenomenon is particularly significant in regard to the landscape because it has rekindled a nineteenth-century ethic that imbued nature, gardening, and landscapes with both spiritual and social virtues.

The result has been a concern for lifestyle, a feeling for place in space and in time. This is the attitude that has elevated the concern for the preservation of the historic landscape to parity with the concern for historic structures, which can now be comprehended as elements in the landscape. For example, today it can be suggested, with credence, that Mt. Auburn Cemetery should be preserved because it had more impact on a whole century of taste and social consciousness than any number of historic buildings.

The point has been reached when we must distinguish between preservation and nostalgic revival. The latter has its own rationale, but must not be confused with preservation, which is the careful conservation and accurate restoration of historic landscapes in order to retain the tactile reality of our cultural heritage, showing us how it was in distinct periods or particular places and revealing environmental lessons that we have forgotten and may well apply anew.

The difficulties in defining the preservation of the historic landscape have been due not to disinterest but, conversely, to the very visceral relationship between man and nature and the nuances and colossal scale differentials from backyard gardens to streets and townships. Architectural structures are simply comprehended and dealt with, when compared to the landscape complex, which is not only structural but organic and cosmic as well. But the awareness is there, and it is this generation that will discover and mend the fabric of our cultural heritage in the land.

Contents

Introduction: Landscape Architecture and Historic Preservation

Robert Z. Melnick, ASLA

The history of a people is drawn on the face of the land, across the landscape. As we settle, control, use, alter, and manipulate the land, we change it and mark it as ours. Once settled, land is never the same, and wilderness disappears. Subsequent generations and users add their signatures, and layers of human input build upon the landscape. Eventually, pieces of this quilt fade, lose their usefulness, their glamour. We search for new, seemingly unique ways to control our land, our territory, our spaces. Often, however, we seem to lose a piece of the past, a piece of our heritage, as we search for new methods and new styles to suit our needs.

Recently, there has developed a spreading interest in the preservation of various segments of the historic and cultural landscape of America. These segments range from backyard gardens, stone walls, and orchard designs to farmstead layout, plantation fields, and regional settlement patterns. Some of these elements are clearly historic: they are the site of a significant event or related to an important person. Some of these places are of consequence because of their place in the cultural development of an area, county, or region. All of them, however, have a common denominator: they are linkages to our heritage, they are connectors to our past, they are physical bonds with those who have come before us. "Past as prologue" has become a common phrase within the historic preservation community.

The increased efforts in landscape preservation represent a substantial new direction within the profession of landscape architecture. For years, landscape architects have been concerned with new development and construction, with sensitive and thoughtful additions within our national landscape. While we have often focused attention on the preservation of "natural" landscapes, historic human elements in our environment have not received appropriate notice. In the nineteenth century, Olmsted, Vaux, Cleveland, Eliot, Weidenmann, and their contemporaries viewed the preservation of natural scenery and natural wonders as a worthy concern for landscape architects. Olmsted devoted a great deal of effort to the preservation of both Yosemite Valley and Niagara Falls. Our nineteenth-century ethic placed more value on natural elements than on human contributions to that landscape—perhaps with good reason. As a nation we still suffered the complex of cultural inferiority when compared with our European forebears. Nevertheless, by the end of the century, although we recognized the relatively short span of our national history, we had begun to mark those places of special historic importance in the development of the nation.

Organized efforts in historic preservation in this country began with two different areas of intent. The first was to preserve historic structures: those places associated with people of national importance. George Washington's home at Mount Vernon was among the earliest of these efforts. The second, less well-known type of preservation was accomplished by the then-Department of the Army at the Civil War battlefields, most notably Gettysburg, Vicksburg, and Antietam. These battlefields were not consciously preserved until the 1890s, and today we are striving to preserve the markers and statues erected then to commemorate war heroes, known and unknown, of the Civil War.

Until recently, the fields of landscape architecture and historic preservation have doubted their mutual bonds. Landscape architecture has been dominated by new design; historic preservation has been dominated by architectural concerns. Both concerns have been necessary. The work represented in this volume indicates the validity of the integration of these fields.

As with the profession and discipline of landscape architecture, landscape preservation has different meanings to those who claim it as a field. There are two convenient ways to divide the field, each with its own segments and parameters.

The first way of looking at this material is by "scale of concern." Some people are concerned with construction details for stone walls, or planting plan details, or the exact location of a specific significant tree. Other people deal with large-scale issues of regional settlement, field patterns, or relationships of one site to another. In between are such issues as farmstead layout, orchard design, or townsite development. All are part of the field, but, as with landscape architecture, all are addressed at varying degrees of detail.

The second way to divide the work is by the types of material investigated. Some focus on the human use of natural elements, while others concentrate on the placement of elements within the natural landscape that are manufactured by humans. Most often these two overlap and intersect each other. But not always. The planning of an orchard may be viewed as a human decision regarding natural materials. A fence in a field is clearly a human imposition in the landscape. The line of trees that gradually developed along the fence-line is the direct result of the fence, but is obviously composed of natural materials. Nonetheless, this division of concern, along with the previous one dealing with scale, may help to differentiate the types of projects undertaken by the group of researchers and practitioners represented in this volume.

The articles, case studies, and projects in this volume represent a variety of approaches to historic preservation.

The value of research as a learning process in and of itself, in addition to its application in landscape preservation, is aptly stated by Catherin Howett: "Most importantly, the process of researching, describing, and explicating is itself a form of conservation, in which we gather together the fragile records of our past and use them to understand it better." Howett's implication that preservation is as much a state of mind as a conscious activity is strongly echoed by Kenneth Helphand's piece on "Magic Markers," when he says that "the marker should reflect a . . . popular and personal concern in its historical information. The marker should have an environmental presence and immediacy."

Taken as a whole, this collection of articles and project reports reflect both of these attitudes towards landscape preservation. Ann Leighton's concern for authenticity in historical plant materials is balanced by Ann Marston's arguments about "landscape interpretation." Marston presents interpretation as but one aspect of the design process in historic environments, and rightly so. The incorporation of historic aspects of our environment into everyday design deserves far more than the lip service it normally receives. In this regard, Suzanne Turner's chapter on "Listening" serves as a clear statement of "meaning" in the historic landscape and the place of written description in the history of ordinary landscapes. Another, larger historical perspective is offered by Darrell Morrison when he refers to "presettlement vegetation" and its place in our growing knowledge of cultural impact on the natural landscape.

Contrasting with Morrison's concerns are the chapters by Richard Macias, Patricia O'Donnell and Steve McNiel, all of whom take as their theme landscape preservation within an urbanized environment. Macias views urban design and revitalization as a process of "directed change" for visual improvement and economic need. O'Donnell's focus is tighter: those great urban parks of the late-nineteenth and early-twentieth centuries, which are now faced with potential deterioration due to limited funding and changing needs. McNiel sees antecedents in Europe, and traces a particular region's commercial storefront design to its background across the ocean. The focus on centers of population, rather than on rural settings, is not unique for landscape architects. We have often extended our efforts to new urban design, town clusters, and residential development. The recognition of the value of relatively large-scale preservation efforts within these communities, however, is recent. The role of the landscape architect in this area is even newer and still expanding.

Finally, there are two chapters which deal with specific situations: battlefields and village greens. Both are particular instances in which some of the previous material has been applied: research, significance, interpretation, design, and plant materials. Rainey's chapter on historic battlefields reflects a clear insight into the place of these landscapes in the national conscience, while Paine's work represents a desire to establish guidelines for preserving (maintaining and using) a unique design element and type for a region of the country.

The second part of this volume consists of a selection of recent historic preservation projects by landscape architects. They range from site studies (Magnolia Mound Plantation and Eleanor Roosevelt National Historic Site) to interpretation (The Buckley Homestead) to cultural landscapes (The Amana Colonies) to urban projects (New Center Neighborhood Rehabilitation) to regional projects (Historic Corridor Conservation) to on-going projects (Black Settlements in America). They represent different concerns, both within the profession of landscape architecture and the field of historic preservation. The intent here is to show a sampling of contemporary work, as well as the range of possibilities.

Landscape preservation might just as well be termed "heritage conservation." It is a conscious activity to positively affect the future through respect and appreciation for the past. As Richard Macias says, we are engaged in efforts towards "directed change." As a nation and as a culture we have often lost the bonds to our past, not through decision but through indecision. As the geographer David Lowenthal puts it:

> The preservation movement opens our eyes and hearts to what lies around us, enhancing our own surroundings by encouraging concern about them. As we save what is good from the past, we realize we need not be passive passers-by, but can be active participants both in securing and in remaking the world we have inherited.*

*David Lowenthal and Marcus Binney, eds. *Our Past Before Us: Why Do We Save It?* (London: Temple Smith, 1981), from the Introduction.

THE
YEARBOOK OF
LANDSCAPE ARCHITECTURE

Part One:
The Theories and Philosophy

Landscape Research: Keeping Faith with Today and Tomorrow

Catherine M. Howett

The growing popular interest in an appropriate philosophy and methodology for the conservation or reconstruction of various "historic" landscapes has made even more seductive the illusion that designed landscapes are like other traditional art forms or like architecture: fully realized at some moment in time and having a final, finished form, a completion that is meant to endure. As in architecture, there are often landscape "plans," two-dimensional diagrams of the designer's intentions for the laying out and furnishing of the site. But while an original plan may contribute substantially to the evolving form of a landscape, it must not be confused with the work itself, which, by its very nature, is involved with process and change.

In no other art do the materials themselves grow, breathe, and change over time. This is true not only of the living plant materials, which may or may not be present, but also of the whole range of continually shifting sensual components that may contribute to the experience of place—the play of light, sounds, smells, the movement of air and of water, and perhaps the random intrusions of people, animals, insects, and birds. If the designer of a landscape has deliberately planned for a hedge of bird-attracting berried shrubs, are the birds' songs and stirrings not a part of the design? Does water in a fountain ever drip or spout, shine or sound exactly the same way on any two days? Is a carefully framed vista not radically different at dawn and at dusk? Pliny the Younger was especially pleased by the effect of the "gloomy shadows" cast by the cypress trees he used to edge an expanse of lawn in one of the gardens of his Laurentine villa; the plan, if there was one, might have said "cypress trees," but "gloomy shadows" was the design intention.

And just as nature and the passage of time continually modify a landscape, so, very often, do the hands and minds not only of the original designers, but of a whole series of subsequent proprietors, gardeners, "improvers," or barbarians. Plants die and are replaced or not. Additions, deletions, revisions are made to the original scheme. Fashions change, so that if a Victorian "gingerbread" porch was added to a Greek Revival-style house, the old rectangular box-bordered beds may have been given a newly fashionable "arabesque" line and in-filled with a variety of exotics. Furthermore, every gardener knows that although there are moments when the experience of a landscape seems fully saturated, when its dreamed-of beauties ravish the eye and soul, a restless yearning comes with the next breath: all-white next year, instead of the mixed reds; watch the groundcover where the oak is extending its canopy; what will be the effect of the new building across the street or across the valley? Thomas Jefferson, that preeminent landscape architect and devoted gardener, epitomized this incessant doing and redoing by his fervid sketching, inventing, and planning that forever outstripped practical possibilities. It is hard to know which serves us better in appreciating Mr. Jefferson's landscape achievements: the painstaking contemporary effort to re-create the original scheme at Monticello, or a passage like this one from his Account Book, detailing possible treatments of the landscape surrounding his spring:

> The ground just about the spring smoothed and turfed; close to the spring a sleeping figure reclined on a plain marble slab, surrounded with turf.... Open a vista to the millpond, river, road, etc., qu[aere], if a view to the neighboring town would have a good effect? intersperse in this and every other part of the ground... abundance of Jesamine, Honeysuckle, sweet briar, etc. under the temple, an Aeolian harp, where it may be concealed as well as covered from the weather.
> This would be better.
> The ground above the spring being very steep, dig into the hill and form a cave or grotto. build up the sides and arch with stiff clay. Cover this with moss. spangle it with translucent pebbles from Hanovertown, and beautiful shells from the shore at Burwell's ferry pave the floor with pebbles. let the spring enter at a corner of the grotto, pretty high up the side, and trickle down, or fall by a spout into the basin, from which it may pass off through the grotto. the figure will be better placed in this. form a couch of moss...[1]

Whether the landscape is new or old, its "ideal" form takes shape like this—in the mind of the designer. We can feel sure that on the day that Louis XIV and LeNôtre had their last conversation about some aspect of the gardens at Versailles or Marly, great plans were still engaging their imaginations.

Moreover because they are so rooted in process, designed landscapes are inevitably vulnerable, even ephemeral. It takes so much energy, intelligent direction, and resources of money, labor, and time to sustain the intended character of a given place that, more often than not, lapses end in losses. There comes a time when no living person even remembers how a particular landscape used to look, much less how it was supposed to look or why it was supposed to look that way. Old spaces are continually put to new uses or abandoned to nature's cyclic encroachment, and the passage of years leaves us with remnants, distorted fragments, or nothing at all that physically recalls places out of the past. The rapid acceleration of this process in modern times has understandably alarmed those who cherish a sense of history, who value the collective memories of family, community, and even nation rooted in familiar places over time. They sense, and rightly so, that the landscape fabric is a most critical part of the built environment, not only as the context for architecture, but also as an important aspect of material culture in its own right. The first passion among the so-called "preservationists" in this country was to save threatened older buildings that had significance for a particular community. In the movement's coming-of-age, the focus of effort has been enlarged to embrace a concern for historically important landscape environments and configurations, whether at the scale of a cultural landscape like the nineteenth-century rice-growing plantation region along the Ashley River in South Carolina, or of a small city garden valued for its ties to a past era.

But landscapes at any scale, as we have observed, simply cannot be re-created or preserved in the way that buildings can. A visitor to an historic house could conceivably enter a room, sit in a chair, and use a pen at a table placed precisely where it stood 200 years before; the view out the window, however, will belong to the fleeting present, not to the past, no matter how carefully its salient forms may have been monitored by enlightened design and administration, as the view from Washington's "piazza" at Mount Vernon to the rural Virginia countryside across the Potomac has been. The failure to acknowledge the impossibility of "freezing" time at some chosen historic moment in the development of a landscape has resulted too often in gross distortions of honest history and in painfully awkward compromises between the realities of the contemporary design program—parking, security lighting, rest rooms, handicapped access, interpretive facilities, etc.—and the client's hopeless determination to recover the mythic "way it really was."

On the other hand, the trenchant criticism of such efforts, voiced by major figures within the landscape professions during the past few years, has not made it easier to develop the needed guidelines for preservation policy with respect to landscapes. Writing in the pages of *Landscape Architecture* in 1976, in response to an inquiry on the part of editor Grady Clay, J. B. Jackson took the relatively extreme position that the only landscape or architectural environments worth saving were those that could justify their existence by serving vital functional purposes in today's society. Jackson said that he found it hard to accept the idea that an environment without a discernible function should be preserved *"because it is a part of our history"* [his italics]:

> It is quite true that much valuable conservation—not necessarily of historically significant environments—is being brought about as a form of recycling: why destroy when a modicum of remodeling can prolong its [sic] usefulness? Yet it is safe to say that many conservation and preservation efforts, especially in small cities and towns, are actually inspired by antiquarian zeal masquerading . . . as historical conscience. Age is the real criterion; an old building, an old environment natural or man-made, must be saved either because it is unique or because it is typical of thousands of others.
>
> In the United States there are scores of museum villages, museum farms, museum streets and alleys and structures, and as tourism becomes big business more and more of them come to the surface. That the public enjoys them is beyond dispute. The public also enjoys Disneyland, and for much the same reason: a "period" disguised as American history is dramatized and illustrated in an attractive manner.
>
> And what is wrong with that? Two things: functional environments, environments which serve as a means to an end—the farm, the factory, the dwelling, the park or recreational area—evolve and change, and the usual preserved historical environment, like Sturbridge Village, excludes not only subsequent developments, but the remoter past. Whether it is a tastefully restored Colonial village, or a ghost mining town, or a Gay Nineties downtown street, the preserved environment is no more typical of its period than is a brand new subdivision, with three model furnished homes on display, typical of American life . . . all of them are essentially sterile.
>
> My second objection is this: a collection of antiques housed in a restored dwelling with attendants in period costumes is not the best place to learn history—even material history.[2]

Jackson ends by quoting a passage from Kevin Lynch's *What Time Is this Place?* (1972), in which Lynch observes that "a sense of the stream of time is more valuable and more poignant and engaging than a formal knowledge of remote periods. New things must be created, and others allowed to be forgotten."[3]

Lynch's book is a brilliant, if somewhat discursive, meditation on our experience of time and change in the physical world and in the built environment; but his proposal that just a few surviving elements from a community's past need be selected for preservation (symbolically resonant fragments, relics salvaged from structures or spaces are quite acceptable) must dismay those who, like myself, are unwilling to surrender precipitously to the bulldozer or the wrecking ball whatever cannot serve some immediate practical purpose, most especially in those instances when a building or landscape *is a part of our history*. Equally perplexing is Lynch's suggestion that within the fabric of a town or city reminders of the community's recent past are to be preferred over vestiges of a more remote time, on the theory that the former are more interesting and relevant to the citizens of today—a notion that seems to me to have been contradicted by the history of any number of artistic and architectural movements. I share Lynch's conviction that "a sense of the stream of time" is both valuable and poignant and should be cultivated in the human community by every resource at our disposal; but I believe that when this kind of sensitivity is not informed by "formal knowledge" of the past, by a solidly grounded understanding of the cultural history of which every surviving building or landscape is a material expression, then what passes for a "sense of time" may be nothing more than a debased sentimentality manifesting itself in the collecting of environmental "souvenirs"—or worse, an arrogant and self-serving faith that what the decision-makers of the moment need or like is all that should be valued of what we have inherited from the past. *Pace* J. B. Jackson, I would rather stand with the antiquarian zealots.

Jackson, that marvelous democrat, has lapsed in not looking more sympathetically at what makes our countrymen travel for miles, stand in line, move slowly through stuffy rooms, looking, listening, and, yes, learning. It is a hunger to discover the past, that strange country from which each one of us senses that we have come. It is an admirable hunger to know the truth of history. And if something less than that is communicated, the fault lies not with the visitors but with the place itself, and with the designers, administrators, and interpreters who have either not done their homework or have preferred a slick stage set to the mysterious palimpsest of places out of the past.

All of this is prologue to the argument that scholarly work in landscape history and the effort to broaden public understanding of landscape traditions have been neglected for too long by design and preservation professionals, and by educators. Thomas J. Schlereth, an historian of American material culture, has accused the academic community in this country of largely neglecting the study of historic environments as potentially rich sources of information and understanding of "linguistic, ecclesiastical, economic, technological, and social history":

> We have not investigated the ways place-names reveal inter- and intra-urban migration and forgotten resources; road systems hint at military policies and former religious alliances; boundaries and courthouse styles recall former political antagonisms; tree plantings document former landownership patterns; or how the vegetation in public parks can reveal nineteenth-century attitudes toward aesthetics, sanitation, or recreation.[4]

By the same token, the profession of landscape architecture has been remiss in not exploring, describing, and interpreting its own remarkable history for the benefit of a larger public. The attention given the achievements of Frederick Law Olmsted since the celebration of his sesquicentennial in 1972—with the subsequent proliferation of books, articles, conferences, and exhibitions—has provided us with a singular model of the way in which scholarly research, educational efforts, and broadening popular interest can come together to enhance our appreciation of inherited landscapes and lay the groundwork for today's planning and conservation strategies. The crusade for greater environmental awareness in the 1960s and the burgeoning movement for historic preservation in the 1970s have together created a climate in which individuals, organizations, and public agencies are actively seeking reliable information and help with questions related to the design of historic landscapes. Precisely because so little scholarly work has yet been done in this country, there is an appalling shortage of expert opinion; consider, just as one example, the absence at this late date of even one reputable history of American landscape architecture, explaining the evolution of regional and national traditions, documenting contemporary theory and practice.

Every landscape older than today is "historic" in a certain sense, and no surviving landscape or landscape remnant can be properly understood, appreciated, or conserved unless an effort is made to ascertain the form it was meant to have, and the reasons why it was meant to have that form. Discovering and describing these things is the business of landscape research, and the need for such research as a prerequisite for planning and/or design decisions is an ordinary, not an extraordinary, one. Without it, we have no way of knowing how to design landscapes that accurately reflect the canons of particular past places and times, and so must either limit ourselves to a contemporary design idiom, regardless of the nature of the site, or else run the risk of creating elaborate and potentially embarrassing landscape lies, monuments to our own ignorance. Without landscape research, moreover, we are unable to analyze and to know, in the fullest sense, even the work of our contemporaries, the most radical of whom must still have had their perceptions and powers shaped by all that has gone before. The geographer David Lowenthal has observed that "we need the past . . . to cope with present landscapes":

> We selectively perceive what we are accustomed to seeing; features and patterns in the landscape make sense to us because we share a history with them. Every object, every grouping, every view is intelligible partly because we are already familiar with it, through our own past and through tales heard, books read, pictures viewed. We see things simultaneously as they are and as we viewed them

before; previous experience suffuses all present perception. . . . Without the past as tangible or remembered evidence we could not function; . . . . It is incarnate in the things we build and the landscapes we create.[5]

We are not in a position, therefore, to bring critical judgment to bear upon the landscape architecture created in our own time unless we have adequately prepared ourselves through study of its sources, intentions, and chosen vocabulary. Even the future development of our profession may be affected by this pressing need for scholarly research; how can we hope for the kind of theoretical dialogue that generates experiment and innovation until more of us take up the task of defining and describing the dialectic of our own discipline's history?

As the need is ordinary, so, for the most part, are the research methodologies by which that need is answered. Their object is simply to flood with light the darkness that closes in behind us with every yesterday, that "dim" past in which records, remembrances, clues, and place-marks have been lost, fragmented, or obscured by the passage of time. There are basically three areas to be explored as part of this effort to recover the history of a particular site at a particular time. The first of these is the cultural context, the whole complex of philosophical, economic, political, social, scientific, literary, and aesthetic factors that together shape the *zeitgeist* of a given age; this is the matrix from which a shared vision of an "ideal" landscape may have emerged, as well as a visual language of forms understood by artist and audience alike. Whatever is eccentric, idiosyncratic, or otherwise seems to run counter to this shaping tide of influence must still be viewed in its negative relation to the larger forces. The major caution to be observed in establishing the parameters of this first area of research is that the community whose values informed a given design must be carefully defined. In a frontier town, for example, there may have been examples of landscapes that primarily reflected adaptive responses to local conditions, and others that were attuned to a "high art" tradition imported from another place. Precise dating, too, may become critical in placing a landscape within its proper context. A study that begins, perhaps, with the cultural history of a whole era must move through deepening layers of discrimination until the special character of each decade asserts itself, and finally individual years. For example, the dates of certain events may be critical—the year of the Louisiana Purchase, the year in which Downing published his *Treatise on Landscape Gardening,* the year in which the World's Columbian Exposition opened in Chicago, or whatever. This aspect of landscape research, the effort to familiarize oneself with the myriad currents at play in a past epoch, is clearly a potentially limitless field of in-

vestigation; and a good researcher is blessed—or cursed—with a spirit akin to the gardener's restlessness, driven in this case by a desire to find out more in order to understand more thoroughly. As compensation, the wide range of resources available for study offers ample rewards along the way: amusement almost as often as edification; frequently, aesthetic delight and intellectual stimulation; always, the pleasure of beginning to really understand some part of the past.

The second area of research is the site itself, whatever survives of the actual landscape that is the object of study. The effort here is to wrest from the physical landscape every possible shred of information, every clue to those earlier configurations we are seeking to discover. Because professional archaeological surveys are scrupulously meticulous and therefore expensive procedures for determining what evidence of former patterns of use the earth conceals, the researching landscape architect needs to be familiar enough with the nature and history of the site to determine the best potential use of any funds available for archaeological excavation. In this way, carefully limited digging may be used to check likely locations for site elements of which vestiges might remain underground—the post-holes from a fence that enclosed a garden, old building foundations, etc. The same judicious appraisal of benefits to be gained versus costs will determine the appropriateness of aerial photographic surveys for a given site; infrared photography may be useful in revealing patterns in vegetation or structural elements that are difficult to read on the ground. There is no substitute, however, for what a trained eye can bring to the task of gathering physical data from a landscape. Every subtle modulation of the earth's contours, every tree, shrub, or flower, every curious pole or hole or pile of bricks may contribute in dramatic ways to the task of deciphering a vanished environment. "Crop marks," for example, changes in the incidence, arrangement, or appearance of certain plant species, can be "read" and interpreted if one knows what to look for:

> Domestic fruits, such as apples and raspberries, which persist for a long time without care . . . indicate the presence of an orchard. Burdock (*Arctium var.*) grows abundantly in especially rich soil, an indicator of the barnyard. Bayberry (*Myrica var.*), a common bush, grows in places where there has been a fire and can often be found growing near fireplace remains, which can aid in reconstructing the floorplan of a house. The lush growth of plant material in a circular form taller and greener than surrounding plants, may indicate the location of a well.[6]

These are standard methodologies for refining the careful inventory of existing natural and man-made features, boundaries, and adjacent land uses that our research of the site embraces. New and more sophisticated applications of science and technology to this data-gathering effort promise to expand still further the scope of what we can hope to know about earlier landscapes.

Finally, research of a particular historic landscape will involve a search for any available documentation of the evolution of the site over time, a venture that may turn out to be the most rigorous, demanding, and occasionally frustrating part of the entire effort. Here, as in the determination of a cultural context rooted in place and time, a staggering variety of possible sources of information presents itself: knowledgeable people can be resources, and books, obviously—not just histories but novels (I once waded through a ponderous two-volume Victorian novel looking for references to a North Georgia residential landscape that was popularly believed to figure in the story), newspapers, poems, photographs, paintings, diaries, letters, maps, advertisements, catalogues, films. The list is endless, and at times the work also will seem so. This is the time to marshal any research help that may be available. In my experience, civic groups who have undertaken responsibility for an historic property can do an excellent job of managing telephone or mail surveys directed to individuals who may be able to shed some light on a set of carefully designed questions related to the history of the site. For that matter, anyone who cares about your project may be willing to help in the search for facts and can be assigned distinct tasks: "Would you find out, please, if any of the libraries in town either purchased or were given books from our man's personal collection, and if so, which titles?" Then when it turns out that the library downtown has a copy of *The Art of Beautifying Suburban Home Grounds* with "our man's" bookplate in the front, you have someone with whom to share the pleasure of that discovery.

Slowly, painstakingly, or in chance revelations that suddenly supply missing information—a rush of "new light" on the landscape we are researching—the answers do come. We need to know the persons involved—designers, clients, users; the means at hand—financial resources as well as natural ones, available technology, materials, and labor supply; the design concepts and criteria that were at work as the landscape took form, whether the designer was conscious of them or not; and finally the chronology of events that either enhanced or disrupted the realization of the original scheme. Our research standards must be high, a requirement that forces us to face squarely the challenge of educating both the profession and the public to the value of this patient and demanding enterprise.

In the end, the "formal knowledge" whose value Lynch questioned is an absolutely necessary precondition for the development of meaningful standards by which to determine which past landscapes can and should be restored or preserved, as well as how the work should be undertaken, supported, and maintained. Expanding the limits of what we know and increasing public awareness of the issues in historic landscape conservation are not necessarily going to create a demand for more restorations; on the contrary, more sophisticated appreciation of the limits of what we can know or do is likely to temper any hopeless enthusiasm for freezing time at some mythic moment in the past. Hard factual information as the basis for sound scholarly interpretation has a chastening effect upon the pursuit of pleasant fictions. But most importantly, the process of researching, describing, and explicating is itself a form of conservation, in which we gather together the fragile records of our past and use them to understand it better. Writing, teaching, talking about historic landscapes, awakening our communities to their significance as prologue to the unfolding story of our own lives, our own environments, invest these places with a new life, a way of surviving in memory and awareness if not in fact. What is discovered about the past is already, in some sense, saved—a vital inheritance for today and tomorrow.

NOTES

1. Betts, Edwin Morris, ed. *Thomas Jefferson's Garden Book, 1776-1824, with Relevant Extracts from His Other Writings* (Philadelphia: American Philosophical Society, 1944), pp. 26–27.
2. Jackson, J. B., " 'Sterile' Restoration Cannot Replace a Sense of the Stream of Time," *Landscape Architecture* 66 May 1976, p. 194.
3. Lynch, Kevin, quoted in J. B. Jackson, p. 194.
4. Lowenthal, David, "Past Time, Present Place: Landscape and Memory," *Geographical Review* 65 January 1975, pp. 5–6.
5. Schlereth, Thomas J., *Artifacts and the American Past* Nashville, Tenn.: American Association for State and Local History, 1980, p. 147.
6. Stewart, John J., "Landscape Archaeologist at Work: How To 'Do Archeology' Without Really Digging," *Landscape Architecture* 68 (March 1978), p. 143.

An Invitation to Landscape Interpretation

Ann L. Marston

Under the broad umbrella of historic preservation falls the activity of "landscape interpretation." This paper examines landscape interpretation in an effort to expand an understanding of possible approaches to preservation projects and to encourage an innovative approach to confronting landscape interpretation problems. With such an approach landscape interpretation can offer not only a means of making a project come to be, but also a means of adding more meaning to the landscape.

BEGINNING CONSIDERATIONS

Terms and their varying definitions continue to cause confusion, particularly to the landscape architect interested in landscape preservation issues. *The Secretary of the Interior's Standards for Historic Preservation Projects* provides definitions of six terms for treatments that may be undertaken on historic properties listed in the National Register of Historic Places. However, the definitions that readily apply to buildings and structures offer much less direction for landscape projects.

In response to the resulting ambiguity, Lisa Kunst and Patricia O'Donnell have drafted working definitions derived from these categories. They have begun to straighten out some of the confusion by providing an umbrella definition for the term *preservation* itself:

Preservation is a process of stabilizing rebuilding, maintaining, or improving the condition and specific qualities of an historic landscape so that the landscape is protected and the design intent fulfilled.[10]

Kunst and O'Donnell next suggest five terms, with definitions appropriate to treating historic landscapes. The first, *restoration*, involves a strictly authentic return of the landscape to its original appearance. Second is *rehabilitation*, which brings the site to a useful, but not necessarily authentic, state. The third, *reconstruction*, involves a reproduction of a landscape setting. The fourth, *conservation*, often referring to natural landscapes, implies stewardship of the site, warding off incompatible land uses, for example. Fifth is *interpretation*, defined as:

the basic retention of the original landscape form with the integration to accommodate new uses, needs, and contemporary conditions. It involves research of the original design intent and use. The design should reinforce historic integrity while integrating a contemporary site program.[10]

This last working definition provides an excellent approach to landscape interpretation applied to site-specific project design but can be broadened to include more options: site-specific design solutions do not always offer the only appropriate response to landscape interpretation projects. as will be discussed in later sections.

Landscape interpretation as a historic landscape project treatment does not have to exclude other approaches. For example, in the project design of the town of New Harmony, Indiana, Kane and Carruth, P. C., combined interpretation, rehabilitation, and conservation treatments in the solution. Kunst and O'Donnell also illustrate several such multiple treatments by using a matrix that lists selected examples to represent a range of historic landscape categories. They suggest eighteen categories, from small- to larger-scale, providing a framework suitable for landscape interpretation projects: residential grounds; monument grounds; public building grounds; garden; minor public grounds; botanical garden; fort; battlefield; cemetery; streetscape; estate; park; working farm; museum village; district; town; prehistoric site; and park system.[10]

This list stems from a survey and study of about 300 carried-out projects. Conceptually, these categories could be continued to complete the framework by including larger regional landscapes, such as states, larger natural-cultural regions, whole countries, and even continents.

Both a broadly based definition and a clear understanding of purposes can be helpful to the design decision-making process in interpretation projects. In no instance should the definition and the purpose of historic landscape interpretation be construed to merely suggest a reinstatement of the past. Rather the emphasis must remain on the communication of the importance of the past to the intended audience. Because of this responsibility, landscape interpretation as a treatment extends an invitation particularly to creative thought and response, wherein lies much of the challenge.

CLASSIFYING THE PROBLEMS AND SEEKING OPPORTUNITIES

Across the broad continuum of project types possible under the approach of landscape interpretation, there may seem to be an intractable number of potential problems, which might serve to discourage some projects from further development. The problems that haunt interpretation projects fall into three categories, stemming from the needs of the contemporary users; the changes to the site over time; and budgetary constraints. Each of the seeming difficulties in these areas may suggest the opportunities, and the areas will be discussed separately before questions are ordered in a design-process approach to suggest possibilities for potential landscape interpretation projects.

Needs of Contemporary Users

Because the needs of contemporary users may differ vastly from those of the original users of a historic landscape, a contemporary designer may encounter several problems. The issue is how to accommodate the contemporary user without diminishing the intended experience in the historic landscape. Conflicts are not uncommon. Typical problems are illustrated by the following hypothetical examples.

Access and Parking

Consider a historic site with limited space for the projected parking needs of contemporary users. Any historic site predating the automobile may not afford ready accommodation, particularly if contemporary visitation is expected to exceed original use. The designer must weight the value of on-site parking versus the possible infringement to the intended experience in the historic landscape. How important is it to accommodate the cars on the site? Is there a less critical part of the site suitable for parking-lot development? Can the automobile approach to the site approximate anything of the historic experience? How important was the approach to the site historically, and is it important enough to warrant a feasibility study for an authentic reenactment? Would contemporary users enjoy a ride in a stagecoach to a stagecoach inn? If this is not feasible, could a contemporary vehicle of comparable size and speed be programmed to simulate the experience? If parking and access pose problems, more thought to and research of the original intent and use of the site may suggest exciting alternatives and possible solutions.

Orientation and Direction

Consider the need to direct the contemporary user of a site. Could this need potentially interfere with the desired experience? By what means will the user know how to move through a historic landscape? Are conventional graphic signs really necessary, and, if so, how can they be designed in keeping with the character of the historic landscape? Care must be taken to avoid the possibility of the sign system becoming an unwelcomed obtrusion in the landscape experience. How did the original users, particularly visitors, find their way about? What were the visual and olfactory cues that guided the sense of orientation? There may not be a great need for traditional signs pointing to, say, a chocolate factory in use. Unobtrusive, yet convenient, paths can suggest the destination, which aromas along the way can confirm. The resulting design may be more sensitive, effective, and interesting than obvious directional arrows and large signs, which can be overwhelming to any historic landscape remnants. Designers who encounter problems in orienting and directing the contemporary user may find solutions by studying and reinterpreting the original patterns of use.

Sense of Experience

Consider a small intimate space once used by a historic figure for private contemplation. Is it even appropriate to consider flooding the small space with hoards of contemporary visitors vying for a split-second glance? To appreciate the experience, seclusion itself may be helpful. Could each visitor be allowed the opportunity to sit alone in the small space? Can the feeling of isolation be promoted in a group-viewing experience? If the logistics do not permit a direct experience with the site, could a group better experience the space in a dark room with a media simulation? Perhaps the need to visit the site could be obviated completely. The experience could take the form of a visual presentation rather than a project design. This idea brings us back to the need for a broad definition of landscape interpretation. Insistence on only site design may eliminate further consideration of appropriate alternatives. The sense of the desired experience should govern the selection.

Changes to the Site Over Time

A second major source of problems in landscape interpretation projects revolves around changes to the site over time. Changes in adjacent land use, loss of site acreage, loss of site features, the addition of historically noncontemporary features to the site and, changes in the state of vegetation are typical examples.

Changes in Adjacent Land Use

For a Victorian residential plot of land, originally surrounded by pastoral landscape scenery, but now hosting a used-car dealership, certain design decisions may be simplified. If the once-existing wraparound porch primarily afforded a view of the pastoral scene, but today offers streamers twirling around the "special deal of the month," the need to reinstate the porch may not be important.

Loss of Site Acreage

If a farm that once measured 500 acres is now a 5-acre land holding, landscape interpretation may attempt to simulate the larger landscape by capitalizing on borrowed views or perhaps by using media simulation. The story of the change in lot size could become an important focus for the interpretation.

Lost Features

If features in the historic landscape have been lost, their importance to the interpretation must be determined. Is the feature itself essential to replace? Was it important in the historic design intent and use? Could a gesture of some type fulfill the role of the future? Could the absence of the feature itself be more telling?

Added Features

What about the addition of features that do not fit into the original historic context? Are they congruous or incongruous, positive or negative? How could they be related to the historic design intent and use? Is it essential for the interpretation to cover only the original development period or is it appropriate to address the evolution of the site over time?

Changes in Vegetation

Changes in the state of vegetation are particularly curious because of the inherent nature of a landscape, which, too, is changing. One question may be what were the initial design intentions for the use of vegetation in the landscape? Were these good or bad decisions? To what state and with what degree of care was the vegetation expected to grow? Have small shrubs, which may have been planted in a low, neat border hedge, become monstrous, ragged specimens obscuring walkways? Should valuable mature vegetation, if not original, be ripped out? Such questions can help justify deviations from original design intent and innovations in programming.

Budgetary Constraints

Just as necessity is the proverbial mother of invention, budgetary constraints may provide a great incentive for innovation. By maintaining a broad definition and a clear purpose, the designer should be able to generate a number of alternate solutions to a historic landscape project that are in keeping with budgetary constraints. Good, sensitive site design should not

have to cost more. If it is not economically feasible to consider a site-specific project design, there are innumerable other ways of providing interpretation: museum exhibits, slide shows, videotapes, movies, portfolios, or books, to name a few. These alternatives can provide the means for undertaking many more historic landscape projects.

Recycling existing materials and finding appropriate uses for available, and affordable, ones are not unique to interpretation site projects, nor are maintenance considerations as part of the design process. The decision to develop a landscape a particular way may depend on the degree of possible maintenance available. It would be fruitless to restore a garden if there were to be no gardeners to care for it. Another means of interpreting that aspect of the site, if it is important, can be found: a pictorial representation or a structure symbolic of a garden might be possible. No project should be abandoned because of budgetary constraints. If the message of the site is important, a form should be sought to express it.

QUESTIONS TO INCORPORATE IN THE DESIGN PROCESS

A design process can provide a logical framework for the approach to a landscape interpretation project; however, raising the necessary questions—although it can be very helpful—cannot guarantee innovative solutions. It is here that the extent to which a designer can think creatively is critical. The six components outlined in this section suggest a design process. The steps, as presented here, are not intended to follow a logical, linear order; in fact, they are often more effective when pursued simultaneously. The questions listed are intended to provide only a beginning context for approaching a project.

Research

During the investigation, the records of the past can be pieced together to construct a picture of the historic design intent and use. What were the initial interests, values, motivations, attitudes, and perceptions that shaped the landscape? How and why did they evolve and change? What may have remained constant, and why? Answers to these questions can help provide guidance and insight to programming.

Site Analysis

The objective here is to "read" the site. What is the story that it tells? What are the positive and negative features in relation to the interpretation goals? Which factors relevant to the study need to be delineated, and to what extent? This analysis must go beyond a mechanical formula approach of analyzing soils, slopes, topography, geology, and the like. J. B. Jackson, William Hoskins, May Watts, and David Lowenthal, whose works are listed in the Bibliography, offer uncommon and innovative approaches to landscape interpretation from which the landscape architect can learn a great deal.

Program Development

During this phase, the problem must be very clearly identified and stated. What is the purpose of the project? What is really important to accomplish, and why? What is the design intent? What are the goals and objectives? A clear definition of the problem and purpose can be invaluable for drafting criteria and establishing priorities. These are, in turn, invaluable to evaluating the alternatives and the effectiveness of the selected solution. What are the user needs? What are the perceptions of the contemporary user? How will the effectiveness of the solution be reviewed and evaluated?

Concept Development

Here the designer must translate the essence of the problem into ideas. The information gleaned from the research, the analysis, and the programming must be interrelated and synthesized. By keeping the ideas on an abstract level, preconceived or unimaginative solutions may be averted; new associations and discoveries may result. It is helpful to question the program needs as stated by a client: a client may express a need for a bench, but may only mean a place to sit.

Schematic Development

What are the most appropriate translations of the ideas into forms? What is the desired character and sense of place? Is site design the most appropriate response? (A study of Prairie Avenue in Chicago by Richard Macias resulted in a museum exhibit rather than a complete neighborhood reconstruction.) Have good criteria been developed to evaluate the effectiveness of the decisions?

Construction and Maintenance

What special protection of the site may be required during construction? Are particular construction techniques necessary and is skilled labor available? Has the maintenance program been considered as part of the design program? Does the way a site was maintained earlier have importance to the program? (John J. Stewart in Canada has considered interpretative maintenance as an integral part of programming his

projects. In one case the whipping of a peach tree, which was historically believed to increase fruit yield, was reenacted.)

Making an effort to raise the right questions and to seek the answers can lead to an exciting and refreshing experience in landscape interpretation. One outstanding example can be found on the National Park Service site of the former Benjamin Franklin house in Philadelphia, an interpretation designed by Venturi and Rausch. Little physical evidence of the house was found. The final restoration design of the house is rendered in only a ghost frame, which re-creates the original sense of space. Further decisions to incorporate exposed portions of the archaeological investigation at the site into the ghost-frame design allow the visitor to read a primary document of the past. Rather than re-creating a period historic landscape or garden, a series of geometric planters and trellises were designed for the site, again to recall the sense of space and organization. An effort to re-create the site with literal accuracy—as what it actually looked like at one particular time or over an evolving period of time—was not considered necessary to the purpose of the historic interpretation. The result is not only innovative, refreshing, and entertaining, but also instructive.

THE QUEST FOR MEANING

The beginning series of questions to ask in the design process and the examples described should only raise more questions and arouse a curiosity to find more examples. The more questions and the more ideas, the richer the alternatives can be for development.

The purpose of landscape interpretation must be emphasized again: it is to communicate the importance of a historic landscape. A designer must first determine what this importance is and next how to communicate that message most appropriately. Through effective communication, the designer plays an active role in enriching the meaning of the landscape from the past in the present. The search for such a meaning is the challenge to the designer and the invitation to landscape interpretation.

NOTES

1. Candee, R. M. "Clio and the Ship of Theseus: The Role of Historians, Architectural Historians, Curators, and Educational Interpreters in Preservation," in *Preservation and Conservation: Principles and Practices.* (Washington, D.C.: The Preservation Press, 1976).
2. Chorley, Kenneth and Jones, Louis C. "Primer for Preservation: What's Wrong? A Look at Historic Preservation." *History News* 19, no. 6, April 1964, pp. 95–98.

3. Hosmer, Charles B., Jr. *Presence of the Past: A History of the Preservation Movement in the United States Before Williamsburg.* (New York: C. P. Putnam's Sons, 1965).

4. Fein, A. "Identifying the Character of the Cultural Landscape." Paper read in the Historic Preservation Lecture Series at Kansas State University, October 1979, Manhattan, Kans.

5. Glassie, Henry. *Pattern in the Material Folk Culture of the Eastern United States,* rev. ed. (Philadelphia: The University of Pennsylvania Press, 1971).

6. Hoskins, William G. *The Making of the English Landscape.* (London: Hodder & Stroughton, 1955).

7. Lynes, Russell. *The Tastemakers.* New York: Harper & Brothers.

8. Jackson, J. B. *The Necessity for Ruins and Other Topics.* Amherst, Mass.: University of Massachusetts Press, 1980.

9. Jackson, J. B. *Landscapes: Selected Writings of J. B. Jackson,* ed. Ervin H. Zube. (Amherst, Mass: University of Massachusetts Press, 1970).

10. Kunst, L. A. and O'Donnell, P. M. "Landscape Preservation Deserves a Broader Meaning." *Landscape Architecture* January 1981: 53–55.

11. Lewis, P. "The Future of the Past: Our Clouded View of Historic Preservation." *Pioneer America* VII, 1975, No. 2: 1–20.

12. Lowenthal, David, "Age and Artifact, Dilemmas of Appreciation," in *The Interpretation of Ordinary Landscapes,* ed. Donald W. Meinig, (New York, Oxford University Press, 103–128, 1979).

13. Meinig, D. W. ed. *The Interpretation of Ordinary Landscapes, Geographical Essays.* (New York: Oxford University Press, 1979).

14. Melnick, R. Z. "Capturing the Cultural Landscape." *Landscape Architecture,* January 1981: 56–60.

15. Morton, W. B. and Hume, G. L. *The Secretary of the Interior's Standards for Historic Preservation Projects* (Washington, D.C.: U.S. Department of the Interior, H.C.R.S., T.P.S.D., 1979).

16. Rapoport, Amos. *House, Form, and Culture.* (Englewood Cliffs, N.J.: Prentice-Hall, Inc., 1969).

17. Sauer, Carl O. *Land and Life: A Selection from the Writings of Carl Ortwin Sauer,* ed. John Leighly. (Berkeley: University of California Press, 1963).

18. Salter, C. L. *The Cultural Landscape.* Belmont, Calif: The Wadsworth Publishing Co., Inc., 1971).

19. Stewart J. J. "Trade-offs: Historic Gardens in the Modern Environment." Paper read at the Historic Landscape Architecture and Gardening Conference, Regional Conference of Historical Agencies, June 1981, Ithaca, N. Y.

20. Streatfield, D. "Standards for Historic Garden Preservation and Restoration." *Landscape Architecture Quarterly* 59, no. 3, April 1969: 198–204.

21. Tishler, W. H. "The Landscape: An Emerging Historic Preservation Resource." *APT* XI, no. 4, 1979: 9–23.

22. Tuan, Yi-Fu. *Topophilia. A Study of Environmental Perceptions, Attitudes and Values.* Englewood Cliffs, N.J.: Prentice-Hall, Inc., 1974).

23. Watts, May T. *Reading the Landscape of America.* (New York: Collier Books, 1975).

Listening to the Historic Landscape: Economy in Image-Making

Suzanne Turner

Seeing is believing, as the saying goes, but the reverse is also true: knowing is seeing.
Arthur Koestler

The genuine voice of the past is exactly what must be safeguarded by preservation.
Paul Philippot

An image arouses deep layers of awareness affording insights into our personal identity, our bonds with nature, and our communion with other men.
Herb Greene

Design is essentially image-making. Design for preservation presumes the power of an image to communicate something about the past. The designer's purpose is to develop an image that will facilitate the site's ability to communicate its unique message, that is, the meaning of its past. Simply stated, a major role of the designer in preservation is to help the site speak.

The predominant technique in landscape preservation for the past half-century has been restoration. Restoration, by definition, focuses on the accurate return of the form and materials of the landscape to their original condition or to their condition at a particular period in the site's history. There are alternatives to restoration. This paper explores one of these: the use of the imagery of the written or spoken word as a means of approaching the historic landscape. Historic landscapes were created and used by "historic" people. By exploring the words of these people, the written and oral accounts of their daily lives, the designer has the opportunity to truly listen to the landscape of the past and, in turn, to make that experience possible for those who will visit the landscape in the present and the future. The image-making potential of the historic record is perhaps more powerful than actually seeing a landscape "in the flesh"; it is certainly more economical in terms of time, energy, and resources.

It is important to understand how each of these approaches, restoration and the use of word-images, relates to the nature of design. Landscapes are designed—and consequently experienced—on two basic levels: the physical and the symbolic. The *physical* level focuses on the arrangement of forms perceived by the user's senses: what the site looks like, what is smells like, what it sounds like, etc. The *sym-bolic* level refers to the meaning that the physical forms represent: the concept behind the design, the emotional and intangible impetus for form generation, the basis for what the design communicates. Restoration addresses the physical level of design, while the use of word-images from the historic record operates in the symbolic realm of design.

The symbolic or conceptual level of design becomes complex when a historic site is considered because the designer is not simply dealing with his or her own personal response to the site and the program but is attempting to identify and communicate those concepts already imbedded within the site through the process of history. The discovery of a site's meaning is often the most difficult part of the design process; it is certainly the major challenge to the designer. To make decisions concerning physical form and materials is basic to the practice of landscape architecture; to decipher and digest the significance of those forms and to incorporate this significance into a proposal for preservation is far more difficult. The archival record provides a direct link to that significance.

Through the use of the archival record, the designer is dealing with those people who gave the landscape meaning, and therefore he or she can begin to see the place through their eyes, to hear and understand how they thought about their landscape, and to recognize how they expressed their landscape ethic in forming their landscapes. Certainly it is not possible to locate either written or first-hand oral accounts for every historic landscape. The more recent the site, the less chance that anything written will exist, since the technology of travel and the telephone has dramatically diminished the role of correspondence. However, the more recent the site, the greater the likelihood that a living person can orally relate his or her experience of the site. If no records exist for a site, they will have survived, in many cases, for another site of the same period. Much period literature, particularly of a local nature, has the same quality of personal expression as is found in private correspondence or journals.

To focus on written or verbal communication is not very popular in a culture that has basically abandoned the written word because of its fascination with "hot" media. Marshall McLuhan defines a hot medium as one that extends a sense to the point of being filled with data. For example, a photograph is hot because, visually, it is highly defined and does not leave much to be filled in or completed by the audience. A "cool" medium, like speech or the written word, on the other hand, is low in definition because so little information is given and so much has to be filled in by the listener or the reader. "Hot media are, therefore, low in participation, and cool media are high in participation and completion by the audience." McLuhan explains that the high definition of hot media engenders fragmentation, that any hot or intense experience must first be forgotten or cooled before it can be learned or assimilated. A result of the new technology, according to McLuhan, is that "more and more we turn from the content of messages to study total effect.... Concern with effect rather than with meaning is a basic change of our electric time."[1]

If we use McLuhan's model and apply it to the historic landscape, the experience of reading the written word or hearing it spoken should be more meaningful than the presentation of a complete image through restoration. The more visually complete the physical image of a historic site, the less involved the user will be in the kind of image-making that makes mental time-travel possible. Whereas the limits of a site that has been restored are precise and fixed, there are no limits to the image of the site as described through the words of people past.

Words from the past need to be utilized by the designer on two levels. The first level involves the development of meaningful site empathy. Once a designer has come to know a person from the past through reading his or her most intimate correspondence or descriptions of daily routine, then that understanding becomes a part of the way the designer approaches the design. For example, the usual approach in the design of an antebellum plantation site has been to embellish the grounds around the house and to screen any remnants of the agricultural past of the site. After a designer (or anyone, for that matter) has read a plantation diary, the landscape of production dominates his or her image and the ornamental landscape becomes a minor feature. The following entries from the *Plantation Diary of Valcour Aime,* a planter in St. James Parish, Louisiana, present an image of plantation life that is far from the white columns and manicured gardens one might see at a restored plantation site:

1832	August:	On the third made 3000 pickets and 1000 posts.
1833	August:	137 watermelons gave 46 gallons of juice which, being evaporated, gave only 3 gallons of thick syrup.
1849	October:	An orange from Mr. J. Roman's place measured 13¼ inches in circumference.
1850	August:	The women have dug new canal in nine days, also widening another.... The women employed to widen canal in Negro quarter.
1851	August:	Cut down 360 large gum trees.[2]

From these typical entries, the designer begins to comprehend the scale of the plantation operation and the diversity of the activities involved. This understanding could lead the designer to try communicating this sense of scale in his or her plan, perhaps through the use of spatial illusion. To treat the landscape of ornamentation without treating the landscape of production would be to grossly distort the true meaning of that landscape.

The second, more obvious level on which these verbal artifacts become important is in the interpretive design for those historic sites whose purpose is to teach the public about the past. Much contemporary design for the interpretation of historic sites employs hot media to communicate the site's history and meaning. Often a movie, slide show, or exhibit of historic photographs introduces the visitor to the site. Granted, many visitors will not read. But many will, if not asked to read too much and if the layout and typeface make the reading easy. The chances that something will be read are increased as the length of the quotation is reduced. Through words from the past, visitors not only get an often quite vivid image, but, more importantly, they become privy to the writer's personal experience of the place. They can participate in that experience and begin to hear (and, by extension, feel) what it meant to be alive and on the land in a particular place in time. Through the words, they are able to listen to the landscape.

One of the best examples of the power of words to create images is the interpretive design for the National Park Service's Franklin Court in Philadelphia. Since little architectural documentation, except the house's foundations, had survived, these were stabilized and exposed for the visitor to see, and a sculptural frame (clearly contemporary) was built to outline the form and scale of the house. Throughout the site, quotations by and about Franklin, which describe or allude to various site features, were inscribed in the pavement, which was located approximately where the feature might have originally been on the site. For example, as visitors view the remains of the foundations of the kitchen, they can read the following passage, taken from a letter written by his wife Deborah to Franklin in England:

Yesterday good Mr. Rhodes, his son Thomas Franklin and wife drank tea with us. We had the best buckwheat cakes that I ever made.[3]

The suggestion is so simple but strong that one almost smells the tea and cakes. Another inscription is an excerpt from the Diary of Manasseh Cutler, which describes Cutler's first meeting with Franklin:

Dr. Franklin lives in Market Street but his house stands up a courtyard at some distance from the street. We found him in his garden, sitting upon a grass plot, under a very large mulberry tree with several other gentlemen and two or three ladies . . . .[4]

Franklin Court is an excellent example of how carefully selected word-pictures, coupled with physical artifacts, can begin to bring the site's meaning to life.

In an age when decisions are inevitably determined on the basis of budget, the economy of words versus actual construction or maintenance of existing features cannot be argued. For example, there are few situations in which the accurate variety of apple tree would affect the experience of the visitor. Horticultural accuracy is a luxury in preservation which seems extremely appropriate for sites significant in the history of horticulture. The academic study of horticultural history is certainly important, and when it is possible to include accurate plant materials without additional cost in terms of research, then their use seems obvious. But for a site with little documentation of plant materials and in which planting was a minor factor in terms of the life style of the people who lived there, it seems imprudent to spend the time necessary to research period plants.

Seeing an orchard in fruit communicates much to the city-dweller or to the child who imagines that all apples come from the A & P. However, the installation and maintenance of an orchard is extremely costly and therefore not possible for many historic sites with limited budgets. The imagined orchard, the one each visitor must paint mentally, carries with it an understanding of what that feature meant to people in the eighteenth and nineteenth centuries. In 1796, Joseph de Pontalba, a New Orleans resident, wrote to his wife, who was in France, about a garden he had planted but had been forced to sell:

I walked all about it [the garden] and everywhere I found something which brought back your presence, or something that I had created. . . . I found all my fruit trees in good shape, all the grafts which I had made are bearing, vines covered with grapes; it has more fruit than leaves. I am persuaded that one could count more than 6000 bunches of grapes on it.[5]

A romanticized vision of a garden, perhaps, but one that gives a tremendous image. Certainly the fact that Pontalba's image is romanticized is significant in beginning to understand the period and the place. Through his words, readers can go beyond simply understanding that orchards existed during the period. They learn that the production of fruit was an impor-

tant aspect of life, that it was pursued with the knowledge of scientific horticultural methods, and that, at least in this case, the efforts were quite successful.

Printed matter from a historic period can be equally descriptive in conveying information about a period landscape. If visitors to a historic site see an orchard, they will assume that fruit was grown there. If, on the other hand, they see pages from an 1851 Mississippi nursery catalog, they will get a much stronger picture of how vital fruit cultivation really was in the antebellum South: the catalog advertises 215 varieties of pears, 177 apples, 54 peaches, 11 nectarines, 7 apricots, 22 grapes, 15 figs, 11 raspberries, and 21 strawberries.[6]

Perhaps the most significant aspect of word images is their ability to portray the landscape in evolution, rather than at a fixed moment in time. In a brief paragraph, the reader can begin to understand a landscape as an evolving phenomenon, providing continuity from generation to generation. A letter from Anna Butler, a 74-year-old gardener in nineteenth-century Louisiana, to her daughter conveys the power of a landscape to connect:

I have worked the strawberries in my garden, which look very well, and Edward made Richmond set out in the old garden a great many plants left over from my bed. It will take days to cut away all of the dead branches on the roses and shrubs and I am so thankful to feel well and be able to be out everyday. I hope your plants from Ellivay's have arrived, also the plants from Gauge and Co. I send you by Mim a root of the old flag, which I found in the old garden. You can divide it into three and when it blooms it will remind you of the days when you were running around here, and gathering the blue and white ones.[7]

Every landscape of the past can speak. It is through listening to these landscapes that we come to understand the meaning of the past and are able to participate more fully in our cultural heritage as well as the shaping of future landscapes. Because the written record is incomplete, it invites designer and user alike to question and to speculate, to use their imagination to fill some of the gaps. It is this involvement with the historic landscape through the word image that is the critical factor. By listening to the landscape of the past through the words of its makers, we not only understand their perceptions and values, but we come to a deeper understanding of our own relationship with the landscape. We establish a sense of connection with those early landscape-makers, and this connection gives us a framework for facing the future.

An image arouses deep layers of awareness affording insights into our personal identity, our bonds with nature, and our communion with other men.

Herb Greene, *Mind and Image*

Notes

1. Affleck, Thomas, "Catalogue of Fruit and Ornamental Trees and Plants Cultivated at the Southern Nurseries," Thos. L. White, New Orleans, 1851, pp. 4–12.

2. Butler, Anna, to "My dear child," March 10, 1899, in the Thomas Butler Family Collection, Louisiana State University Department of Archives and Manuscripts, Louisiana State University Library, 20: 134

3. Deborah Franklin to Benjamin Franklin, November 3, 1765.

4. Diary of Manasseh Cutler, July 13, 1787.

5. "The Letters of Baron Joseph de Pontalba to his Wife," (1796), translated by Henri Sinclair, compiled by Works Progress Administration, 1939 Survey of Federal Archives in Louisiana, Louisiana State Museum Library, #122.

6. McLuhan, Marshall, *Understanding Media: The Extensions of Man* (New York: Mentor Books, 1964, pp. 36–39).

7. *The Plantation Diary of the late Mr. Valcour Aime* (New Orleans: Clark and Hofeline, 1878), pp. 26–147, pass.

Historic Plants for Historic Gardens

Ann Leighton

Despite the growing popularity of preserving and restoring historical aspects of our garden heritage, second now only to the successful restorations of early houses and their interiors, no policy—or even an understood commitment—has yet evolved for achieving historical correctness in plants. The American public is more informed than ever about period furniture styles so that any attempt to slur over dates, materials, and styles of these would rouse indignation and contempt. But the same group will pass a careful architectural restoration of a garden layout without protesting yet one more colorful smothering of the design with the same plants seen in all the other gardens of all the other carefully restored houses.

To date, the accepted formula for landscaping gardens around houses of any period has been to plant the garden seasonally with blocks of the newest hybrid tulips, followed by masses of petunias, which give way, in turn, to scarlet salvia, blue ageratum, and chrysanthemums. Lapses are filled with red geraniums. These provide a season of blooms and inspire the "ah's" from the same visitors who would resent being shown rooms full of synthetic fabrics and bean-filled cushion-chairs.

This is not, of course, to denigrate in any way the plants just mentioned. They all have their places, and not only in our hearts. Almost to a plant, they belong in fancy star-shaped beds cut into the lawn of a bracketed, scallop-eaved, turreted, piazza-encrusted residence of the late nineteenth century. Iron dogs and deer would recognize them instantly.

But Americans are not alone. Travel a bit and you will find the same determination among the French and the English to catch the tourists' breath with extravagancies of modern flowers the distinguished owners of the castles or châteaux or cottages could never have seen, let alone grown. The Portuguese and Spaniards also use exactly the same plants seen everywhere else except that, wherever there are Roman ruins to ornament, they are addicted to the small-but-sure *Begonia semperflorens*. In sheets, on terraces, by pools and fountains where Romans once walked and lounged, the tourist is offered an acre of bright little begonias introduced from Brazil about 1829.

With all the effort and expense that go into creating an effect for hordes of tourists, one may ask exactly to whom the honors really belong. At Versailles, where all these early nineteenth-century South American and Mexican annuals gaily crowd the parterres of Le Nôtre, homage is surely to the busloads and not to Le Nôtre, who meant the spaces to be filled with colored sands and gravel to bring out the design. Hapless the student of gardening and landscaping who, like Rosa Dartle, "asks to know."

The dating of garden flowers has been made easy for us since Roman times. We have Charlemagne's garden list. The Norman Conquest of an England, that until then had been confined to its own wild flowers and the roses, lilies, and cabbages brought by the Romans, introduced carnation, pinks, and more roses as well as new herbs and salad stuffs. Gardens were taken into monasteries and carefully tended for perfection. When the Spaniards took to the seas and the coasts of South America, gardens received fresh material for flower beds as well as for smoking. And with the penetration of the Jesuit missionaries into the wilds of Canada, our wild flowers received their names and places in royal gardens. Finally, when the British came to settle on our coast and found New England trees could make masts of one piece, they brought with them the accumulation of all the cherished and newly discovered garden plants that could be of value to men in the New World. No one needs to do more than study the recipes and remedies and seed bills of the period to get it all right.

For that is the pleasure. It is more rewarding to tend a garden with a reason for everything in it. When Arthur Shurcliff came back from Williamsburg and laid out a simple garden of six raised squares in front of the 1640 Whipple House in Ipswich, Massachusetts, I was told to "plant it symmetrically with authentic material." I asked for a book and, as there was none, I wrote one as I planted the garden with only material for which I had found contemporary documentary evidence. I have tended this garden with pleasure for thirty years because it is *interesting*.

A seventeenth-century garden takes time and work, but so do gardens of later centuries because, as time goes on, so do all the plants introduced. Types of roses increased. Native shrubs were taken in. The western explorations astounded gardeners at home and abroad. The China trade brought its treasures, and Mexico was opened up (to the lasting joy of tourist-trappers today).

It is all there, and, if one knows the background of each plant, it is like going to a really splendid party. For plant backgrounds can be very varied.

There was a gentle craze for "old fashioned" gardens shortly after the charm of affecting to believe in a language of flowers resulted in innumerable little books. The language of flowers had existed, in a rather haphazard fashion, since the use of flowers in the rituals of early heathens was taken over by the church. Early church fathers allowed the rose to represent carnal love and the lily, total purity. The jonquil spoke of lust and, in 1629, was deemed unpleasant for ladies' parlors (In a later, more refined time, the jonquil came to mean "I desire to make your acquaintance"). But as the fancy developed too swiftly into sentimental literature, definitions became so prone to local dictums that misunderstandings must have abounded unless the communicants were using the same book. For instance, in a Boston book, a yellow rose signified "Let us forget." In a Philadelphia book, it meant "Infidelity."

There are simple requirements for researching the restoration of an old garden—any time, any where. The first move is to fix the date, allowing for enough years to make one generation. Within these dates the next moves are nearly automatic. Evidence contemporary to the time is essential and comes first. One has to read what the original planters wrote, read what they read, and, if possible, hear—even if only by a succession of remembered accounts—what they said.

With this accumulation of information carefully recorded, one can start digging for old foundations, fenceposts, border-markers, stumps, and outlines of flowerbeds. The real digging, however, is for live materials that have "escaped" from old gardens and are now blooming in abandoned fields and beside country roads, or even in woodlands and marshes, often having achieved notice and cataloging as local "wildflowers" (the best wildflower books identify flowers not known to be indigenous with comments like "naturalized" or even "escaped from gardens"). It is here that we find our richest sources of plant material for the really old gardens. They can all be checked out by referring to the plant and garden books, complete with pictures, that were contemporary to the dates of the "restoration."

Which brings us to the importance of illustrated, contemporary reference books, an easy problem to solve. For a start, there are good reprints for each of the two vital seventeenth-century reference books used by early settlers: John Gerard's *Herbal,* the 1633 edition edited by Thomas Johnson, and John Parkinson's *Paradisi in Sole, Paradisus Terrestris,* 1629.[5] We know that both these books ranked next to the family Bible as early-American reference books. They are both elaborately and accurately illustrated so that we

can see exactly what the authors were talking or writing about. We know that one of our best commentators, John Josselyn, who wrote from and of New England in the mid-seventeenth century, writes of the plants the settlers brought with them with his copy of Gerard's book beside him, following Gerard's order. So that, when he mentions the "Lilly Convallie growing by the sea," it is actually the common garden lily-of-the-valley we know today.

Research into contemporary reference material of the eighteenth century is also made easy for us. The handsome set of flower prints, Robert Furber's "Twelve Months of Flowers," sold separately and for framing at Williamsburg, Virginia, is actually the first illustrated garden catalogue, published early in the century and handsomely arranged to show the plants available from Mr. Furber's nursery to be grown throughout the year in England.[2] The huge, spectacular groupings of each month's flowers look as if they were all in one gigantic arrangement, like Dutch flower paintings. But little numbers on each bloom refer to a list under each picture, from which one could order seeds. The interest for us lies in seeing how many of our American wild flowers and native shrubs and trees were included, and in discovering from the illustrations what the flowers of the period really looked like. For instance, when Jefferson said "hyacinth," he was not referring to the "florist's flower" we have today (a rounded club of solid bloom) but to a rather frail and drooping one-sided flower more like the wild "bluebell" of the English woods. The eighteenth century abounded in good gardeners and listings.

The nineteenth century is almost as far away from us today as are the others, requiring the same careful reference for each plant. One of the plants we feel most sentimental and loyal about including in a garden today is "bleeding heart" (*Dicentra spectabilis*). Actually, it came from Japan at about the same time as the reliable, public-spirited red geraniums arrived from South Africa. Like them, it goes with bustles and brass beds and not with hoop skirts and four posters. The 1894 edition of *Johnson's Gardener's Dictionary* is a great help to anyone planning an "old-fashioned garden."[4]

Our richest reference books for American gardens in the nineteenth century, however, lie in the masses of printed material put out by the nurserymen, including seed catalogs from all over our country. Landscape architects also abounded by mid-century and their planting advice can be checked in the catalogs of the nurserymen and in the illustrated volumes of William Curtis's *Botanical Magazine.*[1]

So much for reading. Our next resort is listening—to anything anyone who remembers anything pertinent. My longest-lived piece of hearsay came from a very old lady whose mother was a direct descendent of Massasoit, the Indian chief. She related how her mother told her that the Indians always said the only seeds the Pilgrims brought with them were for the plant we call "honesty" or "silver shillings" (*Lunaria annua*), of value only as an ornament when dried. This, I think, is an Indian joke, heartrending, about the lack of equipment the Pilgrims brought with them to a harsh New World.

The third step in restoring any historic garden is to search for material around old cellar holes, in old fields, and at the edges of old woods and walls. The reference book to use in these endeavors is a book of wildflowers of the locality (watching for the so-called "naturalized" or "escaped" flowers). I cannot believe that the New England countryside is so unique that it is the only place where treasured plants of the early settlers took it upon themselves to adventure into the landscape. Often this can be the most interesting part of your restoration: seeing what there is to be had and discovering why the earlier gardeners brought it and grew it. "For meat and medicine, for use and for delight" encompasses all periods, all the way across our country.

And think what a wealth of varied gardens would await the tourists if each area of our country concentrated on presenting its own particular exhibition of the early gardens of its settlers. The little, compact cottage garden of the earliest settlers on the eastern seaboard slowly, slowly traveled west at ox-pace, discarding, substituting, and adopting local remedies and ornaments as it went, finally settling down to speak of the whole historical endeavor of its owners. The Spanish contributed their patios with lasting success and the French their little walled town-gardens. The Swedes and the Germans have contributed fascinating architectural details. And these are only the most obvious evidences of our varied garden heritages. Even opulent copies of European palace gardens by the "Innocents Abroad" at the end of the nineteenth century have their own story to tell.

There are, of course, several words of warning. Don't do anything unless you are prepared to see it through-and do it right. No one will later care for your "inspired guesses" or your theories that since they-were-great-people-and-wanted-the-best, we should give-them-the-best-we-have-today since that-is-what-they-would-have-had-if-they-were-here-now. They are not here now and that is the whole point of redoing their gardens. It is the only way they can come alive again, just as we can feel them presiding in their houses: every garden is a self-portrait.

Notes

1. Curtis, William, "Botanical Magazine," (published by the author from 1787 to 1800) vol. 1–6.
2. Furber, Robert, *Twelve Months of Flowers,* (London, 1732).
3. Gerard, John, *Herbal,* (London; Adams, Islip, Joice & Norton, 1633).
4. Johnson, T., *Johnson's Gardner's Dictionary,* (London, George Bell and Sons, 1894).
5. Parkinson, John, *Paradise in Sole, Paradisus Terrestries,* (London, 1629).

Native Vegetation Restoration: Another Route to the Past

Darrell Morrison

The practice of reestablishing native vegetation in groupings based on the species composition and aesthetic character of presettlement plant communities has gained in popularity during the past decade. Due, in part, to its water- and energy-conserving appeal, this alternative landscape approach has been applied on a variety of scales, ranging from suburban backyards to large commercial and industrial sites.

There are many variations on the basic theme of native vegetation restoration. They all represent attempts to emulate certain characteristics of indigenous, naturally evolved plant communities, albeit to varying degrees of detail and integrity.

To begin our discussion of native vegetation restoration, two definitions are submitted. The first is a strict definition; the other is a modified, practical one.

Strictly defined, native vegetation restoration is the reintroduction and reestablishment of presettlement plant communities on sites previously occupied by them, but from which they have been removed by human activity; the diversity and density of reestablished plant species are equivalent to that which occurred in the original presettlement plant communities. As defined above, native vegetation restoration is a practical impossibility.

A modified, more achievable form of native vegetation restoration is defined as the reintroduction and reestablishment of community-like groupings of plants on sites that possess the environmental characteristics to support them, incorporating key plant species and distribution patterns that will, over time, emulate those of the presettlement vegetation.

Even this modified, practical definition may include a variety of practices, depending on the restoration goal. If the primary goal is an educational one, a wide array of plant species may be of chief importance in order to maximize opportunities to see and to identify a broad cross section of species. On the other hand, if the primary goal is to capture the "visual essence" of a plant community, the distribution of forms, colors, and textures in characteristic patterns may be the highest priority in the restoration. Either approach may be valid in a given situation, and both may "fit" within the modified definition.

Whatever the goal, native vegetation restoration, as it will be discussed here, does not take a hands-off, laissez faire approach; it is, rather, an active and ongoing process. For example, in initial implementation of a restoration, it may first be necessary to eliminate or suppress any highly competitive, nonnative vegetative cover that would interfere with the reestablishment of native species. Next, plants or seeds of native species might need to be reintroduced because there may no longer be any "parent" plants of those species in the vicinity to provide propagules. Once the initial planting of native species is accomplished, continued management may be required to suppress nonnative invading species or to emulate presettlement phenomena that once perpetuated the "original" natural community. A prime example of this is the use of fire as a prairie management technique.

A BRIEF HISTORY

While native vegetation has gained new attention in the recent past, there are certainly precedents for this approach in the history of American landscape architecture. Following is a brief exploration into some such earlier examples of native restoration activity.

Probably the best-known advocate of the native landscape and its reintegration into the designed landscape was Jens Jensen. Throughout his career, Jensen, a Danish-born landscape architect whose work spans the period of about 1890 to the 1940s, increasingly utilized native materials and natural processes in designing landscapes in the American Midwest. As a landscape architect in the Chicago Park System and as a private consultant, Jensen demonstrated his facility in the use of native communities of plants on a variety of scales, ranging from one-acre residential sites to large parks.

Among the latter are his designs for Humboldt Park and Columbus Park in Chicago, developed in the early years of the twentieth century. In each of these, Jensen incorporated a "prairie river" theme: a curving lagoon bordered by wetland and prairie plants, with large open "meadows" adjacent to them. This use of native Illinois prairie grasses and flowers, and cattails, reeds and other wetland plants led to symbolic, rather than literal, re-creations of nature. Nevertheless, they suggested the power and movement of the native landscape that inspired their design.

In the 1940s, Jensen's plan for Lincoln Memorial Garden in Springfield, Illinois, converted former rolling farmland into a series of community groupings with a network of mowed pathways of varying widths and "sun openings" providing spatial diversity. Designed for the Garden Clubs of Illinois as a memorial to Abraham Lincoln, it contained various associations of trees, planted as seedlings or even seeds by volunteers. Thirty-odd years later, the impression gained by the casual visitor is that the paths and openings were carved out of a natural complex of woodlands and prairies.

In the same midwestern region in which Jensen practiced, Wilhelm Miller of the University of Illinois advocated "The Prairie Style of Landscape Gardening" in a 1915 publication with that title. This document encouraged both preservation of remnant native landscapes and their restoration in parks, home grounds, and on roadsides. It listed woody and herbaceous species appropriate to different types of sites, but did not go as far as to provide techniques for implementing the restorations.

In 1929, a book by Dr. Edith A. Roberts, a plant ecologist, and Elsa Rehmann, a landscape architect, entitled *American Plants for American Gardens,* recommended the use of native groups of plants based on natural communities of the northeastern United States. This book represented a landmark in that it combined botanical information with aesthetic characteristics of the various plant communities.

There is little evidence that the native landscape philosophy and information generated by people like Jensen, Miller, or Roberts and Rehmann were widely accepted or adopted by the landscape architectural profession during the period of the 1930s through the 1950s. Related work, however, was underway by botanists and ecologists at a number of arboreta. Among these were John Curtis and Henry Greene at the University of Wisconsin Arboretum and William Niering at the Connecticut Arboretum. They were actively engaged in pioneer restoration and "renaturalization" of sizeable tracts of land. The original documentation of planting and establishment procedures, as well as the restoration plantings themselves, continue to provide useful information to present-day restorationists.

Today, with water and energy concerns supporting the case for native vegetation restoration, the approach has acquired a degree of acceptance in the profession. This acceptance, however, is not without some barriers, preventing widespread adoption. Obstacles include the difficulty of obtaining native plants and seeds in many areas and the need for localized information on native species and how to grow them.

Another obstacle is related to the time required to reestablish the aesthetic character of the natural landscape. While many people find the "true" natural landscape to be quite acceptable visually, they understandably have difficulty with the visual character of "natural plantings" in their early stages of establishment.

More broadly, there still exists a carry-over of the pioneer attitude that suggests taming the threatening wilderness represents "progress." But the farther chronologically removed we become from our pioneer past, the more likely we are to accept the reinstatement of pre-settlement vegetation to some small part of our surroundings.

RATIONALE FOR RESTORING NATIVE VEGETATION

Many reasons for restoring community-like groupings of native plants are advanced by proponents of that practice. These can be categorized as ecological/environmental, economic, educational, and aesthetic.

Ecological/Environmental Factors

In this category, a central argument is that a plant native to a specific geographic area has become adapted to the climatic and edaphic, or soil related, conditions of that region. While there are exceptions due to extreme man-induced changes in those conditions, it is usually true that species native to an area can be reestablished and will grow without benefit of "artificial" watering and feeding, winter protection, or other cultural practices that may be required to grow certain nonnative or exotic species in that same area.

Similarly, community-like groupings of diverse native species are often less dependent on the application of chemical herbicides and pesticides than are exotic plantings—particularly monotypic plantings such as single-species hedges and lawns—which become prime targets for insect and disease infestations. Landscapes that utilize few or no chemical fertilizers, herbicides, and pesticides constitute less of a threat to water quality in adjacent rivers, streams, and lakes than do conventional high-maintenance landscapes. In the "standard" designed landscape, a certain portion of these chemical "additives" may be carried to surface water as runoff, or they may infiltrate the soil to pollute groundwater.

Energy demands may be lessened—relative to "standard" plantings—on a "renaturalized" landscape by reducing the amount of mowing and clipping that is done, although there are obviously places where the most appropriate and functional vegetative cover is mowed turf. In any case, lawn areas are often larger than necessary and are essentially nonfunctional; less energy-demanding groundcovers, such as a diverse mix of native groundlayer plants, provide a positive alternative.

Economy

There are obvious economic benefits associated with the reduced inputs of chemicals, water, energy, and labor. The cost of maintaining "high quality" lawn areas—irrigating, fertilizing, and mowing frequently—may cost in the range of $500 to $1000 per acre per year. On large sites, it is obvious that substantial savings can be realized by replacing even a portion of extensive lawn with much less intensively managed groupings of native plants.

An additional economy results when natural processes are permitted to occur. An example of this is the vegetative spreading and/or reseeding of existing plantings; the number of plants is thereby increased without adding to the installation cost. This approach is in marked contrast to much traditional planting, in which the number of plants is not permitted to change over time. This is because the primary goal in the management of these traditional plantings is the *maintenance* of a predetermined number and distribution of plants. Management of a native community restoration, on the other hand, implies *guided change*, with plant numbers and distribution shifting over time. But the net result is often a higher density of plants and greater diversity at low cost.

Education

There are many instances in which the landscape serves direct educational purposes. Arboreta and botanic gardens are the obvious examples of this. They often include collections of native plants, either as labeled specimens or as assembled community-like groupings.

Less obvious, but potentially effective, opportunities for educating the public about ecological concepts and plant communities exist on school grounds, parks, historic sites, industrial sites, and home grounds. Such settings may provide people frequent and regular contact with native species and communities, thereby making the seasonal and long-term changes that occur therein an integral part of the observers' daily experience. The physical extent of native plantings on such sites may range from borders and islands to extensive zones planted with species that are adapted to the specific soil/moisture/sunlight conditions.

Aesthetics

In a world where there is an ever-increasing tendency toward standardization and sameness, the incorporation of native plant community groupings in the

22

designed landscape serves (1) to provide a regional or local identity; and (2) to expand the palette of forms, colors, and textures in that landscape.

Buildings, highways, and even directional signs have contributed to the environmental homogeneity. Typical "landscaping" has likewise become more similar, with a small palette of the same widely tolerant plant species used seemingly everywhere. Even the distribution patterns are repeated, with trees scattered about in the ubiquitous mowed lawn and with shrubs clustered in carefully defined beds. Even where very different microenvironmental conditions exist, there is no appreciable change in planting or distribution patterns. Thus, homogeneity prevails within a region as well as between regions. Using the limited array of plant species and the same or very similar arrangements of them, "landscaped" hillsides look very much like the adjacent floodplains.

Local, indigenous vegetation, on the other hand, provides a unique source that can be used to visually differentiate between regions. Native plant community groupings matched to specific site conditions create different colors, textures, and patterns in these different microenvironments. Yet they are not "jarring" contrasts because there is usually a transitional zone between them where blending occurs, just as it does when two naturally evolved communities meet.

Besides the region-to-region and within-region differences that can be perpetuated with native community restorations, proponents point out that such plantings, per se, tend toward greater visual diversity than do traditional or typical plantings (this again relates to the fact that such a limited range of life forms and plant species are typically incorporated into the designed landscape in standard commercial practice). A native community restoration—even a stylized one—is likely to include plants that provide greater color and textural diversity as well as the quality of movement. Examples include the linear leaves and freely swaying grass seedheads of the native prairie; reeds and rushes of the wetland; and a wide variety of wildflowers and ferns of the forest. As a "bonus", there is likely to be a greater variety of insects, birds, and butterflies attracted to the diversity of plant species, adding their own element of ephemeral color and yet another type of movement to the landscape.

NATIVE VEGETATION RESTORATION TECHNIQUES

As defined earlier in this chapter, native vegetation restoration is not a laissez-faire procedure. Instead, it implies active implementation and management practices to "return" a restoration site to a condition that approximates a presettlement "natural" state. To do this, there must be some understanding both of the restoration site and of the natural community models upon which the restoration is based.

Natural Model Data

Information that should be gathered about the natural community or communities upon which a restoration will be based includes the following:

1. *Species composition and distribution.* The first prerequisite to the successful execution of a native community restoration is the identification of the numerically important plant species in the natural version of the community, as well as the assessment of their approximate density and distribution patterns. Also important are the relationships of the species with each other and with microvariations in environment: soil depth, texture, pH and nutrients, topography and solar orientation, and drainage and moisture characteristics.

2. *Aesthetic character.* In most restoration work, the emulation of a prevailing aesthetic character is important, as well as a resemblance to the botanical composition. However, some simplification in the botanical composition is often a practical reality

Fig. 1.   Wetland planting at Lincoln Memorial Garden, Springfield, Illinois. It shows the national character of Jen Jensen's design three decades after it was planted.

Fig. 2.   Prairie backyard at the author's house in Madison, Wisconsin. The plants in this island of Indian grass, showy goldenrod, and little bluestem grass wave vigorously on a south-facing slope.

Fig. 3. Woodland groundlayer in area shaded by the author's house. The border includes maidenhair fern, interrupted fern, wild geranium, bloodroot, maypole, and yellow lady's-slipper.

in restoration plantings. In making these simplifications, it is important not to sacrifice the "visual-essence" species, which provide an important visual quality to a plant community, whether or not they are of greatest numerical importance. Examples might be trees that provide an important bark texture (e.g., shagbark hickory); plants with memorable flower color (e.g., fringed gentian); or plants with contrasting leaf form (e.g., prairie dock in a field of grasses).

3. *Community dynamics.* A natural plant community is a dynamic, changing complex of organisms interacting with each other and their environment. A knowledge of successional patterns and changes over time in the natural model may help in predicting the sequence of change in a restoration, both for the spread of individual species and for the likely change in species composition over time.

Probably the best sources of information on the natural prototypes are extant stands of community types in the same region. Field study of these remnants can yield information for all three of the above categories. In cases where there are no remaining examples of the community in the region, references to written work on local vegetation and plant communities may have to provide the basis for planning

species selection and placement, as well as for subsequent management strategy.

Site Information

Just as a thorough understanding of natural community(ies) is helpful in planning a successful restoration, so is a thorough familiarity with the physical characteristics of the site itself. To a greater degree than in "standard" landscape design, restoration design suggests fine-line distinctions in species selection, closely reflecting soils, moisture, temperature, and light conditions. In addition to the purely "natural" site characteristics, there may be elements relating to earlier human activity, for example, buildings that create new microclimates, or overly competitive nonnative plants that need to be suppressed before native restoration can occur.

Using the information on the community(ies) to be emulated and the restoration site analysis as a base, plans for implementation can be developed. A logical approach is to identify all the plant communities that could theoretically be accommodated by the physical characteristics prevailing on different parts of the site. These can then be matched with various use requirements. For example, if solar access is a need, then an open, noncanopied community planting can be installed and subsequently managed to keep it open. Or

Fig. 4.   Prairie planting at the site of CUNA Mutual Insurance Society in Madison, Wisconsin. Sweeping, curving forms of prairie plantings adjacent to a traditional mowed lawn symbolize the vastness of a tallgrass prairie that probably occupied the site in presettlement times.

Fig. 5.   CUNA Mutual's prairie planting in winter. This shows the textural effect of such plantings emerging from snow.

Fig. 6. A portion of the prairie planting at General Electric Medical Systems Division near Waukesha, Wisconsin. This illustrated the potential of using native plantings on industrial sites and roadsides.

if shading is a requirement, a strategy that will lead to a woodland community over time can be developed; this could involve a "successional" approach, whereby an initial planting of fast-growing pioneer trees (e.g., trembling aspen) might provide both initial shade and an environment in which a more permanent forest community could develop (e.g., a maple-basswood community).

NATIVE VEGETATION RESTORATION AND HISTORIC PRESERVATION/RESTORATION

Linkages between the native vegetation restoration approach to landscape development and historic landscape preservation and restoration are self-evident. In a sense, a return to presettlement vegetation—or a visual emulation of it—is the epitome of historic restoration, taking us back to an era that may have lasted several thousand years prior to European settlement of this country. In restoring or preserving sites adjacent to historic structures, native community-like plantings may or may not be appropriate. For instance, if the structure was originally at the frontier of settlement, a backdrop of seemingly native presettlement

vegetation might be very appropriate; on the other hand, if the building was originally placed in an already-modified landscape, the site should probably reflect those human/cultural changes.

There are a variety of reasons for considering a native vegetation restoration alternative in designing a variety of sites. Furthermore, there is a growing body of knowledge to support this activity, although there are still many important gaps. There have been sufficient examples of restoration carried out to assure us that it is possible to emulate natural presettlement plant communities, both botanically and aesthetically. The illustrations that accompany this chapter provide some evidence that this is indeed a viable approach and a route to past landscapes.

NOTES

1. Miller, Wilhelm, "The Prairie Style of Landscape Gardening," University of Illinois Extension Service, Urbana, Champaign, Illinois, 1915.
2. Roberts, Edith A. and Elsa Rehmann, *American Plants for American Gardens,* 1929.

Urban Design: Catalyst for Comprehensive Revitalization

Richard Macias

We have been told that we are both the beneficiaries and the victims of change: beneficiaries because our needs and our technologies have come together to improve our lives in many obvious ways, and victims because, at the same time, we have allowed change to erase certain values looked upon as barriers to progress. We have allowed change to become a criterion for the so-called improvement of our urban areas. Mistakenly, we have interpreted the role of design in urban evolution as a cyclical requirement to start over.

There are countless examples—both successes and failures—of urban improvement throughout this country. The attempts in the 1960s to create downtown malls resulted in many well-designed, attractively appointed spaces intended to generate economic gains. Some succeeded, but many failed, in a fruitless effort to bring economic recovery to Main Street. Similarily, we have lamented the visual chaos that typifies the entry corridors of many of our communities. We criticized the lack of design only to realize that these strips of development represent economic successes.

In recent years there has been an increasing awareness of the importance of combining visual improvement with economic need. We can point to several recent events that have heightened this awareness of value in the built environment. Among these are the Historic Preservation Act of 1966; the incentives brought about by tax reform, favoring improvements to historic buildings; the National Main Street Program; and the countless conferences and workshops that have served to educate city officials, property owners, merchants, and designers to the benefits of preservation in the many forms that it takes.

It is important to say that, while preservation may be an understood concept, its subcategories create confusion in the overall understanding of dealing with change. In our context, revitalization refers to the improvement of the well-being of the residents of the community through a process of *directed change*. This is the only legitimate goal of revitalization. Of course, there are different ways of perceiving and of achieving this goal and, as a result, two basic approaches have arisen: the economic approach and the environmental approach. The economic approach sees new development, new business, and the influx of funds—whether private or public—as the main determinant of prosperity and, thus, the quality of life. The environmental approach emphasizes the importance of beautification efforts and the quality of environmental experience enjoyed by residents and users alike. These two approaches overlap somewhat in most revitalization programs; however, most programs usually stress one to the detriment of the other. Because the political process directly affects both economic and environmental issues, the failures of many revitalization efforts fall into three general categories: political, economic, or environmental.

The designer's challenge has become obvious: strive for directed change that can offer economic gain through the existing, albeit short-lived, political process (long-range planning is characteristically influenced by the attitudes of a political body that changes every four years).

With the problem and the challenges in mind, the needs for urban design become more apparent and, therefore, a process for directed change must emerge. The following offers one approach.

COMMITMENT TO CHANGE

The commitment to change is the commitment to growth and to the acknowledgment of a fundamental principle.

Fig. 1. Economics and design in combination should judge the success or failure of an urban commercial area.

Although the type of sprawl or unstructured growth associated with highway development has convinced many towns that growth can only occur at the expense of community identity, the notion is somewhat misleading. A Wonderbread commercial of some years back—the figure of a child shown growing to maturity in a matter of seconds—illustrates the point that growth can be defined as a change in form over time, without loss of identity.

Successful community growth likewise encompasses a period of cultivating and nurturing certain qualities and influences and of screening others, all the while allowing for the incorporation of new impulses. This is achieved, ideally, in a conscientious program of development that has specific short- or long-term objectives consistent with the perception of an emerging or ongoing identity.

In preparing for a process of directed change, which is the basis of revitalization, the following questions can lead to a clearer articulation of the components of community identity:

1. What have we been in the past? Are there attributes worth preserving or is there a longstanding problem to be overcome?
2. What are we now? Is this what we want to be at present?
3. Where are we going if we continue on our present course? Do we want to go in this direction?
4. Where do we want to go? What do we want to become?

Although these are simple and fundamental questions in the majority of cases, the revitalization effort has not usually been preceded by—or founded upon—this type of assessment, which is the keystone of any managed development process. The failure to conscientiously screen objectives is apparent, for example, in the half-conscious and inappropriate desire of cities to become towns and vice versa.

PRESERVATION IN REVITILIZATION

A few years ago preservation meant saving buildings for specific visitation purposes, which resulted in numerous museum-like expressions. In the last five years, however, the concept of preservation has changed dramatically to include social issues, issues of neighborhood displacement, and the economic and environmental realities of urban change.

In a certain sense the preservation movement is beginning to outgrow some of the original blind spots of its early years in the same way that urban design has outgrown the urban design myth of the 1960s. This myth—urban design as the solution to declining business—is evident in the downtown malls that sprouted up all over the country.

However, despite the maturing of the preservation movement, we can still, in a certain sense, say that the urban design myth of the 1960s has been translated into the preservation myth of the 1970s and 1980s in that the focus of preservation, when taken narrowly, is

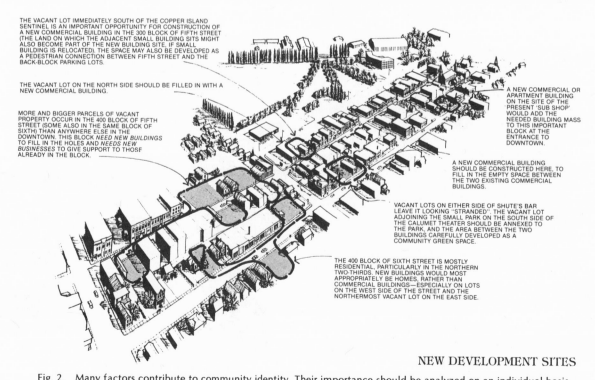

THE VACANT LOT IMMEDIATELY SOUTH OF THE COPPER ISLAND SENTINEL IS AN IMPORTANT OPPORTUNITY FOR CONSTRUCTION OF A NEW COMMERCIAL BUILDING IN THE 300 BLOCK OF FIFTH STREET (THE LAND ON WHICH THE ADJACENT SMALL BUILDING SITS MIGHT ALSO BECOME PART OF THE NEW BUILDING SITE, IF SMALL BUILDING IS RELOCATED). THE SPACE MAY ALSO BE DEVELOPED AS A PEDESTRIAN CONNECTION BETWEEN FIFTH STREET AND THE BACK-BLOCK PARKING LOTS.

THE VACANT LOT ON THE NORTH SIDE SHOULD BE FILLED IN WITH A NEW COMMERCIAL BUILDING.

MORE AND BIGGER PARCELS OF VACANT PROPERTY OCCUR IN THE 400 BLOCK OF FIFTH STREET (SOME ALSO IN THE SAME BLOCK OF SIXTH) THAN ANYWHERE ELSE IN THE DOWNTOWN. THIS BLOCK *NEED NEW BUILDINGS* TO FILL IN THE HOLES AND *NEEDS NEW BUSINESSES* TO GIVE SUPPORT TO THOSE ALREADY IN THE BLOCK.

A NEW COMMERCIAL OR APARTMENT BUILDING ON THE SITE OF THE PRESENT 'SUB SHOP' WOULD ADD THE NEEDED BUILDING MASS TO THIS IMPORTANT BLOCK AT THE ENTRANCE TO DOWNTOWN.

A NEW COMMERCIAL BUILDING SHOULD BE CONSTRUCTED HERE, TO FILL IN THE EMPTY SPACE BETWEEN THE TWO EXISTING COMMERCIAL BUILDINGS.

VACANT LOTS ON EITHER SIDE OF SHUTE'S BAR LEAVE IT LOOKING "STRANDED". THE VACANT LOT ADJOINING THE SMALL PARK ON THE SOUTH SIDE OF THE CALUMET THEATER SHOULD BE ANNEXED TO THE PARK, AND THE AREA BETWEEN THE TWO BUILDINGS CAREFULLY DEVELOPED AS A COMMUNITY GREEN SPACE.

THE 400 BLOCK OF SIXTH STREET IS MOSTLY RESIDENTIAL, PARTICULARLY IN THE NORTHERN TWO-THIRDS. NEW BUILDINGS WOULD MOST APPROPRIATELY BE HOMES, RATHER THAN COMMERCIAL BUILDINGS—ESPECIALLY ON LOTS ON THE WEST SIDE OF THE STREET AND THE NORTHERMOST VACANT LOT ON THE EAST SIDE.

NEW DEVELOPMENT SITES

Fig. 2. Many factors contribute to community identity. Their importance should be analyzed on an individual basis.

exclusively on resources and their retention without the other ingredients of urban design. The result has often been historic "theme towns" that, in some cases, convert a nicely detailed Victorian rivertown into a Bavarian village. Add to this the "miracle, low-maintenance" transformations that are very much in evidence in many small towns today. These panel-and-screen cover-up solutions were, in their own way, attempts at revitalization; details of an earlier generation were cleaned up into what we have found to be faceless commercial districts.

A PROCESS FOR REVITALIZATION

To achieve the necessary attention to both scope and detail and to address the common confusion as to where to begin revitalization, a viable planning analysis and implementation process is necessary. In somewhat simplified terms, this process involves: (1) assessing the areas physical characteristics; (2) considering the market area as it typically extends well beyond the downtown commercial zone; (3) coordinating these with the suggested improvement; and (4) determining and implementing a strategy.

We can break the strategy or revitalization process down into four specific phases. These are: (1) the *preplanning phase,* in which the awareness and need for change is recognized, appropriate help sought, and the general revitalization objectives defined. (2) The *planning phase,* in which conditions and resources are inventoried and analyzed and a course of action is determined; (3) the *implementation phase,* when the accepted plan of action is embarked upon, with specific players assuming their predetermined roles; and (4) the *post-project phase,* in which the project is monitored, maintained, and adjusted or revised periodically over the long-term. For our purposes, we will concentrate on the second, or planning, phase

Fig. 3.

because it is at this level that the designer's skills take into consideration local participants, translate their concerns into a plan, and offer both the elements for implementation as well as post-project management and monitoring.

The Planning Phase: Existing Conditions and Opportunities

After the general objectives have been set and the necessary expertise obtained, the planning phase is embarked upon. The major elements of this stage are the inventory and anlaysis of existing conditions and resources and the formulation of a specific recommended plan for action. It is important to realize that the emerging plan for action—and the specific projects of which it consists—will ultimately be determined by the inventory and analysis of community conditions and resources. This plan may vary from the original, very often unspoken, preconceptions held by community members regarding the exact nature of the project. This happens because these preconceptions usually predate a thorough review of the community, which may provide new data, and because people tend to confuse objectives, goals, and methods.

INVENTORY

A number of attributes contribute to the character of an area. The accompanying diagram (Fig. 4) presents characteristics that give form to an area—its edges, voids, focal points, and so forth. Basically, all of these physical components fall into one of an area's two major zones: the public and the private. These relate to responsibility as well as to ownership, and the boundaries, features, and responsibilities of the two zones must be agreed upon for effective implementation to occur. It is often the zone of public responsibility that is ignored, not so much in the design sense as in the way in which its changes affect the true opportunities for economic survival.

Identification of resources thus includes not just facades, but the voids, spaces between buildings, intersections, views, traffic patterns, and focal points and edges. These patterns of open space are important elements of the public zone and they relate to the way an area is used and perceived. An area may be profiled, for example, on the basis of pedestrian circulation opportunities and lengths of walk. Research suggests that people will not walk more than 300 feet from their parking space in a downtown area; but placed in a shopping center, they will walk two miles with little hesitation. The challenge in the downtown area is to make people feel that they have walked less without the need to preempt close-in space for additional parking. Providing conveniences and enhancing linkages can make downtown areas appear closer to

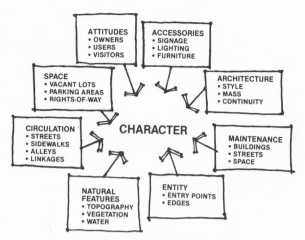

Fig. 4. The character of an area is the result of many influences.

one another through the process of sequential improvements. Alley-ways can be overlooked as resources in the evaluation of a towns pedestrian circulation. The innovative use of inner building areas to provide shopping is another way convenience has been gained while preserving the area's existing continuity and character.

Many approaches have been developed to inventory the public and private property zones within commercial areas. Blockscape analysis is an approach that evaluates facades and assigns different values to buildings in terms of their design participation in an

overall urban revitalization. Depending on the scale of actually implementable change, this approach targets the priority areas and gives a basis for incremental choices to be made should full-scale treatment prove impossible due to economic or policy limitations. This is an important consideration because each facade represents one owner or merchant who is going to effect recommended changes. So although for aesthetic reasons it is appropriate to assess the entire block as a unit, for purposes of implementation, a building-by-building approach is necessary. For this reason, facades are separated into cost zones, giving further definition to the scope of private responsibility (Fig. 7).

ANALYSIS

Once the physical characteristics of an area are assessed, these are related to the actual consumer market. Market considerations include an identification of the true area that utilizes the specific urban core in question. Additionally, it pinpoints where consumers come from, attitudes of buyers and sellers, and also the recognition by merchants that they have a responsibility to create a shopping environment buyers will wish to use (this may include new displays, increased inventory, changes in store hours, and so forth.)

For most small communities, once the market area has been assessed and a reasonable understanding of the attitudes of the shoppers has been determined, it is possible to identify the various levels of use of the

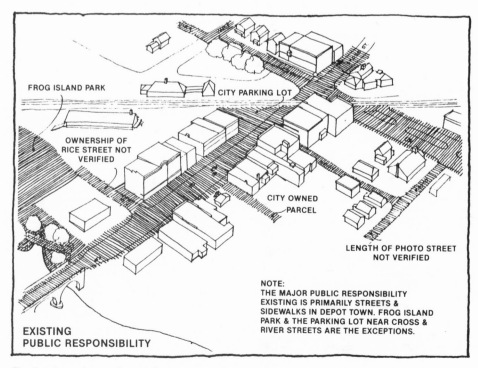

FROG ISLAND PARK   CITY PARKING LOT

OWNERSHIP OF
RICE STREET NOT
VERIFIED

CITY OWNED
PARCEL

LENGTH OF PHOTO STREET
NOT VERIFIED

NOTE:
THE MAJOR PUBLIC RESPONSIBILITY
EXISTING IS PRIMARILY STREETS &
SIDEWALKS IN DEPOT TOWN. FROG ISLAND
PARK & THE PARKING LOT NEAR CROSS &
RIVER STREETS ARE THE EXCEPTIONS.

EXISTING
PUBLIC RESPONSIBILITY

Fig. 5. An understanding of the overlaps between public and private responsibility can assist implementation of urban improvement programs.

Fig. 6.   The contribution of individual buildings should be viewed in the "blockscape" context.

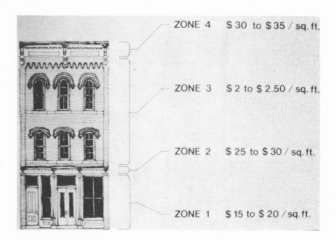

ZONE 4	$ 30 to $ 35 / sq. ft.
ZONE 3	$ 2 to $ 2.50 / sq. ft.
ZONE 2	$ 25 to $ 30 / sq. ft.
ZONE 1	$ 15 to $ 20 / sq. ft.

Fig. 7.

"Main Street" area (Fig. 8). These include convenience, comparison, and general shopping, and the influence of the merchant as a user; The employee, the person on business, and the "captured" person who may be there unintentionally, perhaps lost, should also be considered. The attitudes of each of these market audience segments will determine the type of use and will combine to determine an appropriate marketing strategy for the area.

From the marketing strategy come suggested improvements at four levels: region, city, downtown, and public/private ownership. These divisions have been termed within the design community as "grains" and in

this process of revitalization they are useful in determining recommended improvements at four easily identifiable scales of any given commercial zone (Fig. 9).

At the regional level, strategies might include highway graphics or advertising campaigns, based on the knowledge of those towns, which contribute to the downtowns regional market area. This assumes that the improvements at the city and downtown levels have been reviewed. The fourth level—where the relationship between public and private use is determined—is crucial in assessing the nature of funding opportunities and responsibilities.

- SELLER

- BUYER

SELLER		BUYER
• window displays • signs on buildings • hours of operation • impulse buying orientation	CONVENIENCE SHOPPING	• Arrives Downtown for short duration • Shops for immediate needs • Walks minimal distance-parks at street meter • Knows where things are downtown
• overall appearance • merchandising technique - sophisticated • price range • product lines	COMPARISON SHOPPING	• Arrives Downtown for long stay • Walks more • Parks in long term areas • Influenced by displays, signs and sequence improv.
• special image • non-traditional shopping hours	GENERAL SHOPPING	• Makes special purpose trip for personal or "car" care • Long time frame influence (day and night) • variable duration • food-drink orientation
• none	EMPLOYEE	• sales/service/governmental • influenced by hours of employment for shopping • variable circulation • lunch hour and closing time peaks
• impulse orientation	ON-BUSINESS	• Property owner/non-merchant • service oriented • Sales person • often not prone to buying
• displays	CAPTURED	• visitor • passer-by going north • downtown resident • lost

- USER PATTERN DIAGRAM

Fig. 8.   Understanding the needs of the user will help in reaching urban design conclusions.

31

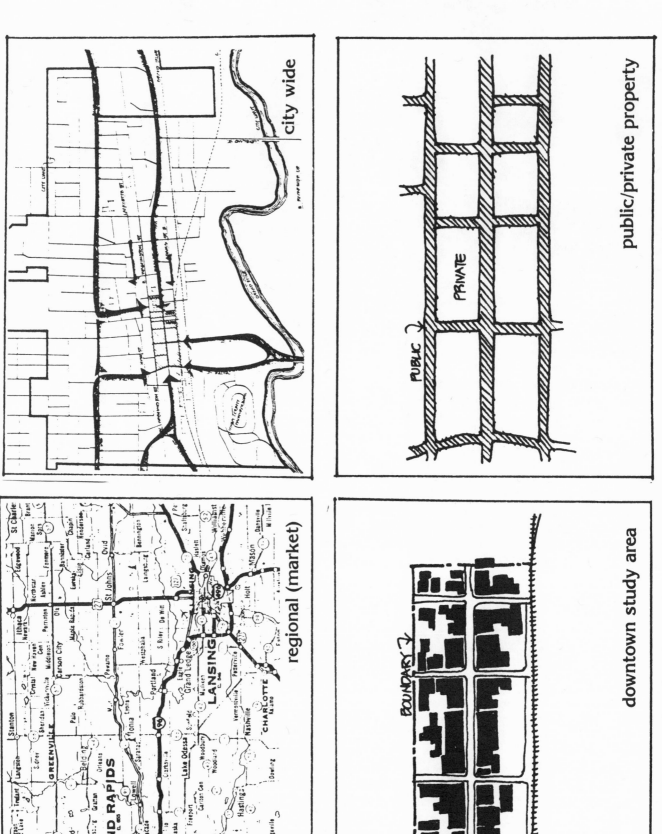

city wide

public/private property

regional (market)

downtown study area

Fig. 9.   The study area begins at the regional level so that specific urban design solutions can be responsive to the "sequence of moving through a community."

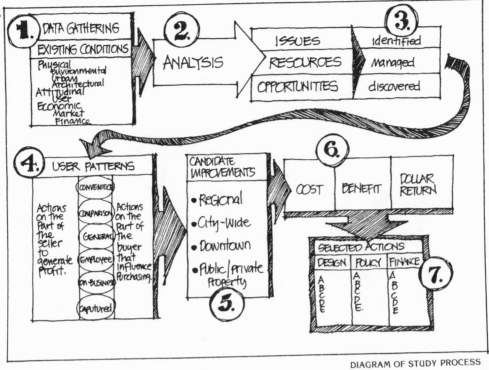

DIAGRAM OF STUDY PROCESS

Fig. 10.   The revitalization process considers all conditions of the study area so that the benefits of any single action are in proportion to the effort.

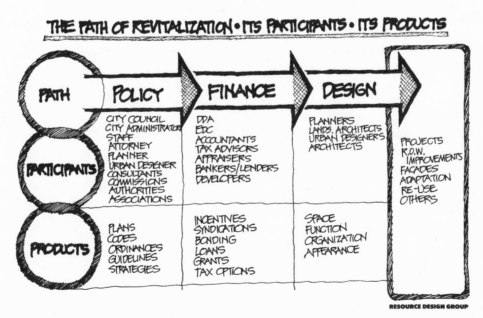

Fig. 11.   The design "product" of revitalization is dependent upon a sequence of involvement by many groups and individuals.

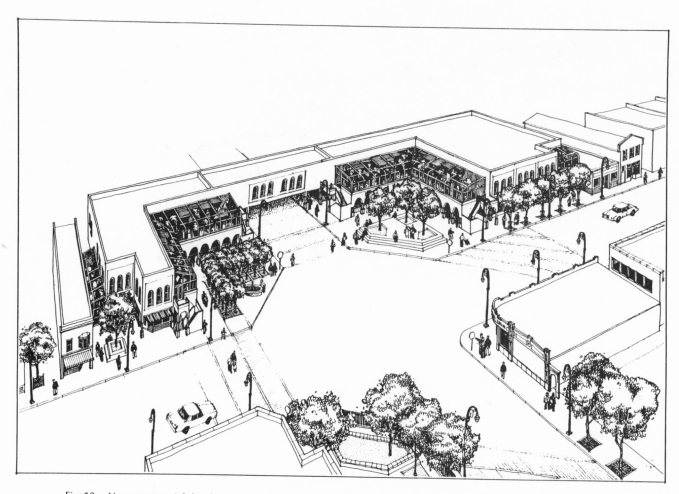

Fig. 12. New commercial development can become part of a revitalized area based on an analysis of market demand.

IMPLEMENTATION STRATEGY

From the four levels of suggested improvements, an implementation strategy is then determined. Improvement, and the related attitudes, are dealt with under three categories: policy, finance, and design. For example, in the area of facade improvements, the pivotal implementation factor for a city would prove to be in the policy area. This might be because improvements are dependent upon the policy decisions an administrative body would make in supporting either loan or grant programs for local property owners.

In recognizing that design is dependent upon those decisions that emerge from policy and finance, it is important to understand the individual participants that become involved along the path of revitalization. The accompanying diagram (Fig. 11) shows the participants and the products that emerge from the categories of policy, finance and design. For example, the design expression of a preservation plan can be an obvious expression of the decision-making process. However, the intangible success of revitalization—changes in property ownership from absentee to owner-occupant or the increased income a business might have through the improvement of the buildings facade, for example—can only be understood in a long-term evalua-

tion as part of the post-project phase. The participants must be similarly recognized so that the sequence allows for appropriate decisions in the correct project sequence. In a healthy economy, the local bank might be in the position to loan revitalization funds; however, their decision will be based on an appraisers recommendation, hopefully one that understands the resource value of existing architecture and the influence of architectural character.

CONCLUSION

The process outlined here is an attempt to further clarify the little-understood concept of urban change. The process recognizes that evolution has taken place in our urban areas and that it has been a gradual process of improving, embellishing, or discarding the "fixtures" of earlier improvements.

The influence of historic preservation today is to put those "fixtures" into focus, through the process of resource analysis, so that the designer's role can be one of directing change amid the influence of needs, attitudes, economics, resources, politics, and the elusive, but attainable, qualities of life.

Historic Preservation as Applied to Urban Parks

Patricia M. O'Donnell

Historic urban parks represent a commonly held, highly visible part of our landscape legacy. Over the past decade, sparked by the environmental movement, the nation's bicentennial, and blatant infringements on historic parklands, active private citizens and local government officials have begun to work for the preservation of historic urban parks. Landscape architects and other professionals working on these parks are faced with concerns for historic integrity as well as with the multiple levels of considerations normally required in park planning. Few guidelines exist for this work.

In defining a historic urban park, let us refer to the criteria for evaluation provided by the Secretary of the Interior for the National Register of Historic Places. The urban park in question would need to possess the quality of significance in the areas of American history, landscape architecture, or culture as well as "integrity of location, design, setting, materials, workmanship, feeling, and association."[1] The site may also represent the work of a recognized master or possess high artistic value, and it should be over fifty years old. The qualities of integrity, that the landscape embody its original intent, and significance, that it hold a unique place in our history, are the essential ingredients for listing on the National Register. In this article, the term *historic urban park* will be used when referring to an urban landscape that meets this criteria and has been or could be listed on the National Register.

This article will explore the beginnings, chronology, and current status of historic urban parks; detail some park preservation projects; and propose an approach to the planning and design process that is especially suited for projects of this type.

BACKGROUND

Nineteenth-century American urban parks were designed for two complementary purposes: to reinstate the natural world in urban surroundings, and to provide recreation for city dwellers. These parks varied in size and proposed use, ranging from public squares and traffic circles to block-size airing grounds, larger neighborhood pleasure grounds, and large city-wide parks. Often a number of parks and grounds were connected by a system of parkways, designed for leisurely travel between them.

Access to truly natural landscapes was severely limited for the majority of urban dwellers during this era. The landscaped park was designed by early professionals to contrast directly with the city, allowing the visitor to shut out the hustle and bustle of town life. Frederick Law Olmsted and his contemporaries thought that the landscape park would soothe the spirits of park goers and refine their coarse lives.

A park, according to Olmsted, could only be called so if there was enough ground, formed in such a way as to create a totally natural experience; it had to be 150 acres or more to achieve the proper effect. In the preceding paragraph the range of different sizes and types of open spaces included in a nineteenth-century park system was noted. Today we call all open lands developed for recreation "parks." The distinction between Olmstedian terminology and contemporary usage is an important one. It lies at the root of a common misinterpretation that the only purpose of the nineteenth-century urban parks was to embody the pastoral, soothing landscape and that the parks were meant to be used in relatively passive ways. Many of the larger parks, by Olmsted and others, did match this purpose, but the smaller ones—not called parks but rather neighborhood pleasure grounds, airing grounds, and playgrounds by Olmsted—were designed for active recreational pursuits. The plans of such parks included baseball fields, running tracks, exercise equipment, playground equipment, and other sports facilities. The larger landscape park was meant to provide the experience of nature for all city residents, while the smaller grounds provided for the recreational pursuits of nearby residents. In the best possible situation, enough parks, both large and small, were set aside so that the full range of uses was accommodated without attempting to fit everything on one piece of ground.[3]

RECREATION, THEN AND NOW

Urban parks developed in the late-nineteenth and early-twentieth centuries make up a great portion of close-to-home recreation acreage available to city dwellers today. Many of these landscapes have some historic significance. When the parklands were first developed, desirable frontage properties were often built up with upper class residences. While real estate adjacent to some city parks has maintained high values, it has experienced significant decline in others. Theories of changing urban cores demonstrate a gradual shifting from upper to lower class inhabitants in central city areas. The combination of a changing set of nearby users and changing recreational pursuits has compounded the potential conflicts between historic integrity and contemporary use.

Some people consider historic parks worthy of preservation simply as works of art. However, while these parks are often indeed exemplary works of landscape art, their recreational value is their most important quality. The quality of urban historic parks that has endeared then to the public and has contributed most heavily to their continued existence is their use for the recreation of many people in the ways that they choose. The vast majority of people who use them have no knowledge of the origins, artistic value, or historic significance of these parks. A brief examination of the meaning of recreation in urban historic parks, past and present, is therefore necessary for any discussion of urban parks preservation.

Have recreational styles changed radically from those practiced in the nineteenth century? In an effort to respond to this question, the author investigated the recreational use of parks in three ways. First, design documents and annual reports from 1870 to 1915 of the Buffalo Parks Commission (Fig. 1) and selected reports from Chicago, St. Louis, New York, Brooklyn, Boston, New Jersey, and Seattle parks were studied. Second, historic and contemporary plans, drawings, photographs, and aerial views of a number of parks were reviewed. Third, existing use and conditions in individual parks in Chicago, Seattle, Buffalo, St. Louis, New York, Brooklyn, and Boston were analyzed by walking through the parks themselves. A good working knowledge of the chronological development of recreational styles in historic urban parks has been acquired through this investigation.

Olmsted's writings detail a separation of park use into two major classes: exertive and receptive. *Exertive* recreation was meant to stimulate any part of the body needing it. This class of recreation included athletic sports, such as baseball and swimming, and games requiring mental skill, such as chess. With the exception of the mental-skill games, exertive recreation, as defined by Olmsted, is the same as *active* recreation today. The second class of recreation was the *receptive,* which included activities not involving physical strain. This group encompassed recreational pursuits that are currently classified as *passive* recreation. The receptive class was further divided by Olmsted into gregarious and neighborly recreation. The *gregarious* type was characterized by settings where large numbers of relative strangers could walk, talk, meet, sit, or promenade in a pleasant, light-hearted manner

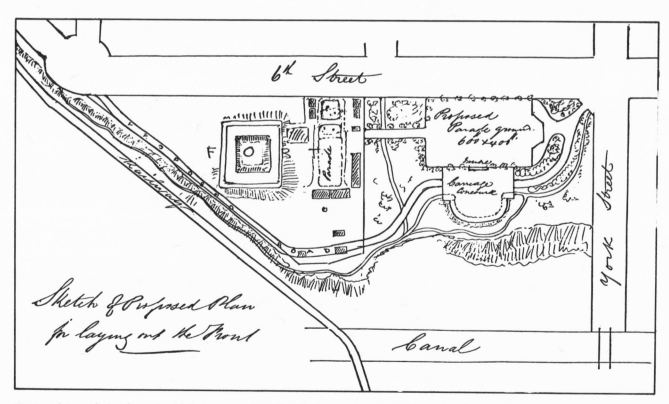

Fig. 1. This rough sketch was found during a search for Buffalo System plans in the Olmsted Archives in Brookline. Although unsigned, the writing is similar to that of Calvert Vaux, and it was probably drawn in 1869 or 1870. The drawing serves to authenticate the origins of the plan for the Front, one of Buffalo's first parks.

(Fig. 2). A good example of a setting for gregarious recreation is the Bethesda Fountain and Mall in New York's Central Park. The *neighborly* type was characterized by a landscaped ground with picnicking and refreshment facilities, where small groups of families, friends, or lovers could pass the time privately in fresh air and relaxing scenery.[4]

Today when we inquire about the recreational preferences of people, we often consider only those types that would be called active. Two park-user surveys conducted by the author afforded the opportunity to respond to both passive and active pursuits in parks. The resulting responses showed as great a tendency toward the passive recreational pursuits as toward the active ones. In one study of frequency of use, the greatest positive response was given to passive behaviors. The activities chosen as most frequent were, in order of preference, walking in the park, watching others play, "hanging out" with friends, and relaxing on the grass (Fig. 3). The park as a green, open space and a landscape of other people as well as nature were the most important ingredients. In addition, the author investigated the active/passive use dichotomy, hypothesizing that active users would make up one portion of park users and passive users another. The opposite was found to be true: in general, those responding to the survey used the parks in both ways.

As a result of both historical and contemporary research, it is the author's contention that the recreational pursuits of nineteenth-century park users were not radically different from those of today. The Olmstedian vocabulary translates fairly well into contemporary terminology, and the theory of providing a number of grounds, varying in size and use, is equally valid.

One of the most notable differences between park users then and now may be found in the quantity of users. While use was great in past decades, the number of people using urban parks today seems even greater. The areas surrounding many historic urban parks are more densely populated than ever before, and decreased mobility, due to skyrocketing transportation costs, has created greater demand for close-to-home recreational opportunities. Problems of poor maintenance, vandalism, and fear of crime, however, do act as deterrents to use in some urban areas.

An increase in the diversity of recreational pursuits accounts for another major difference between past and present park use. While the same general classifications of recreation seem to apply, the number of different active pursuits has increased. Any municipal parks commissioner would be able to recite a long list of organized groups of sports enthusiasts lobbying for more or better facilities. The problem is not only that the requests by joggers, golfers,

Fig. 2. Gregarious recreation is shown in this sketch from an illustrated report on a proposed park for Buffalo writted by Fredrick Law Olmsted in 1888. (Reproduced courtesy of the Buffalo and Erie County Historical Society)

Fig. 3. An example of passive recreation in urban historic parks, this recent view of Front Park in Buffalo, New York, shows a pleasant shady path enjoyed by pedestrians. (Photograph by the author)

canoeists, swimmers, tennis players, baseball, football, and soccer teams, etc., are equally valid, but that each group wants each support facility in their nearby park. The development of numerous facilities in historic parks over the years has often seriously compromised the integrity of the original design. When planning for parks today, difficult decisions about what should go where and why it should go there must be made.

THE FORCES OF CHANGE

Urban historic parks have been altered in a number of ways over the decades. An exploration of the dynamics of change may aid the landscape architect in understanding the conditions found in parks today. By recognizing the forces that have contributed to current conditions, more appropriate strategies for the preservation and enhancement of historic urban parks can be found.

In numerous cities, legislation at one time allowed for the placement of public buildings on park lands, especially if they were to house cultural institutions and/or were privately endowed. Parks often contain art, science, or historical museums, public libraries, hospitals, senior citizens centers, community build-

ings, bath houses, concession stands, maintenance sheds, and other structures. The elaborate fairs and expositions held around the turn of the century left a legacy of neoclassic buildings in parks. The Museum of Science and Industry in Chicago's Jackson Park is a remnant of the World's Columbian Exposition of 1893.

In addition, parks were thought to be fitting places for monuments. Those who died in wars, great public figures, ethnic heroes, or prominent local citizens were often memorialized in stone or metal in a historic park. A proliferation of monuments within the park landscape created the impression of a cemetery ground (Fig. 4), an impression that the original designers were attempting to counteract.[6]

In many cases, historic parklands have changed through the unplanned accretion of recreational facilities and support structures. A greater emphasis on health and physical development brought pools, bath houses, and playgrounds into city parks during the recreational-reform movements of the early 1900s. Lawn tennis, lawn bowling, and golf were popular around 1915 and public demand saw these sports accommodated on the landscape of public parks. To these, add all the possible facilities for horseshoes, shuffleboard, flycasting, badminton, croquet, soccer, handball, tennis, ice-skating, tobogganing, basketball, baseball, jogging, and other sports that have been—or

Fig. 4. Monuments placed haphazardly in the park landscape create a cemetarylike effect. This one, in Cazenovia Park, is marred by graffiti. (Photography by the author)

are now—popular, and you will find that the nineteenth-century rural retreats, neighborhood pleasure grounds, and small nearby parks have been overlaid with numerous recreational facilities (Figs. 5 and 6). As an example, Detroit's Belle Isle has suffered from the philosophy of ''more is better'' as city officials have attempted to provide for the gamut of recreational needs by squeezing them all into one park.

Many historic parks are more than a century old, and park plantings, past their prime, are seriously declining. Shrubs, trees and flowering plants are found in less quantity and quality than they were in earlier days. Fear of crime resulted in the removal of numerous shrubs and low-branching trees during the 1960s. The scourges of Dutch elm disease and American chestnut blight drastically altered the image of parks and parkways in many areas. When trees have been replanted, varieties have not always been carefully chosen, or placement carefully made.

The most recent and devastating intrusions on parklands were wrought in the 1950s and 1960s, when inner-city expressways plowed through the land. In the original planning of park systems, right-of-ways, which were. often 100 to 200 feet wide, were secured for parkway routes. In thoroughfare developments, street-widening projects, or cloverleaf placements, park-lands have been traditionally easier to steal than property in private ownership. As more visitors came by car to parks, portions of parkland were paved for parking lots. In all, a vast number of green acres have been lost under seas of asphalt (Fig. 7).

The passage of time has taken a toll on subsurface and overland drainage systems, original stonework in bridges and retaining walls, and circulation routes for walking, bicycling, or riding. Normal deterioration and haphazard changes have compromised the function of these elements. Continually restricted budgets have led to decreased availability of equipment, materials, and work forces. The resulting deferments of needed repairs and improvements have caused a slow deterioration of all aspects of historic urban parks. This slow deterioration is the beginning of a downward spiral. Desirable park users come less often to parks in ill-repair. Undesirables migrate to parks that few people frequent. Frustration with unfunctioning equipment leads to abuse. Signs of vandalism and the presence of undesirables decreased use even further. Boston's Franklin Park in the 1960s, feared by neighborhood residents and providing a haven for drug dealers and criminals, is a good example of this type of deterioration and the resulting social problems.

In other parks, faults in the original designs have

Fig. 5. This photograph and the one in Fig. 6 give two views from opposite sides of the same area, taken 80 years apart, and illustrate the changing nature of historic urban parks. Shown here are an aquatic plant basin and a large wading pool in Humbolt Park around 1899. (Photography courtesy of the Buffalo and Erie County Historical Society)

Fig. 6. Humbolt park in 1979. Here the basin has been replaced by an ice-skating rink, and a bathhouse blocks the views to the same wading pool. (Photograph by the author)

Fig. 7.   Accommodating the need for faster travel, Humbolt Parkway, graced with six rows of maples, was replaced with this depressed expressway. The only remnant of the parkway is this terminal piece at the entry to the park. (Photograph by the author)

also led to marked alterations. While members of the Olmsted firm were more than competent, they were not infallible and portions of some designs have proven to be disfunctional over time. Such was the case with Cazenovia Park in Buffalo. In the 1896 plan of Olmsted, Olmsted and Eliot, Cazenovia Creek was widened to form an irregular lake with three islands. Spring flooding and the resulting silt and gravel deposits filled in portions of the lake within a few years of the initial excavation. After continued, unsuccessful efforts to reestablish the desired water feature, the plan was abandoned.[7]

All of the changes in park landscapes, caused by the various forces described above, should not be categorically negated. In some cases, adaptation has resulted in the conservation of a landscape. For example, the development of a public golf course surrounding South Park Lake in Buffalo has preserved, in an uncluttered shape, both the original lake edge and the adjacent meadows and plantings. Competition from flying golf balls, however, may discourage casual strolling.

Some historic urban parks have escaped radical change. A few have been conserved through benign neglect. Investments required to carry out major changes were not secured or a status quo policy was followed, carrying the historic parks unscathed through the decades.

In rare cases, historic landscapes have been well-maintained and carefully altered. Seward Park in Seat-tle is such a case. Designed by the Olmsted brothers in 1912, the 192-acre peninsula provides a range of water-related recreation and a well-preserved and enhanced natural landscape. Tower Grove Park in St. Louis is another such case. Planned and endowed by Henry Shaw in 1872, it has been well-treated and carefully altered. The recent integration of an exercise course and plans for a new senior citizens center, incorporating a Victorian period styling to match other park structures, show the same level of sensitivity operating today.

PLANNING FOR PRESERVATION

When undertaking work on an historic urban park or park system, the best initial step is a comprehensive survey. Planning for the preservation of parks operates most effectively in five areas: identification, evaluation, protection, preservation, and enhancement.[8] A comprehensive survey is primarily concerned with the first two and may suggest strategies for the third.

Comprehensive Survey

To carry out the identification and evaluation processes, original documents that detail the design and development of the historic park in question need to be obtained. An archival search of the local park department, public libraries, historical societies, and records of the design professionals involved should be conducted. This search would secure both graphic and verbal records of the park-development history. A further investigation of chronological records and current conditions would allow an assessment of the integrity of the existing landscape. These initial steps form the basis of all further work toward the protection, preservation, and enhancement of the historic urban park.

During the summer of 1979, the author conducted a comprehensive survey of the Buffalo Olmsted Park System.[9] The survey involved the steps noted above and resulted in a written and graphic report. This report contains a catalog of the professional plans developed for the parks and parkways, recent aerial views of the grounds, and a photographic record, in color and black-and-white, of the system as it existed in 1979. The written portion of the report details the development of the parks system, traces the chronology of change, and evaluates the integrity and significance of the parks and parkways. Appendices of valuable information uncovered in the survey process complete the document. The original purpose of the work was to gather widely spread, critical information to form the basis of a thematic nomination of Buffalo's Olmsted Park System to the National Register. In addition, the report is a useful resource for future consideration of any part of Buffalo's system. The nomination written by Frank Kowsky was accepted in April of 1982.

Spurred by threats of drastic alteration to Branch Brook Park, designed by John C. Olmsted and currently encompassing 360 acres, in Essex County, New Jersey, members of the Newark Cherry Blossom Festival, Inc. researched the relevant documents and prepared a National Register nomination. Listing on the National Register provides a measure of protection for historic landscapes in that plans for alterations funded with federal monies must be reviewed and approved. The nomination, submitted in May of 1979, was approved in June of 1980 and Branch Brook Park is now protected as well as eligible for preservation funds as a result.[10]

In the spring of 1981, the City of Chicago Department of Planning issued a request for proposals to conduct a historic park features study. The study was to include a survey of landscape, architecture, and sculpture within 65 historic Chicago parks. This extensive survey is currently underway.

The work of identification and evaluation is continuing elsewhere. Local chapters of the American Society of Landscape Architects (ASLA) have promoted surveys of historic landscapes with some success. In 1981, the National Association for Olmsted Parks (NAOP) initiated a national inventory and assessment of Olmsted legacy parks. This work, only partially funded at present, is moving forward in Massachusetts, New York, and Illinois. The resulting documents, when completed, should provide a rich base of information. It will function as an important tool in the processes of protection, preservation, and enhancement of these historic urban parks.[11]

If one considers the limited progress to date, it becomes obvious that there is a massive amount of identification, evaluation, and protection work that could be pursued by interested landscape architects for some years into the future.

Preservation and Enhancement

A number of philosophical approaches are possible when addressing the preservation and enhancement of urban historic parks. The most conservative viewpoint would favor complete restoration. Following this philosophy, a thoroughly researched, painstakingly detailed, and precisely dated restoration of the historic park could be attempted. The extension of this approach would create a park museum, fixed in time and protected from change. While some people may advocated this conservative approach, carrying it out would be very expensive. Practically speaking, it may be an impossible treatment for a living landscape.

At the opposite end of the spectrum, a wholly contemporary perspective might embody the notion of "from today, onward." Following this philosophy, the historic value of the landscape is disregarded and is replaced with a statement of goals and objectives that addresses current and future recreational needs. If competently handled, this approach can create an appropriate landscape for urban recreation, but a valuable historic resources is lost in the process. Funding for this approach has not been readily available, and, as a result, the complete recycling of a park has rarely occurred.

Generally, preservation work carried out in historic urban parks will fall into three categories: reconstruction, rehabilitation, or adaptive use.[12] By virtue of the fact that parks are public landscapes, and that responding to the needs of today's park users may include the integration of elements not present in the original plan, the strict restoration of a park landscape as is appeared near the time of development is not recommended. The best approach to the preservation of historic urban parks is one that strikes a sensitive balance between the desire for historic integrity and the necessity of adaptation for full contemporary and future use.

There are a number of interesting, recent projects in historic urban parks that reflect the range of approaches taken today. In Chicago's Jackson Park, a Japanese Garden and Pavilion has been reconstructed in an area of the Wooded Isle that contained a similar garden and pavilion during and after the 1893 exposition. Improvements to the basketball courts, wading pool, and picnic area have been made in Martin Luther King Jr. Park (formerly Humbolt Park) in Buffalo (Fig. 8) as the initial steps toward implementng an updated master plan for the park. The Dairy and an adjacent open pavilion, delightful Victorian Gothic structures, were fully restored in New York's Central Park, and a landscape rehabilitation for the surrounding area is now proceeding. In other areas of Central Park, a study has been conducted on the potentials for restoring the Ramble, and a team of professionals is currently at work on plans for the Mall and Bethesda Fountain. In the South, Cherokee Park was reconstructed after a devastating tornado destroyed much of the park, and the entire Olmsted Legacy of Louisville is being documented in a local media project. An intensive research and planning process for Long Meadow in Brooklyn's Prospect Park holds hope for the eventual rehabilitation of this important park feature (Fig. 9).

Fast-moving traffic has been rerouted out of Buffalo's Delaware Park through the completion of an internal loop road and the elimination of an expressway on-ramp. Small stone bridges have been constructed in the Back Bay Fens of Boston, improving pedestrian access to portions of this river park. Extensive improvements to a deteriorated trail system and blockage of internal automobile access have enhanced pedestrian use at Boston's Franklin Park. The separation of bicycle, roller skating, jogging, and pedestrian traffic around Seattle's Green Lake has improved safety for all the many users of this pleasant circuit path.

PRESERVATION PROJECTS

During the 1970s and the early 1980s, the activism of dedicated citizens brought the plight of their beloved historic parks to the attention of often-complacent local officials. This exposure, coupled with the availability of sources of funding, resulted in increased government support for park-related projects.

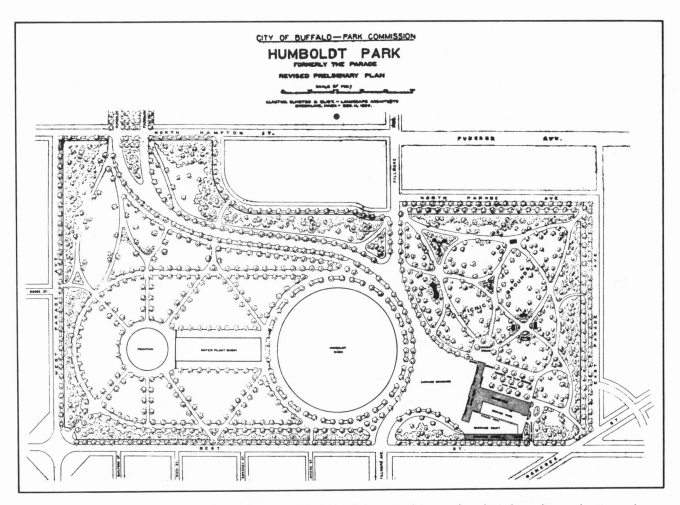

Fig. 8. The preliminary plan for Humbolt park by Olmsted, Olmsted and Eliot, 1896, features a large basin for wading, toy boating, and promenading around, a large picnic grove, a playground, and a concert grove. A plan of this type, with a number of facilities, was suitable for a neighborhood pleasure ground, providing recreational opportunities for nearby residents. (Reproduced courtesy of FLONHS, National Park Service)

Fig. 9. This early view of the Long Meadow in Prospect Park shows the pastoral quality of this landscape. Planning is currently underway for the restoration of this park feature. (Reproduced courtesy of the Library, Archives of the University of Illinois at Urbana-Champaign)

Various projects in historic urban parks were undertaken as a result. In this section, recent preservation work in several parts of the country will be discussed.

These projects vary in scale, expenditure, and quality of implementation. Many of them began with the development of a comprehensive plan that provided a philosophical basis for specific solutions. Such a plan is sometimes a disappointment to community members and public officials who expect detailed solutions to pressing problems. A comprehensive plan, however, is meant to provide a framework for the hundreds of individual decisions that are made throughout a lengthy implementation process. In order to gain a better perspective on recent work, activity in several historic urban parks will be discussed in greater detail.

Delaware Park, Buffalo, New York

Delaware Park, designed by Olmsted, Vaux and Co., is the largest park in the Buffalo system. Over a decade of continuous effort has been expended on behalf of the park by committed citizens who have served as a catalyst for the efforts of a team of design professionals and for the support of public officials. In July of 1973, after several years of activity, the Delaware Park Comprehensive Development Plan was completed and submitted to the Delaware Park Steering Committee, a group of private citizens, design profes-

sionals, and representatives of pertinent city departments. The plan set forth 59 separate proposals in a six-year action plan, stressing development of the park into a varied, relevant, recreational facility. Relatively little historical research was conducted, and, while reconstruction of some parts of the park was proposed, the emphasis was placed on development. In the eight years since the submittal of the plan, a good portion of the proposals have been implemented. They include installation of two neighborhood tot-lots; extension of the park into the Black Rock Community; rehabilitation of the rose garden and pergola; development of a new soccer field; improvement of the basketball and tennis courts and baseball fields; and removal of dead and damaged trees. Less tangible, but equally significant improvements have been made in the communication between public officials and concerned citizens, as well as in the coordination of large events and the management of the park in general.

The polluted condition of the park lake was one of the most important problems to solve. The final solution rerouted the flow of Scajaquada Creek and city storm sewer runoff underground, separating them from the lake. The lake, reduced in size, is now fed by nearby springs. The engineering portion of the work has been completed, but, unfortunately, the services of a landscape architect and an ecologist to oversee the treatment of the lake edge and to restore a balanced ecology to the water feature were eliminated from the budget. The result is a barren, sharply sloped, streamlined lake edge that is far from Olmstedian in character.[13]

Cherokee Park, Louisville, Kentucky

The redevelopment of Cherokee Park presented a unique set of circumstances and opportunities. In 1974, a devastating tornado passed through the center of the park, splintering or destroying over 2,000 mature trees in the 300-acre park. Extensive historical research of park documents in the Brookline Archives was conducted by Olmsted Associates. The firm of Johnson, Johnson and Roy utilized this research in the development of a comprehensive reconstruction and management plan. The Federal Disaster Assistance Funds available for the work were qualified by the stipulation that they could be used only to return the site to its former condition. The intent and purpose of the plan was, therefore, to restore the planting and character of the park to the Olmsted design as it had evolved into a community recreation resource. The landscape architects developed guiding principles for their efforts, based on the original philosophy and spirit of the park design; however, no specific planting plan was prepared for the reconstruction process. Field studies showed a variety of topographical, soil, and drainage conditions; field locating of 2,500 trees and 4,600 shrubs was conducted to best match the varied conditions. The initial planting, completed in 1976, was carried out using small materials. Strong management recommendations were made for their care and maintenance and for further supplemental plantings in the future. An interesting result of this work is that the citizens of Louisville today see the park in a condition similar to its appearance after original construction. A generation of proper care will be required, however, for the park to resemble the pretornado state.[14]

Back Bay Fens, Boston, Massachusetts

Frederick Law Olmsted, Sr. served as landscape architect on the improvements of the Back Bay of Boston, commonly known as the Fens, in 1879. The Fens was designed as a continuous, twisting river park around the tidal pools of the Muddy River. The watercourse in the Fens stagnated after the installation of a dam in 1910. Landscape architect Arther Shurcliff redesigned and adapted the park to these new conditions in the 1920s. During the next five decades, motor vehicle pressure resulted in major alterations, cutting the Fens off from the Charles River Basin, destroying some original stone bridges by H. H. Richardson, and filling a portion of the watercourse for a parking lot. The Fenway Project Area Committee (FenPAC),

formed by interested citizens in 1973, became the organized voice for improvement of the Fens. In 1976, after three years of pressure on the city, Carol R. Johnson and Associates was retained to produce a master plan for the battered Fens. The plan was meant to address historical, ecological, and sociological issues. When completed, it had explored such questions as: Which improvements would be most consistent with Olmsted's concepts, or, if inconsistent, still worthwhile? Which projects would be most important to arrest further deterioration? and to what design and material standards should the city adhere, from an historic preservation standpoint? Accurate historical research formed a sound preservation basis for the plan and the original intentions of the designer were referred to throughout the document.

The major recomendation of the master plan were: remove some existing streets and return the right-of-ways to parkland; remove the parking lot built on filled watercourse land and reexcavate the Muddy River in this area; rehabilitate and strengthen the plantings and control the invasive aquatic plants; replace derelict footbridges and improve pedestrian circulation in general; and improve the athletic fields and the Mother's Rest playground. It is interesting to note that the victory gardens, established during the war and still in use, were retained. These gardens were seen to be a meaningful and useful addition to the park that was thought worthy of retention.

The master plan did not strongly address the critical issue of water quality in the park. The text referred to a 1973 water-quality study, but failed to make a forceful case for improvement of this important element of the Fens.

Progress has been made towards implementing the plan. To date, decorative gates have been restored, tree and water's-edge rehabilitation has moved forward, and two new stone footbridges, designed to be in character with the original Richardson bridges, have been constructed. FenPAC has worked with the landscape architect on the implementation of the plan and continues to be a leading voice for the complete restoration of the Back Bay Fens.[15]

Franklin Park, Boston, Massachusetts

Franklin Park is the last and largest park in the Boston Park System. Designed in 1885 by Frederick L. Olmsted, Sr., the 500-acre retreat was actually composed of two distinct parks. The front portion, along a formal promenade, The Greeting, was to remain open day and night and contained such features as the Little Folks Fair, the Music Court, the Deer Park, Sargent's Field, and the Pergola. The second, Country Park, was to be closed at night and featured the Wilderness, Scarboro Hill, Canterbury Hill, School Master Hill, and

Nazingdale, an open meadow. Today, Franklin Park is known as one of Olmsted's greatest large urban parks.

By 1968, the park had deteriorated badly, which prompted Miss Emma Lewis, a concerned neighbor, to initiate the Franklin Park Advisory Council. The Council lobbied with city departments for a substantial clean-up, as well as for a master planning effort. The Council became the Franklin Park Coalition in 1975, broadening its base of support. Finally, under pressure, the City of Boston began a physical and social clean-up, retaining V. Michael Weinmayr Associates in 1978 to prepare a revised general plan for Franklin Park. The landscape architects wrote their plan on a firm historically and chronologically researched base, reactivating Olmsted's dual park plan. When the initial draft of the plan was presented, it met with a great deal of criticism from the Franklin Park Coalition. The plan, based on a premise of underuse, sought to increase the popularity of the park through substantial physical improvements. The Country Park landscape was to retain its scenic beauty and, with the development of an extensive trail system, become more accessible to park visitors. Access to the park was also to be improved, with the construction of three pedestrian overpasses. Other elements of the plan included the decreasing of the golf course to nine-hole size; the initiation of selected new plantings; the restoration of several overlooks, with one as an outdoor theatre; the adaptive reuse of the bear dens; the blocking of vehicular access to the interior; and the screening of structures with appropriate plantings. The Franklin Park Coalition assisted the landscape architects in refining the draft document and has since continued to work with them on the first phases of construction. The reconstruction of Scarboro Hill, the rehabilitation of the trail and drainage systems, and the placement of granite blocks for vehicular control have all progressed. Although the Franklin Park Coalition is not entirely satisfied with the final plan, it is working toward its implementation.[16]

Ravenna/Cowen Parks, Seattle, Washington

The city of Seattle has a system of Olmsted legacy parks and parkways that encompasses 2,000 acres. The Olmsted Brothers designed the system, beginning in 1903, to take advantage of the existing parks and the wealth of distinctive topographical features, including hills, shorelines, and mountain views. Two of these parks, Ravenna and Cowen, have a history that chronicles dual pressures: preservation of the natural environment and provision of various recreational opportunities.

Two contiguous parcels of a forested ravine, purchased by private citizens late in the nineteenth century in order to preserve their wilderness quality, were included in the Olmsted Brother's 1903 proposal for a comprehensive park system. By 1911 the Seattle Parks Department had acquired this sixty-two acre urban forest, creating Ravenna and Cowen Parks. However, the original stand of trees was cut, amid public outcry, to provide timber for rebuilding the city after a massive fire; and as time went on, some areas of the steeply sloping ravine were filled and leveled to create playing fields, tennis courts, wading pools, and picnic grounds.

By the 1970s, after several decades of only routine maintenance, serious problems had emerged. The ravine, now covered with second-growth forest and fern understory, was plagued by erosion, caused by informal trails on unstable soils. Playfield, picnic area, and playground turf required improved drainage, and reseeding. The comfort station and picnic shelter required rehabilitation and the path system and stream course needed reworking.

Unlike the citizen-based activism seen in other cities, in Seattle the officials of the Department of Parks and Recreation were the activists for the renewal of these public landscapes. In 1979 the department, aided by Ravenna community participation, issued a design program for the improvement of Ravenna/Cowen Parks. This program sought to extract the best from both the preservation and the recreation approaches to improving the parks.

In response to the design program, Ed Macleod and Associates were hired to develop a comprehensive improvement plan. The landscape architect in charge of the project carried out historical research, behavioral observations, and communication with members of the Ravenna-Bryant Community Association during the planning process. The summer of 1981 saw much of the proposed work completed. Of special note is the careful treatment of an historic sulfur-spring source on the ravine floor and the revegetation of eroded slopes.[17]

Colman Park, Seattle, Washington

When the Olmsted Brothers laid out Lake Washington Boulevard, one portion of the lakeshore could not be secured for that use. Two small parks, Colman and Frink, were designed to route the traffic back to the lakeshore from the displaced boulevard. Encompassing 27 acres, Colman Park was designed as a circulation corridor providing pedestrian paths, stairs, and underpasses to carry those on foot from nearby residential areas to the lakeshore and a winding, scenic roadway for carriage and equestrian traffic. At three points along the twisting boulevard, ornamental bridges allowed the passage of vehicles above and of pedestrians below.

By 1978 the once well-used pedestrian circulation

system had become derelict and impassable. In August of that year, the Department of Parks and Recreation issued a program for the improvement of the Colman Park walkways. The objectives of the improvements were to restore the original pedestrian circulation system; to rehabilitate over-used and poorly drained areas; to eliminate unauthorized vehicular access and parking; and, in general, to regain the intended character of the park.

No research or consultation with private groups contributed to the project, although local residents communicated their desire for park improvements through city officials. A landscape architecture firm produced the planning documents; an engineering firm was contracted to produce construction documents and to oversee the construction phase. During the summer of 1981, the work of regrading, draining, and surfacing the pedestrian system was completed. Greater funding will be required in the future to restore missing portions of the ornamental stone bridges and to complete the park rehabilitation.[18]

Bryant Park, New York, New York

Bryant Park is located in midtown Manhattan, adjacent to the Fifth Avenue branch of New York Public Library. Set aside as a breathing space when the library was built, this block-size park was designed by Gilmore Clark in the early 1930s. According to Clark's plan—formal in tone—the park rose in elevation from the street level, with granite walls, benches, balustrades, rows of trees, and a low hedge surrounding a fountain and central lawn.

The reputation and condition of Bryant Park had declined substantially by 1980. Poor visibility into the park, due to walls bordering the street and the overgrown hedges, had turned the park into a perfect environment for undesirable and illegal activities. Supported by the Public Library, private foundations, and business concerns, the Bryant Park Restoration Corporation (BPRC) was formed and began to work toward improving conditions in the park. Seeking specific solutions to the problems of under-use by the general public and misuse by drug peddlers and derelicts, BPRC retained Project for Public Spaces (PPS) to study the conditions and detail a park rehabilitation program. PPS sought to increase Bryant Park's attractiveness to office workers, library users, shoppers, students, and residents of and visitors to the city; additionally, they wished to ensure that these potential users would feel secure and comfortable when in the park. The long-range goal of the project was to supplement the city's resources for maintaining the park with the development and funding of a capital improvement and maintenance program. Although Bryant Park is considered to be an urban historic park, no historical research was conducted. However, a comprehensive program of behavioral research was undertaken by PPS to gain an understanding of the drug-dealing patterns, the recreational use, and the cultural activity use of the park. The perceptions of nonusers from nearby office buildings as well as of users found in the park were recorded in a survey to provide a balanced perspective.

The recommendations of PPS were directed toward redressing the balance of users in the park and included the widening of entryways and the removal of hedges to increase visibility; the relocation and improvement of vending and concession operations to attract users; the restructuring of the circulation pattern to eliminate dead-end corners; and the staging of more events in selected areas to encourage greater use. The PPS report ignited a great deal of controversy which is still unresolved. Thus far, management strategies for the park have been improved and several vending and concession operations have been relocated and augmented. Structural alterations of entry stairs and balustrade are awaiting capital funds.[19]

PROJECT COMPARISON AND A PROPOSED METHODOLOGY

Each of the projects discussed were similar in their main objective: the enhancement of an urban historic park. The groups involved, the planning processes, and the recommendations that characterized these projects did overlap, to some degree, but were often unique. Since the deteriorated condition of urban parks is being explored and counteracted for the first time in roughly a century, and since such action may not take place again for decades into the future, the manner in which this work is conducted and the recommendations it yields should be the soundest possible.

In the optimal situation, a consistent group of elements would be combined for an historic urban park preservation process. All of these critical elements were seen in one or more of the projects discussed, but were not found as a whole in any one of them. Inadequate attention to any of these elements may compromise the quality of the project. The ten consistent elements of an optimal process are:

1. commitment and involvement of a private group or groups
2. commitment and involvement of local government officials and staff members
3. awareness and input of the general public
4. carrying out of thorough historical research that details the original design and chronological development of the park

5. complete analysis of existing physical conditions
6. documentation of current use, perceptions, and preferences through behavioral research
7. synthesis of historic and contemporary research findings to form a philosophical basis for the design approach and subsequent recommendations
8. proposal of design recommendations that balance historic integrity and contemporary use
9. proposal of management strategies that will retain the public landscape in good condition, while recognizing limitations of manpower and materials
10. implementation of the recommendations through the continuing commitment of design professionals, private groups, and local government

In order to develop a clearer picture of current practice, the seven projects discussed have been compared for each of these ten elements Fig. 10. The scores given range from one to five and signify levels of performance in each category, with one being the worst and five the best possible score. These scores are judgments made by the author on the basis of information available to her. They are intended to point out areas where gaps are apparent in the process of historic urban park preservation and not to offend

those involved in such work. All of the scores are assigned with regard to the author's opinion of an optimal historic urban park preservation process. This optimal process is one that provides for a better-than-adequate performance in each of the ten elements included and, therefore, produces a plan for the park that balances historic integrity and contemporary use. In terms of a preservation treatment, the result of this optimal process could be termed a landscape adaptive use.

Turning to an analysis of the project comparison chart, a glance at the total row shows where performance is adequate or better and where it is definitely lacking. Private group and local government commitment columns both yielded high scores. Local government involvement has often been the result of pressure by the exemplary commitment of a private group. The case of Seattle, where government has taken the lead, is a rare situation.

The level of public involvement in most of the projects was low. One dilemma for the professional working on an historic urban park project is defining the client relationship; the paying client is generally not the using client. In this type of project, there are actually four clients groups that need to be considered. The first is the local government officials, who are often the paying client. The second consists of local-

Key:
1—None
2—Minimal
3—Adequate
4—Better than Adequate
5—Exemplary

Delaware Park Buffalo, New York	5	3	3	2	3	2	2	2	2	3
Cherokee Park Louisville, Kentucky	3	4	2	5	4	1	1*	3	4	4
Back Bay Fens Boston, Massachusetts	5	3	1	4	4	1	4	4	3	3
Franklin Park Boston, Massachusetts	5	3	1	4	4	2	3	3	3	3
Ravenna/Cowen Parks Seattle, Washington	3	5	1	4	4	3	3	3	3	4
Colman Park Seattle, Washington	1	5	2	2	3	1	2	3	2	3
Bryant Park New York, New York	5	3	3	1	4	5	2	2	4	2
TOTALS	27	26	13	22	26	15	16	20	21	22

* Not applicable in this project because of legal mandate to replace pretornado landscape

Fig. 10. Historic Urban Park Project Comparison Chart.

government employees, who maintain the parks and who bring a view of the day-to-day operations. The third group is the identified private organization that actively pursues the betterment of the park; and the fourth is the general public. This last client is comprised of unidentified park users and of potential users who do not currently utilize the park but may when improvements are made. The first three of these client groups are often—and should consistently be—consulted during the planning process. The general public can, in part, be reached through behavioral research. In addition, awareness and input can be obtained through media summaries and public meetings at several intervals during the development of the plan. Public involvement is seen as a costly, time-consuming addition by some, but the greatest group of potential park users should not be omitted from the planning process. Generating public involvement may serve to meet legislative guidelines for government funding and to broaden the support for implementation of recommendations.

In the area of historical research, we see a range of scores, demonstrating inconsistency of performance. In historic park preservation, the quality of the historical research is understandably important (Fig. 11). An exemplary level of both original-design and chronological-development research should be attained in order to provide an adequate basis for the synthesis and subsequent steps. Research of the original designs is often more than adequate, while the tracing of changes, and their underlying reasons, is less well done. A thorough understanding of the alterations of a park is essential to avoid re-creating old problems when attempting the restoration of original features.

In analyzing existing conditions, a traditional task for the landscape architect, the total score was high, showing a good level of performance in this part of the process. The behavioral research category, however, showed a range of scores and a low total. Gaining an understanding of the existing use of the park through research methods such as formalized observation, analyses of physical traces, and self-reported perceptions, preferences, and use of the park through interviews or questionnaires, contributes invaluable information to the planning process. Landscape architects should not assume that others use parks as they would or that all users are the same. Variations in life style, sex, age, class, ethnic origin, and other factors all contribute to a diversity of park use. The landscape architect may become familiar with the unique qualities of particular park users through behavioral research.

Most critical in the process of planning for the preservation of historic urban parks is the synthesis step. This is the point at which a balance between historic and contemporary agendas is sought, and hopefully achieved. The reason for low scores in this category may be due to a lack of sufficient data from historical research, behavioral research, or public involvement. The best synthesis of competing requirements cannot be made unless complete base information is secured. This information should then be fully utilized in establishing the philosophical approach to park preservation and enhancement. The suitability of the design and management recommendations are dependent on the quality of synthesis achieved.

Judgments must be made in determining which features to retain, reconstruct, alter, or eliminate. A multitude of how-to questions addressing the restoration of plantings, minimization of conflicts in use, integration of desirable facilities, and other important issues need to be responded to in a systematic way. An approach that could prove useful in sorting out these issues, and thus creating a sound synthesis, may be the adaptation of the philosophy and resulting design principles of the original designers and the application of these to the current situation. The historical research phase should yield, from graphic and written sources, required information about the original park design. The behavioral research phase and input from the four client groups should define contemporary goals and objectives. The stance of the landscape architect would best be one of sensitivity to historic integrity, balanced by current needs and preferences. The original design construct could then be applied to the existing landscape.

The following are the critical design qualities of Olmsted legacy historic parks; these qualities can be activated in the preservation and enhancement of the parks.[20]

1. *Profuse Plantings* were developed in all spaces from casual to formal, and small to large. A broad palette of materials was used, with foliage in varying shades of green. Plants included trees of all sizes, shrubs, vines, wildfowers, ferns, aquatic plants and grasses, but no showy hybrids. Selection was not restricted to native materials but included all plants adaptable to the region. The qualities of each setting were created with plantings; trees were spaced singly or in small groups on a grassy meadow to produce a pastoral effect; stepped materials were composed in masses to enclose and direct views while defining spaces; dense, varied materials were planted on rough ground creating a dappled light and shade to simulate a wild, mysterious environment.

2. *Spatial extension* was achieved through the opening, obscuring and closing of views, forming broad vistas and intimate outdoor rooms. The landscape was seemingly enlarged by leading the viewer

PLAN FOR A PUBLIC PARK

ON THE

FLATS SOUTH OF BUFFALO.

To the Park Commissioners:

Sirs,—We have the honor to submit drawings showing a plan for a park adapted to a site on the shore of Lake Erie, south of the city, as contemplated in a resolution of the Common Council of February, 1887, and in subsequent action of your Commission, recorded in its last Annual Report. For distinction's sake, we shall refer to the proposed park as the South Park, and to your present park as the North Park.

It is believed that many citizens of Buffalo are of the opinion that discussion of the subject of this report might better be deferred until it has been more maturely considered whether the city just now wants to engage in another park enterprise, and whether if it does so, the required park had better be in a place naturally so unattractive within itself as that which you have had in view. Mature consideration can be given to neither of these questions, without a much more definite statement of the project than has hitherto been possible, and a better knowledge than has hitherto been had by

Fig. 11. The written documents of design professionals can contribute greatly to historical research efforts. Pictured is the first page of a report written by Frederick Law Olmsted for the Buffalo Park Commissioners in 1888. (Reproduced courtesy of the Buffalo and Erie County Historical Society.)

through a continually changing experience, often in a circuit route.

3. *Separation of circulation modes* was provided through the development of distinct systems for as many as five uses; pedestrian, bicycle, equestrian, slow pleasure driving and faster through traffic. Safe intersections of the different modes were designed through the use of grade changes to create overpasses and underpasses. In informal areas gently curving roads and paths were characteristically used.

4. *Separation of activities* was provided through physical distance and/or screening with landforms and plant materials. Provision for varied uses and the clustering of similar uses minimized potential conflicts in use through design for separation.

5. *Structures and site amenities were integrated* into the landscape through careful placement and emphasis on overall effect. Modest frame or stone comfort stations, maintenance structures, stables, picnic shelters and rustic shelters were blended into the park setting. Bridges, retaining walls and drainage systems were designed with natural or picturesque character. Benches, light standards, drinking fountains and other site amenities of appropriate design and materials were placed in the landscape.

6. *Gathering spaces* were designed for large numbers of people. These spaces were often more formal and were designed in linear or geometric shapes. They were more decoratively appointed than other parts of the parks, with terraces, balustrades, statuary, mosaic paving, intricate light standards and other ornate features. Formal spaces were often edged with rows of trees, which blended away into an informal landscape.

7. *Natural spaces* were created where park visitors could seem to be completely removed from the artificial and man-made. Naturalistic landscapes containing plant materials and water features were composed to provide this type of setting.

8. *Active recreation settings* were provided. Pools for swimming or wading, gymnastics equipment, running tracks, tennis courts and baseball diamonds were among the sports facilities included in the design of parks.

9. *Design for harmony* of all elements was the overall consideration. Each park functioned as a whole, without attention being drawn to individual elements.

Although this approach to historic urban park planning may have been taken before, it has not been explicitly stated. The application that is of importance here is the use of historic principles to bolster integrity and respond to current use simultaneously. What is be-

ing suggested is not simply the use of the original plan to restore lost elements, but the use of the original design principles to mediate between historic integrity and contemporary use.[21] As an example, the principle of separation of activities could be used to place a visual and aural barrier between a picnic area and nearby tennis courts. A planted berm, dense on the picnic side and used for informal seating on the tennis side, would provide an appropriate solution. The form of the berm would be irregular, with plantings varied, applying the planting principle in their selection. In another situation, a new soccer field might be placed at the edge of a meadow, in an area where the ground is relatively level, and the uprights placed carefully so as not to obstruct the vista. Minimal grading or vegetation removal would be necessary and the quality of the space would be retained, satisfying the spatial extension and harmony principles. The landscape resulting from this application of original design principles would not be a restoration, rehabilitation, reconstruction, or conservation treatment but, rather, an interpretation of an historic landscape in an adaptive use process.

The design and management recommendations categories show adequate, but not exemplary, scores. The performance level in these categories is directly linked to the quality of synthesis achieved and is judged on that basis. In both these areas the consistent application of original design principles can improve the results. Management recommendations, sometimes overlooked by landscape architects, are important in establishing continuity and promoting longevity of the park work.

The final step in the process, implementation, is also the final unknown. When the landscape architect or project team completes the planning document, city officials and community members become critical allies in the struggle to carry out the plan. Within the current economic situation, parks improvements do not reach a high-priority level unless citizens make their demands known and city officials listen. An exemplary solution to the preservation of urban historic parks will satisfy preservationists, recreationists, managers, and everyone in between. The broad base of support that can be generated with an excellent plan will provide a greater opportunity for full implementation.

Conclusion

Each historic landscape, as we see it today, is a composite of all the forms it has taken over the years. One role of the landscape architect in historic urban park work is to make visible the layers of time in such a way that the park becomes more understandable to those who use the spaces now. There is, and will continue to be, pressure to redefine the role of historic parks in urban life. Utilizing the approach outlined in this article, the design professional will be better able to undertake this redefining process. The resulting plan should provide an urban landscape with recreational value and historic meaning. As the historic value of these landscapes becomes more tangible and respected by park users, their appreciation of the parks will be the tool that secures historic urban park preservation now and into the future.

References

1. National Park Service, Department of the Interior, *The National Register*, U. S. Government Printing Office, 1975–211–308/20. This publication describes the National Register program and details the criteria for evaluation in the text.
2. Charles E. Beveridge, "The Olmsted Legacy of Public Design," Incidental Publication No. 1, 2nd Edition, April 1, 1981, National Association for Olmsted Parks. This thirteen-page compilation contains a list of parks, parkways, public recreation grounds, and public places designed by Frederick Law Olmsted Sr., his partners, and successors between 1857 and 1961.
3. Frederick Law Olmsted, *Public Parks*, Brookline, Massachusetts, 1902, pp. 47–53. This consists of two papers read before the American Social Science Association in 1870 and 1880, entitled, respectively, "Public Parks and the Enlargement of Towns" and "A Consideration of the Justifying Value of a Public Park."
4. Ibid., pp. 36–46 and pp. 88–91.
5. Patricia M. O'Donnell, *Houghton Park User Survey Report*, City of Buffalo, 1980. The survey included the responses of 401 park users ranging in age from 9 to 79 years. O'Donnell, Patricia M., *User Survey for Martin Luther King Jr. Park: A Report on the Findings*, unpublished manuscript. Three hundred and nineteen park users were surveyed.
6. The first public, park-like settings in this country were found in landscape cemeteries, like one in Mount Auburn near Boston. Olmsted, thinking the cemeteries a dreary place disapproved of using them for recreation. Olmsted refers to his disapproval of monuments in parks in *Public Parks*, pp. 92–95, as well as in other park reports.
7. Buffalo Parks Commission, *13th Annual Report* through *23rd Annual Report*, Buffalo, New York, 1883 through 1893. These contain selected references to the condition of Cazenovia Park, Creek, and Lake.
8. Advisory Council on Historic Preservation, *The National Historic Preservation Program Today*, Washington D. C., U. S. Government Printing Office, 1976. The use of these terms as definers of procedures in historic preservation is applied primarily to architectural preservation in the cited text. The author has used them in referring to historic landscape preservation.
9. Patricia M. O'Donnell, *Survey of Buffalo's Olmsted Parks*, The Landmark Society of the Niagara Frontier, and the New York State Department of Parks and Recreation, Division for Historic Preservation, Buffalo, New York, 1979.
10. The National Register nomination for New Jersey's Branch Brook Park was submitted by Kathleen P. Galop and Ron Rudin. It was approved by the Keeper of the Register in June of 1980 and is on file at the National Park Service.
11. The National Association for Olmsted Parks announced the undertaking of a national inventory and assessment in 1981. A report on the progress of the inventory was published in the *NAOP Newsletter,* January, 1982.
12. Lisa A. Kunst and Patricia M. O'Donnell, "Historic Landscape Preservation Deserves a Broader Meaning," *Landscape Architecture,* Vol. 71, No. 1, January 1981, pp. 53–55. In this article, the authors have proposed definitions for the treatment of historic landscapes. Ms. O'Donnell has refined and expanded these definitions in the document cited as (21).
13. Building Science Inc., Planning Consultants; Castle, Hamilton, Houston Lownie, Architects; Decker and Borowsky, Architects and Planners; Schnadelbach Braun Partnership, Landscape Architects; *Delaware Park Comprehensive Development Plan Summary Report*, Buffalo, New York, July, 1973. Delaware Park Steering Committee, *Delaware Park Comprehensive Development Plan: Summary Outline*, March 1976. The author served on the Delaware Park Steering Committee from 1977 to 1979, and in this capacity learned a great deal about the plan for the park and was active in its implementation.
14. Allen J. Share, "Restoration of a Tornado Ravaged Park," *Landscape Architecture,* Vol. 66, No. 5, September 1976, pp. 456–462. The information on Cherokee Park Restoration was also drawn from the author's notes on a presentation given at a seminar conducted by the Alliance for Historic Preservation at Williamsburg, Virginia, in June of 1980.
15. Carol R. Johnson, "Master Plan for the Back Bay Fens to be Presented at NAOP Conference," *National Association for Olmsted Parks,* Spring/Summer, 1981, Vol. 1, No. 2, pp. 12–13. Richard Heath, "Two Master Plans for Boston's Park System Brings Olmsted into the 20th Century," June, 1980. Unpublished paper given to the author by Mr. Heath, president of the Franklin Park Coalition. The information on the Back Bay Fens was also drawn from the author's notes from a presentation given by Carol R. Johnson at the NAOP 2nd Annual Meeting, April 23–26, 1981, held in Boston, Brookline, and Cambridge, Massachusetts.
16. V. Michael Weinmayr, "Working with Local Pressures," *Landscape Architecture,* Vol. 71, No. 1. January 1981, pp. 50–51. Information on Franklin Park was also drawn from a paper by Richard Heath, cited above, and from a presentation of the plan by V. Michael Weinmayr at the NAOP 2nd Annual Meeting.
17. City of Seattle, Department of Parks and Recreation, *Ravenna Cowen Parks Improvements: Design Program*, April, 1979. Additional information on the Seattle Parks was gained from a visit to Seattle in August of 1981, a tour of the parks, and conversations with Donald M. Harris, Director of Development, Department of Parks and Recreation, Seattle, Washington.

18. City of Seattle, Department of Parks and Recreation, *Colman Park Walkways: Revised Preliminary Program,* August, 1978. The author saw work in progress on this project during her August 1981 visit to Seattle.

19. Project for Public Spaces, *Bryant Park: Intimidation or Recreation,* New York, 1980. Information was also drawn from the program development proposal for Bryant Park made by PPS and from discussions with Ed Lubienecki and Fred I. Kent who worked on this project.

20. The author derived these design principles from the study of numerous Olmsted legacy park plans and a familiarity with a large number of parks from field study. A similar construct, which views the Olmsted landscape from an historians perspective, has been developed by Dr. Charles Beveridge, Dr. Beveridge's "Seven S's" were presented at the NAOP 2nd Annual Conference and in the *NAOP Newsletter,* January, 1982.

21. Patricia M. O'Donnell, *Preservation of Urban Historic Parks: A Balance of Historic Integrity and Contemporary Use,* submitted in partial fulfillment of a Master of Landscape Architecture Degree, University of Illinois at Urbana-Champaign, June, 1982. The concepts presented in this section of the article are more fully explored in this thesis document.

Commercial Streetscapes

Steve McNiel

The current small town vernacular for Main Street storefronts in the United States includes a metal-clad pole structure and is essentially the same as barn architecture. How different this is from the original concept of Main Street architecture, which was urban in character and existed in a form similar to row houses, with no separations between buildings, and often constructed as commercial blocks, thereby enclosing several storefronts under one architectural identity. The new structures are utilitarian in their ease of construction and relative low cost, and the form of these buildings relates fairly well to the older farm architecture of stone and wood, but this style is not in keeping with the boom-town, flat-faced front and the protruding, richly ornamented cornice of the older Victorian forms. The largest departure from traditional rural buildings is the lack of careful and often-original details that articulated and individualized both farm and commercial architecture of the past.

We have begun to address these issues by developing a local inventory and statistically based description system. The system facilitates the clustering of buildings based on a multi-variable analysis, which considers elements of general location; the relation to street and surrounding or attached buildings; the massing of the structure; the way it meets the sky and the ground; the extent of fenestration, including the rhythm of the windows and doors; and, finally, the use of materials and ornament. To accomplish this analysis, it was essential to try to understand Main Street in its historical context.

Our work, while considering the larger rural landscape, has focused primarily on downtown commercial architecture (Figs. 1 and 2). Recognizing that several authors have documented the history of farm architecture, it is our feeling that, given the great activity going on at the present time in the restoration and revitilization of the small town in the United States, the time is right for study of what remains and what the past might tell us about the heritage and the potential legacy of commercial architecture on Main Street. This seems even more important given the massive demographic changes of the last twenty years, where one finds a large outmigration from major urban centers and the resulting phenomenal growth in small towns.

Our intent is to describe some of the historical context for the forms we have found on Main Streets in Dane County, Wisconsin. Looking at the commercial architecture that is still extant, one finds that the buildings taken together exhibit a full range of styles, from the simplest, most basic vernacular structures to some well-crafted high-style examples.

On the high-style side of the scale, an effort was made to piece together an understanding of the history of high-styled storefronts, since the majority of our samples were trying to represent high-styled structures. Highlights in the evolution of two types of shopping environments in Europe will be presented and some suggestions will be made about the influence that these European antecedents had on Main Street, U.S.A.

However, before we do that, it is important to establish the role of the storefront in its context, as a functional part of the streetscape of the village or town in which it existed. Historically the storefront in Europe took a variety of forms, including the early itinerant traders—whose "storefront" often consisted of the side of the road where he stopped his horse—up through the relatively elaborate structures of the Greek Agora in Athens and Trajan's Market in Rome.

THE EVOLUTION OF STOREFRONTS

The classical form of the storefront can be seen in examples from early Greek and Roman markets. This form includes a facade that creates a frame for displaying the merchandise and services offered within. It is basically transparent, allowing for the maximum display of goods and ensuring an adequate supply of natural light into the rear of the store. This transparency was originally articulated as an opening that could be covered at night by wooden doors, such as those used at Trajan's Market (Figs. 3 and 4). Centuries later, in other storefronts, this space was filled with small panes of leaded glass to create a weatherproof shield; however, this treatment reduced the visibility from the street and forced the customer to go inside in order to view the merchandise.

By the time the Victorian storefront was being built in the Midwest, the small panes had given over to huge

Fig. 1.   Main Street 1912, Village of Cambridge, Wisconsin. The village still retained abundant greenery and a modicum of garish signs in this early part of the automobile age, but the signs for the Chevrolet dealership and the garage mark the beginning of large-scale automotive advertising.

Fig. 2.   Main Street 1979, Village of Cambridge, Wisconsin. What has the Main Street lost in the last 67 years? A good many trees and diagonal parking. What has it gained? A few new buildings, paved roads, and more and larger signs.

Fig. 3. Trajan's Market, Rome (ca. 100 A.D.). In this upper level, each storefront facade is basically the same but interior spaces vary widely. Each doorway has two long tracks carved into the stone to carry the massive wooden doors that were used to secure the shop at night.

Fig. 4. Trajan's Market, shop interior. A representative shop consists of a rectilinear space with a vaulted ceiling and a standard facade. Several variations on this plan are scattered throughout the complex. Most show evidence of special needs: a kiln for pottery, a trough for water as well as a forge for a blacksmith or jeweler, a firepit for cooking.

sheets of plate glass, leaving goods and services once again in full, unobstructed view of the customer. Strolling and window shopping became a popular activity in response to this transparency in form. The frame, which contained and marked this image of the sales space, consisted of structural walls and columns covered with symbolic ornament reflecting the tastes of the times.

The structural portion of the facade varied only slightly throughout the years and this variation was almost always dictated by the building's style and materials. For example, the Romanesque facade utilized massive masonry or stone arches, while the delicate Italianate and Gothic forms utilized cast-iron structural members.

What follows offers a more detailed overview of the evolution of the storefront in Europe and connects these structures to American Main Street storefronts.

Early Markets

There exists a long-established form division between the indoor shopping center, or "enclosed mall," and the traditional Main Street shopping area. Both types seem to have coexisted for a very long time. Our description will deal briefly with both forms.

The Greek Agora was an area that evolved over a period of time from earlier prototypes; it was, in its final form, a series of stone columns and a long, gabled roof with a collonade on both sides surrounding the shops, which were open stalls. It was not only used for selling, but also an area used by politicians and townsfolk as a location for political debate. The market area, however, lost the function as an open meeting space by medieval times. The early classic architectural forms of the Greeks have been admired and emulated for thousands of years in the western world. Even today the influence is still considered important, as evidenced by Faneuel Market in Boston. Faneuel Market is an important revitilization project preserving a vital example of neo-classic style.

Trajan's Market in Rome, located directly across from Caesars Forum and next to the Forum of Augustus, existed as a sophisticated shopping center and included hundreds of stalls or shopfronts, each identical in the form of the facade. The complex is characterized by five different levels and by the small passageways that wander through the labyrinth of shops (Figs. 5 and 6). These elevated shopping streets opened out onto a major plaza that included temples and platforms. This market was built around the time of Christ and, with the Agora of Greece, represented a prototype for the Main Streets we find later in the form of many individual shops existing side by side within a single architectural facade. These commercial blocks became common in the United States after the Civil War and achieved full expression in the 1880s and

1890s. Later, the unified Main Street gave way to the democratic principle of individual entrepreneurism and one finds contiguous shop fronts exhibiting individual stylistic characteristics, while generally resembling each other in mass and structure.

The Middle Ages

After the collapse of Rome, merchandising came to a virtual end. During this feudal period, everything belonged to the landowner and the peasants had little or no spendable income and a limited amount of trade goods. During this time, the small villages that had grown with the Roman military outposts began to decline because of repeated invasions from the east and north. Physical protection led to fortresslike villages with narrow spaces and high densities. Lewis Mumford, Eliel Saarinen, and J. B. Jackson have all commented on the medieval city and the role of merchants in that environment; they are great proponents of the medieval city, believing that in many ways they were more liveable and supportive environments than contemporary examples.[1] J. B. Jackson has traced briefly the redevelopment of the marketplace in the medieval city, with an emphasis placed on the role of the street as an organizing element for marketing. This easily leads to an understanding of Main Street as a shopping environment, it being highly dependent on the street for identity and structure. According to Jackson:

> Perhaps the first evidence we have of this change—of the city evolving from a fluid assembly of legally defined groups or orders into a composition of well defined spaces—is the appearance in the 11th Century in one northern European town after another of a recognizable, permanent marketplace. In earlier times merchants periodically offered their wares for sale in the *vicus* or in any sufficiently wide street, and local craftsmen joined them, though their production was scanty. But a combination of economic and political circumstances fostered the creation of distinct, centrally located spaces for this sort of activity. . . . Thus the marketplace came into existence. At first little more than a widened street or open space in the *vicus,* it then moved into the town itself to be nearer its customers and sources of supply; and finally in the 11th Century, in many of the numerous new towns laid out in central Europe and France and England, we see a rectangular public place, often in the very center, where regular markets could be held. And eventually there are several markets—livestock market, grain market, crafts market, even hay market, wood market, etc.[2]

This development of market spaces continued to evolve through the Renaissance and culminated in the contemporary commercial district, separated into zoned-use areas of heavy and light industry, manufacturing, and commercial sales.

Fig. 5. Trajan's Market, main facade. The semicircular, multitiered facade of Trajans Market is constructed of unusually thin bricks. Several temples and platforms filled the space that the market surrounds. Although only a portion of the market is visible, one can sense the classic regularity that came to characterize many American Victorian commercial blocks. In this view, the newer structures behind the market visually overpower it and contrast greatly with its strict classical spacing.

Fig. 6. Trajan's Market, indoor shopping mall. Two levels of shops face a pedestrian street. The view out the far end is of the Roman Forum and the Palatine.

Marketing in the medieval city went through a transition from practically no activity to weekly markets typically found in small squares or plazas. This was accompanied by the rise of a merchant class and, finally, by the creation of a commercial district. These districts were mainly filled with warehouses, dock facilities, and the elements of an overland transport system for moving goods. It must be recognized that patronage was still relatively small in the Middle Ages because of the predominance of a peasant society that had no disposable income. One does, however, find at this time the development of the artist's or craftsman's studio, where services as well as goods could be sold. Mobile marketing in the form of pushcarts and horse-drawn wagons also expanded during the late Middle Ages as roads became safer to travel and trade goods, both local and exotic, became more popular and commonplace.

The Renaissance

In the architectural transition from the gothic forms of the medieval townscape, the massive stone walls and parapets gave way, in the Renaissance, to a more delicate and varied architecture. Many of the styles harkened back to early classical Greek and Roman forms and developed combinations of several styles and classical orders.

The city of Florence offers a particularly interesting example of Renaissance townscape because of its relatively unchanged fabric. The early structures of Florence retain vestiges of their late medieval heritage in the characteristic massive Tuscan forms, materials, and colors. The Palazzo Vecchio in Piazza Della Signoria and the Ponte Vecchio, the market bridge, retain the transitional styles of the early Renaissance (Fig. 7). The beautiful, multicolored dome of the Cathedral of Santa Maria Del Fiore makes the transition to architecture of the high Renaissance. In terms of the commercial architecture of Florence, many of the older forms still exist, including the open street market, where vendors bring in mobile carts. This remains one of the most popular types of marketing today, but is only one of the many surviving forms. The lower court of the Uffizi Gallery is still an active trading area, today primarily inhabited by artists and craftspersons. It remains—two long colonnades surrounding a pedestrian street, which connects the Piazza della Signoria and the Arno River near the Ponte Vecchio (Fig. 8).

Other types of older surviving markets include the Basket, or Straw Market, which is housed in an open, free-standing portico consisting of a massive roof held up by very high arches of stone (Fig. 9). One of the most interesting shopping streets in Florence is the Via Romana, which crosses the Ponte Vecchio built by Neri di Fioravanti in stone on an earlier wooden con-

Fig. 7. The Ponte Vecchio, Florence (1345). Designed by Neri di Fioravanti, this structure is representative of the market bridges that were frequently built in the late Medieval and Renaissance periods. The Rialto Bridge in Venice is another surviving example.

struction. The storefronts that exist there today, while being of later construction, nonetheless reflect a style of storefront that was characteristic of many locations in Europe in the early Renaissance. These are tight, self-contained storefronts, often utilizing a bay window that projects out into the street to intercept shoppers. At night, these are covered by heavy wooden doors that are hinged at the top and become awnings during the day when they are open for business (Figs. 10 and 11). The streetscape has a totally closed-down appearance when these doors cover the display cases, revealing very little of its real function to those who pass by. When the shops open, the bridge functions as a small pedestrian node and center of activity.

The Renaissance in northern Europe developed a slightly different form of storefront because of the extreme weather conditions found there. In Zurich, for example, some commercial buildings dating back to the seventeenth century are being maintained and look no older than their twentieth-century counterparts because they have been restored periodically. The storefronts we see today are not those of the seventeenth century, but the buildings unmistakably retain the original style in their overall appearance, including small window panes, thick walls, and the use of heraldry below the classical cornices and string courses (Figs. 12 and 13). It is not at all difficult, when viewing these storefronts, to see an affinity with those of the American Midwest since the overall elements of mass, scale, and materials appear to be the same.

One sees another important similarity to American Main Street architecture in the Renaissance house-

Fig. 8.   Uffizi Galleries, Florence. For centuries, vendors have used these colonnades for a market area—a transitional form between the open air market and the commercial street.

Fig. 9.   The Basket Market, Florence. This market, still quite active today, represents an intermediate stage between open air markets and commercial malls.

Fig. 10. Closed Shops on the Ponte Vecchio.

Fig. 11. Open Shops on the Ponte Vecchio.

Fig. 12.   Typical shop in the old quarter of Zurich.

Fig. 13.   Typical shop in the old quarter of Zurich.

shops of Amsterdam. They used a high, decorative parapet wall to create a new way for the building to meet the sky. This form was picked up and used very heavily by American pioneers (The boom-town fronts, as they are often referred to, existed as a gabeled roof behind a parapet wall; these walls were often designed in fanciful patterns, including stepped pyramids and rounded pediments of several types, and usually exhibited exaggerated proportions and little detailing.) The large house-stores of Amsterdam were built by an entirely new class of merchants, made rich by their connection to a canal system and their important position on the North Atlantic seaboard. They used dramatically new forms at the top of the building where it meets the sky and, in so doing, transformed the appearance into an infinitely varied one, but still possessing a new and exciting unifying theme. But the more unique contribution is probably the scale of the fenestration in relation to the overall area of the facade. The amount of glass on these buildings was proportionally larger than was common. Because of the low amounts of natural light in these latitudes, it was important to let as much natural light as possible into the building; therefore, a style evolved that featured large windows in the fronts of buildings facing the canals, where they could gather reflected light as well as direct light. This proportion of glass can be seen later in the Chicago-styled commercial structures of the early twentieth century and eventually in the all glass-and-steel high rise form and also in some of the cast-iron facades that one finds on Victorian Main Street.

Possibly one more example from the late Renaissance will help us understand the storefront as it had evolved up to the beginning of the Industrial Age. The Marais is one of the oldest neighborhoods in Paris, a city that has torn down all but a few of their older buildings. However, within the Marais there are still vestiges of the sixteenth, seventeenth, and eighteenth centuries in the form of Second Empire buildings. A representative example is the single building containing several storefronts on the bottom with apartments above. The patina of the building shown in Fig. 14 reveals the wear-and-tear of a life of active trade in a market area of services and crafts. This building obviously has been a party to hundreds of years of active trade, as evidenced by its deteriorated physical state. It reflects a time when craftsmanship was still the main element in manufacturing and sales and when small shops served the public through an open facade or one filled with small panes of glass. The period itself was characterized by a new prosperity and an increased urban sophistication, especially in Paris. Customers were more affluent and enjoyed the reputation of Paris as the style-setter. The shop forms appear to have the characteristics of the now-familiar universal form, especially in the symmetry of door and windows. The use of high transomed windows that allow the sunlight to penetrate deep into the storefront also relates them to American forms. Only the overly high and narrow facades are significantly different. In this example in the Marais, we also see the use of heavy wooden doors to close off the shops at night or in inclement weather. France, it will be remembered, was quite a volatile

Fig. 14.   Typical second empire building containing shops and apartments in the Marais, Paris.

theater of social reform during the period this architecture was formed, adding insight into the use of the heavy doors which were undoubtedly for protecting merchandise and self as well.

We have reviewed the early and the late forms and find, up until the Renaissance, an expression of original forms. But as one progresses through the Renaissance, one finds an emerging movement that based its ideals on the classical forms of ancient Greece and Rome. They were trying to get back to the essence of a classical life-style, as they perceived it. They imagined a return to the pinnacle, to the old truth, only doing it in a more delicate and advanced way. Finally, the full flowering of commercial enterprise in the Renaissance and the individual expression of an awareness of the psychology of selling were translated into physical form in the storefronts.

Modern Times

In seventeenth-, eighteenth-, and nineteenth-century England, one finds forms evolving that served as direct prototypes to colonial American shops and even a few similar to what our sample finds in Dane County, Wisconsin. The later forms included the Gothic Revival and the styles of the romantic age, culminating with the Queen Anne Style, that most eclectic of all Victorian styles since it borrowed from a number of other "pure" styles to synthesize a unique blend of architectural forms. These styles were popularized in England and the Continent and quickly spread to North America.

In the Midwest, the individual nineteenth-century storefront followed the vernacular of the day. It was first of all an urban form, transplanted to the village. It evolved through a long history of utilitarian structures designed to attract customers and to serve the needs of product sales and service delivery. Structurally, the storefront was most often a wood or masonry structure with an ornamented or stylized facade.

By the time the Midwest was building its storefronts in the 1860s through the 1880s, Americans had forsaken the earlier Federal Style that characterized colonial buildings on the East Coast, and by the time of the Civil War they had adopted a group of styles for storefronts, the most popular of which was the Italianate, characterized by a heavily bracketed cornice and hooded, tall, narrow windows. Also built at this time were the classical Greek Revival forms, which were a very popular style for residences. A few Gothic Revival and Second Empire storefronts were also built at the end of the Civil War. Still later, the heavy Romanesque Style became very popular, especially for banks and civic structures. In Dane County, however, our inventory has shown the greatest quantity of extant storefronts dating from before the turn of the century to be of a vernacular form of the Queen Anne Style. According to D. J. Stith, "the Queen Anne Revival, also called Neo-Jacobean, Free Classic, was initiated by the English architect Norman Shaw in the 1870s and reached Wisconsin around 1880. The name Queen Anne is thoroughly misleading, the style being an American version of a popular contemporary English style that actually owed almost nothing to the earlier architecture associated with the reign of Queen Anne."[7]

Around the turn of the century and through the first two decades, the eclecticism of the Victorians produced a few examples of what John Wells has called the Victorian Renaissance style and the Beaux Arts style; however, the majority of the storefronts from this period seem to reflect a form that Wells calls Victorian Functional, a less ornate version of the typical symmetrical facade that, as with the Queen Anne Style, blended individual ornamental elements in a free eclectic composition which responded to the individual aesthetic of the store owner more than it did to any formal sense of a high style. But even as the styles of the storefront changed as did their proportions, the basic ingredients of the facade remained the same: plate-glass windows with high transom windows above, the symmetrical organization of the facade with the recessed doorway entering between two small display windows (Figs. 15 and 16), or an asymmetrical arrangement, where a corner door allowed for a more continuous show window.

J. B. Jackson has said that one of his greatest pleasures is noting the slip from high-style architecture to locally produced crude imitations, which, in their own way, establish the character of that particular village. We found that the storefronts of Dane County, Wisconsin, were, for the most part, constructed by local masons and carpenters. They picked up forms from pattern books and magazines available at the time; or they copied extant high-style examples, for instance those seen by businessmen on trips to Milwaukee or Chicago. These travelers brought back ideas and instructed the local carpenter to proceed with a design close to what their memories dictated. We recognize that perception plays an important, but as yet unqualified, role in this transporting of high-style Chicago architecture into the vernacular of the small town.

In the earliest stages, pioneers most often used wood. Commercial spaces evolved from early log beginnings through frame and finally to masonry and cast-iron structures. At first, stores seemed to be located in houses. These "parlor stores" usually contained a tavern as well. The C.P. Moseley log cabin serves as an example of such an early commercial beginning in south-central Wisconsin. This structure stood on high ground about five blocks from what became the center of the Village of Oregon, Wiscon-

Fig. 15. The Klein Block, Deerfield, Wisconsin (ca. 1910). The storefront retains the high transom windows and retractable awnings typical of its period.

Fig. 16. The Klein Block, Deerfield, Wisconsin (1981). The storefront has been modified in the recent past by covering the transom windows, providing a fixed awning, and painting the bricks. Nevertheless, the basic transparency remains.

sin. In 1843 it was a simple wooden structure, possibly evolving through the usual progression from log house-store to a frame dwelling with a salesroom in the parlor. In each case the wood would have been cut and milled locally. As Main Street developed, other bonafide storefronts began to appear. These were almost invariably constructed of wood and used oil lights and coal or wood heat. Like the first log house-stores, few of these original storefronts remain. They have fallen to fire or obsolescence. The structural frame of such buildings evolved finally into masonry walls or wooden columns covered with masonry and, in a few cases, cast-iron columns and panels. Cast iron was also used extensively for decorative features after the Civil War, and pressed tin was used in an effort to make commercial structures fire resistant.

The structural frame was covered to a greater or lesser degree with ornament, which carried its own symbolic meaning and often reinforced the building's style. Styles in Dane County were established for the most part during a long period of storefront construction when forms and ornament were borrowed from the past. The styles themselves carry names such as Greek Revival, Neo-Colonial, Romanesque and Gothic Revival, each one indicating the classical aesthetic vocabulary being borrowed. The ornament reflects a wonderful diversity of form and symbolic content. Some early catalogs illustrate hundreds of different patterns available to the turn-of-the-century builder. (Figs. 17, 18, and 19).

As has been illustrated, all of these forms have antecedents in the commercial architecture of Europe and generally follow the same basic formulas for product and service sales established over two thousand years ago.

NOTES

1. Mumford, Lewis. *The City in History, Its Origins, Its Transformations, and Its Prospects,* Chap. 9, "Cloister and Community," and Chap. 10, "Medieval Urban Housekeeping."
   Saarinen, Eliel. *The City, Its Growth, Its Decay, Its Future,* Chap. 1, "The Medieval Case."
   Jackson, J.B. *The Necessity For Ruins,* pg. 58.
2. Jackson, J.B. *The Necessity For Ruins,* pg. 57. "This merchants' village was known in northern Europe as a *vicus.* In western Europe the usual term for this merchants settlement was *portus,* from which of course we derive our word for harbor."
3. Ibid. pg. 58.
4. Mumford, Lewis. *The City in History, Its Origins, Its Transformations, and Its Prospects,* pg. 146.
5. Jackson, J.B. *The Necessity For Ruins,* pg. 59.
6. Rifkind, Carole. *Main Street, The Face of Urban America;* pg. 73.
7. Stith, D.J., et. al. *Design in Wisconsin Housing, A Guide to Styles,* pg. 10.

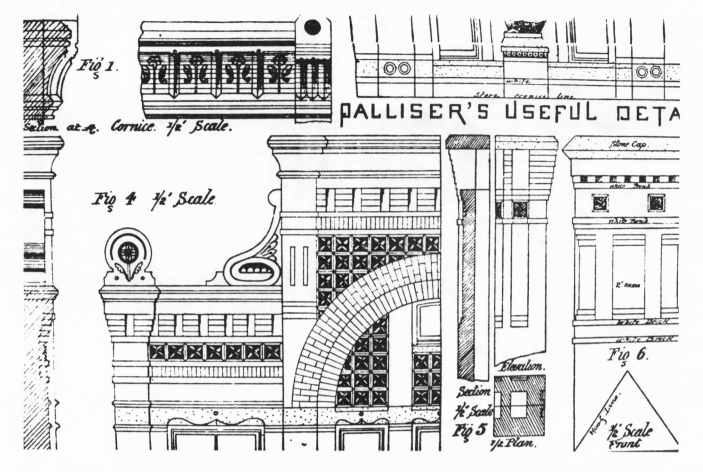

Fig. 17.   Storefronts with cast-iron pillars and galvanized cornices and window cap. Modest one at upper left is representative of many Midwest examples. Architectural details in a particular style supplied by Palliser & Co., Architects and Publishers of Fine Architectural Works, Bridgeport, Conn., 1890.

BIBLIOGRAPHY

Bayley, William, *William Bayley & Co's Catalogue of Architectural Iron Works,* Republican Sentinel Co., Printers: Milwaukee, Wis., 1882.

Bicknell, A. J., *Wooden and Brick Buildings With Details,* A.J. Bicknell & Co., Architectural Book Publishers, New York, 1875.

Brucher, Gene, Edt., *Two Memoirs of Renaissance Florence, The Diaries of Buonaccorso Pitti and Gregorio Dati,* Harper & Row, Publishers, New York, 1967.

Buckley, Ernest R. Ph. d., *The Clays and Clay Industries of Wisconsin,* Wisconsin Geological and Natural History Survey. Bulletin No. VII (part 1), Economic Series No. 4. Published by the State, Madison, Wisconsin, 1901.

Burckhardt, Jacob, *The Civilization of the Renaissance in Italy,* Vol. II, Harper Colophan Books, Harper & Row, New York, 1929 edition, with illustrations.

Cummings, M. F., and Miller, G. G., *Architectural Designs for Street Fronts, Suburban Houses, and Cottages,* Young and Benson, Publishers, Troy, N.Y., 1865.

Cummings, M. F., *Architectural Details, for Houses, Stores, Cottages, and Other Buildings,* Orange Judd & Co., New York, 1873.

Decorators Supply Co., *Illustrated Catalogue of Plastic Ornament,* Decorators Supply Co., Archer Ave and Leo Street, Chicago, Ill.

Depew, Chauncey M., *One Hundred Years of American Commerce,* Vol. II, D. O. Haynes & Co., New York, 1895.

Diamonstein, Barbaralee; *Buildings Reborn, New Uses, Old Places,* Harper & Row, Publishers, New York, 1978.

Foley, Mary Mix, *The American House,* Harper Colophon Books, Harper & Row, Publishers, New York, 1980.

Glassie, Henry, *Pattern in the Material Folk Culture of the Eastern United States,* University of Pennsylvania Publications in Folklore and Folklife, University of Pennsylvania Press, Philadelphia, Pa., 1969.

Glassie, Henry, "The Double-Crib Barn in South Central Pennsylvania." Pioneer America, 1:1 (Winter, 1969), 1:2 (July 1969), 11:1 (Jan, 1970) 11:2 (July, 1970).

Glassie, Henry, "Structure and Function, Folklore and the Artifact", Semiotica VII:4 (1973).

Glassie, Henry, *Folk Housing In Middle Virginia,* University of Tennessee Press, Knoxville, Tennessee, 1975.

Jackson, J.B., *The Necessity For Ruins.* University of Massachusetts Press, Amherst, Mass., 1980.

Keyes, Elisha W., *History of Dane County,* Madison, Wis, 1906. (no publisher listed).

Kniffen, Fred, "Louisana House Types," in Annals of the Association of American Geographers XXXI, 1936.

Kniffen, Fred, "Folk Housing: Key to Diffusion", Annals of the Association of American Geographers, 55:4 (Dec. 1965).

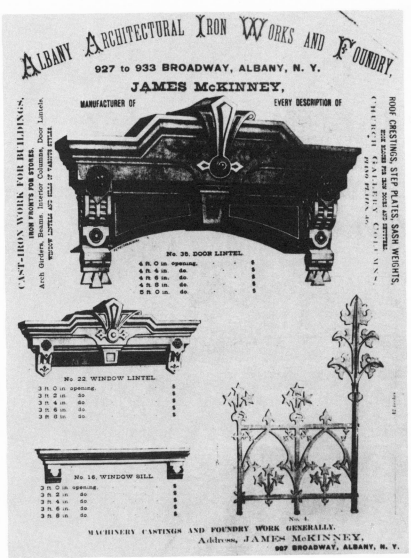

Fig. 18. Cast iron parts available in 1865, from *Architectural Designs For Street Fronts, Suburban Houses and Cottages.*

L'Orange, H.P., *Art Forms and Civic Life in the late Roman Empire,* Princeton University Press, Princeton N.J., 1972.

McKee, Harley Jr., *Recording Historic Buildings: The Historic American Buildings Survey,* U.S. Department of the Interior, National Park Service, Washington, 1970.

McNiel, Edward S. and Koop, Michael, "Planning in Dane County, Wisconsin: A regional perception of historical development in five communities", Pioneer America Society Transactions, (forthcoming), 1981.

Milwaukee Business Directory-, 1891, 1900, 1906, 1911, Milwaukee, Wisconsin.

Mumford, Lewis, *The City in History, Its Origins, Its Transformations, and Its Prospects,* Harcourt, Brace and Jovanovich, New York, 1961.

Palliser, *Palliser's Useful Details,* Palliser, Palliser and Co. Architects and Publishers of Fine Architectural Works, Bridgeport, Conn., 1890.

Pen and Sunlight Sketches of the Principal Cities in Wisconsin, Phoenix Publishing Co. Chicago, 1893.

Rapport, Amos, *House Form and Culture,* Foundations of Cultural Geography Series, Prentice-Hall, Englewood Cliffs, N.J., 1969.

Rifkind, Carole, *Main Street, The Face of Urban America,* Harper & Row, Publishers, New York, 1977.

Saarinen, Eliel, *The City, Its Growth, Its Decay, Its Future,* The M.I.T. Press, Cambridge, Mass., 1943.

Sloane, Eric, *An Age of Barns,* Ballantine Books, New York, 1967.

Sloane, Eric, *I Remember America,* Ballantine Books, New York, 1971.

Speltz, Alexander, *The Styles of Ornament,* Dover Publications, Inc. New York, 1959. (original in German, 1904).

Stith, D. J., Meyer, R. P., Dean, J. M., *Design in Wisconsin Housing, A Guide to Styles,* University of Wisconsin-Extension, Madison, Wisconsin, 1977.

Waite, Diana S., *Architectural Elements, the Technological Revolution,* Scribner and Sons, The Pyne Press, Princeton, N.J., 1973.

Wells, John, *Victorian Commercial Architecture of Indiana,* Historic Landmarks Foundation.

Woodword, George E., and Thompson, Edward G., *Woodwords National Architect,* De Capo Press, 1975, reprint.

Venturi, Robert; Scott Brown, Denise; Izenour, Steven, *Learning From Las Vegas,* The MIT Press, Cambridge, Mass., 1972.

Fig. 19.   Cornices available from the Decorators Supply Co., Chicago, as late as 1929.

The Memory of War: Reflections on Battlefield Preservation

Reuben M. Rainey

At first glance it looks like a blend of Central Park and the Blue Ridge Parkway. The gracefully aligned one-way road with its spiral curves and carefully maintained turf shoulders melting into the hardwoods leaves little doubt one is in a precinct of the National Park Service, where road-making is still practiced as an art. Meandering through the mixed hardwood forest, the road connects a series of closely cropped grassy meadows clearly defined by forest edge, linked outdoor rooms reminiscent of Olmsted and Vaux's greenswards at Central Park or the Long Meadow at Prospect Park. Joggers, picnicking families, strolling couples, and flying frisbees underscore the park-like ambience. On a beguiling Virginia spring Sunday, when the dogwoods bloom, the procession of autos celebrating the spring rites creates a bumper-to-bumper *passeggiáta,* which may necessitate the temporary closing of the road.

Yet aside from the obvious declaration of the entry markers, there are sure signs we are not in an ordinary park. There are cannons in the meadows, floating icons on a vast sea of lawn; and there are stone monuments, an obelisk and less finely dressed blocks of granite, which lend a certain funereal air, as if one might be in a nineteenth-century rural cemetery, a Mt. Auburn or Greenwood transposed to the undulating uplands of central Virginia, except the monuments are not nearly so numerous. (Some teenage couples are perched high on the cannon barrels, totally absorbed in one another's conversation and occasionally stealing a kiss, but this is strictly against the rules of those who supervise the area.) There is also an abundance of historical markers, speaking a precise and didactic West Point prose about troop positions, battle tactics, types of fortifications, and battery emplacements. Here and there we even find battle paintings, encased in weatherproof frames, with accompanying recordings inviting us to re-create in our imaginations the actual events of battle that a little over a century ago shattered the quiet of these pastoral surroundings and left the well-groomed lawn strewn with the dead, the wounded, and the debris of battle. These paintings are little marked by artistic license. Philippoteaux's Gettysburg cyclorama may depict Union troops charging across poppy fields punctuated with the stucco farm-houses and haystacks of Normandy, outfitted with the breeches and bandoleers of the French army, with the painter himself gazing serenely on the battle like a donor in a Renaissance altarpiece. Not here. The work we see is the product of a collaboration between painter and military historian, who have sought to honor to the letter Leopold von Ranke's dictum that history is "what actually happened."

In the summer there is even what the Park Service calls "living history," staged troop encampments at re-created fortifications and an artillery demonstration complete with galloping steeds and the live firing of a field piece. These living history personnel, clad in meticulously accurate uniforms, are articulate and courteous. Well-instructed in both history and safety (live cannon are indeed hazardous), they respond to our questions authoritatively and pose patiently for the inevitable photographs. Finally, there is a striking two-level brick visitor center, whose octagonal form, we are told, echoes the actual fortifications of the battlefield, referential architecture at its finest. The core of the center is a cylindrical "war room" whose overhead projectors mark troop positions on a three-dimensional model of the battlefield—providing a brilliant display of audiovisual virtuosity which orients us for the visit. So captivating is the presentation, it may well remain in our memory long after the features of the battlefield itself have faded. The courteous ranger informs us the building was designed to house its display, which was created first, and not vice versa, which is the usual case. In the dim twilight of the interior, we note one portion of the floor has been peeled away to reveal beneath our feet the debris of battle; it is ersatz debris, to be sure, but it looks surprisingly real in the penumbra. Around the perimeter of the walk, well-lighted photo-murals, a diorama, and display cases, while depicting the technology of war and key episodes in the battle, are devoted in large part to presenting the life of the common soldier—the same archetypal figure whose sculptural image adorns the courthouse greens and boulevards of much of North and South.

The place we are visiting used to be classified by the War Department, which supervised it from its inception in 1926 to its transfer to the National Park Service in 1933, as a "military park," yet another modification of that term which has been used to characterize much of American space—national park, landscape park, pocket park, theme park, amusement park. It is now called a "national battlefield." We are at Petersburg National Battlefield, Petersburg, Virginia, whose seige warfare prefigured that of the First World War. Indeed, in the glow of the patriotism and prosperity that followed that war, the funds were appropriated by Congress to establish this park, bringing to fruition the efforts of many private organizations dating back to the late nineteenth century. Petersburg Battlefield is a space of no small extent. 1518.76 acres of it are in federal ownership. While it is one of the more recent battlefield preservations of the federal government, it bears a family resemblance to its older siblings—Antietam National Battlefield, and Gettysburg, Shiloh, and Chickamauga-Chattanooga National Military Parks—all of which were taken over by the federal government in the 1890s.

The space we are in is not devoted to the preservation of priceless and unique natural scenery for future generations, nor is it intended to provide relief from urban stress. It is a space devoted to the memory of war, an attempt to create a memorial in the classic sense, a place that evokes reflection on the meaning of the tumultuous events that transpired within its precincts. One scarcely finds this concept of an *entire* battlefield landscape set aside as a memorial in the rest of the world. Europe is, of course, filled with war memorials, cemeteries, ossuaries, tombs of unknown soldiers, and battlefield markers, but rarely is an entire battlefield itself preserved.[1] The National Trust in England, which is, of course, a private organization, has preserved a few, and one suspects they were inspired to do so by American precedents, in the same fashion the national park idea has been emulated by many nations. Waterloo is a considerable tourist attraction, but it contains nowhere near the number of markers, monuments, or interpretive facilities that the typical American national battlefield does.

When private citizens in Gettysburg, led by Gettysburg attorney David McConaughy, formed themselves into the Gettysburg Battlefield Memorial Association, in September 1863, soon after the battle, it was probably the first time anywhere in Western civilization that a preserved battlefield landscape was to be employed as a memorial. As McConaughy remarked:

> There could be no more fitting and expressive memorial of the heroic valor and signal triumph of our army, on the first, second, and third days of July 1863, than the battlefield itself, with its natural and artificial defenses, preserved and perpetuated in the exact form and condition they presented during the battle.[2]

Just as many nineteenth-century American painters turned to the natural landscape as their proper subject matter, American citizens were beginning to create memorials out of the very landscape itself. When the federal government became involved in the process in the 1890s, the great national parks of the West were being formed to preserve unique natural scenery. Indeed, for a period of time, preserved battlefields such as Gettysburg were referred to simply as "national parks." At present there are 24 of these battlefields in the United States set aside for preservation, comprising a total of about 52,000 acres.[3]

Battlefields pose difficult problems for those who would preserve them. The oft-repeated litany, "historic preservation has come of age," has no doubt much to support it, yet that maturation is sorely tested when one engages these unique memorial landscapes. Little has been written which deals with their preservation—and, like most landscape preservation projects, the issues they pose are legion.[4] This inquiry will address four of these issues which are of fundamental importance: Why preserve battlefields? What should be the visual appearance of a preserved battlefield? What are the advantages and pitfalls of "living history" in battlefield interpretation? And how should battlefield interpretation deal with atrocities or other modes of behavior repugnant to members of a civilized society? We will approach these four questions in part by an analysis and critique of existing examples of battlefield preservation. These questions do not admit of finality. We shall explore their implications and state a tentative position on each of them. Our basic intent is to raise significant questions and stimulate further inquiry into this complex and oft-neglected mode of landscape preservation. Of course, the issues touched upon here transcend the specialty of battlefield preservation. Many, if not all of them, emerge when one confronts the task of preserving a cultural landscape, whether it be seventeenth-century Jamestown, an eighteenth-century Virginia Tidewater plantation, or a nineteenth-century New England industrial town.[5]

Why Preserve Battlefields?

The question "Why preserve battlefields?" may appear on first glance to be rather academic since some 52,000 acres of battlefields are already preserved by the federal government and there are additional ones under state jurisdiction as well.[6] Perhaps the more appropriate question is not *why*, but *how* should we continue to preserve these sites? Yet it should be obvious that the way we preserve something is determined by our reasons for preserving it. Furthermore, this rationale must be subject to constant examination lest we lose all understanding of what we are doing. Preservation is not a once-for-all event; it is an ongoing process in which each generation (or should we say, decade?) reinforces, revises, or expands its cultural memory through interaction with the artifacts and landscapes of its past. A shift—conscious or unconscious—in preservation rationale may bring about a decisive change in the treatment of a site. An unconscious rationale is to be avoided at all costs since it can easily spawn initiatives that might destroy the very thing we are striving to preserve, usually through the saccharine alchemy of nostalgia. Thus the question of why preserve battlefields is both necessary and perennial.

An informed reply requires the perspective of history. Why were the battlefields initially preserved? How were they used and by whom? Has their mode of preservation changed? If so, how and why?[7]

As noted above, the concept of setting aside an entire battlefield as a memorial originated with Gettysburg attorney David McConaughy in September 1863, a scarce five weeks after the battle had ended and before Lincoln's address at the Soldiers National Cemetery, which was founded through a separate citizens' organization. The citizens whom McConaughy addressed formed themselves into a private organization, the Gettysburg Battlefield Memorial Association, which was chartered by the state of Pennsylvania in April 1864. The primary goal of the association was to

> hold, and preserve, the battlegrounds of Gettysburg . . . with the national and artificial defenses, as they were at the time of said battle, and by such perpetuation, and such memorial structures as a generous and patriotic people may aid to erect, to commemorate the heroic deeds, the struggles, and the triumphs of their brave defenders.[8]

At this stage of its evolution, Gettysburg was envisioned as a memorial solely to the Union troops, and the lands purchased for the memorial were a portion of those occupied by the Union army during the battle. The Civil War was to rage for two more bloody years and the setting aside of the field was no doubt intended to inspire the continuous war efforts of the various Union armies.

Thus the Gettysburg preservation, the first of its kind, originated from patriotic motives, which have throughout history inspired many a culture to preserve its tangible past. It began as what Robert M. Utley calls an "associative monument," a monument identified with a particular event in a particular place, whose preservation is intended to be educational, inspirational, and patriotic.[9] Gettysburg became the archetype for other preserved battlefields, so an examination of its development is in order.

Gettysburg evolved as a memorial to contain monuments. The battle landscape itself became a depository of individual monuments erected to commemorate the valor and sacrifice of individuals and of

Fig. 1. Monument to the First Brigade of the First Pennsylvania Cavalry, Gettysburg.

particular units of the Union army (Fig. 2). This is what gives much of the present-day battlefield the look of a sculpture garden or rural cemetery, a vast sweep of greensward dotted profusely with granite and bronze shafts and sculptural images. This came about in the late 1870s, when the Pennsylvania branch of the Union veterans organization of the Grand Army of the Republic held a reunion at Gettysburg and decided to initiate the erection of monuments. The Grand Army of the Republic soon controlled the stock of the Gettysburg Battlefield Memorial Association and elected its officers to the board of directors. By 1888, the twenty-fifth anniversary of the battle, various private associations, some backed by state funds, had erected about 200 major monuments in the national cemetery and on the battlefield.[10]

The erection of a monument occasioned considerable ritual celebration: parades, speeches, a reunion of veterans, and a dramatic unveiling of the monument, which evoked applause and cheers from the gathered throng (Fig. 3). Often the speeches were given by the commanding officer if it was a memorial

Fig. 2. A typical example of an early battlefield monument at Gettysburg, the 14th Connecticut monument erected in 1884. The plaque provides a detailed description of the activities of the unit during the Civil War and is erected on the precise spot where the unit was deployed on the third day at Gettysburg.

veterans. It had become a great ritual ground of reunion and celebration of their sacrifices and heroic deeds. Sculptural images were thought, in particular, to be especially effective in giving visual reality to the individuals who performed heroic deeds and in serving to leave a more lasting impression on future generations. As noted art critic S. R. Koehler remarked in 1886:

We are still capable of feelings of gratitude, of admiration of noble deeds, of legitimate pride in our common country, of the veneration of martyrdom and self-sacrifice, and we experience the need of giving out-ward expression to these feelings. It is quite natural that for this purpose we should turn to art. For it is art only . . . that can give shape to an idea in a way which will appeal to the multitude.[12]

Indeed, it was the image of martyrdom and sacrifice that was used most frequently to characterize the deeds of the Union soldiers at Gettysburg and in other battlefields. As Horace Bushnell addressed the Yale alumni in 1865:

From the shedding of our blood have come great remissions and redemptions. In this blood of our slain our unity is cemented and sanctified. The sacrifices in the field of the Revolution united us but imperfectly. We had not bled enough to merge our colonial distinctions, let out the states rights doctrine, and make us a proper nation. . . . We have now a new and stupendous chapter of national history.[13]

J. Howard Wert, who in 1886 wrote a guide to Gettysburg that moved the visitor from monument to monument, commented on their aesthetic merit, and provided a historical narrative of the events each commemorated, noted in his guide:

The more this field is decorated with these works of art, the more powerful becomes the impetus of the traveller and patriot to visit or revisit the field of glory. . . . Those who have traversed with us these rock-crowned cliffs have gone over the most consecrated ground this world contains, except the path of the Savior of the world as he ascended the rugged heights of Calvary.[14]

Wert reflects how most individuals viewed these spaces; they were sacrificial ground, sanctified by the blood of martyrs. They had the look of sacred space: set apart, marked with monuments, a sacred precinct like those at Delphi or Olympus to honor heroes. The penchant for memorials during the 1880s had created very distinct spaces unlike any others in the country, although resembling in part a landscape park or a rural cemetery. The emphasis on memorials tended to radically transform the original appearance of the battlefield, despite the intention of the Gettysburg Battlefield Memorial Association to maintain the field in

to a brigade or battery, and much of the speech was a stirring reminiscence of the heroic action of the unit itself. The monuments had to be approved by the Memorial Association and were required to be of granite and/or bronze, to be placed exactly on the spot where the unit went into action, and to contain historically accurate details of such matters as the actions of the unit, its members, and its casualties. Most of the monuments were the work of anonymous stonecutters working for such businesses as the Smith Granite Company of Boston or the local firm of J.W. Flaharty, which also sold tombstones and other mortuary monuments.[11]

It is clear that at this stage the battlefield, while serving as a memorial in the classic sense, to remind us of significant events of the past and to inspire dedication to patriotic ideas, had a special meaning to the

Fig. 3. The dedication of the First Bull Run monument, June 10, 1865. Such dedications were accompanied by considerable ceremony, especially parades and stirring addresses by veterans. This form of battlefield commemoration reached its peak in the late nineteenth century. (Courtesy of the Library of Congress)

its "original condition." This is particularly true of Gettysburg and Antietam, where most of the memorial-raising activity was directed, perhaps because both of these battles turned back Confederate attempts to invade the North. Battlefields that were preserved later are not so profusely decked in monuments; typical of these are Petersburg, Fredericksburg, Chancellorsville, and Spotsylvania Courthouse.

Preserved battlefields passed from the hands of private citizens' organizations and individuals to the federal government, and within the government from the War Department to the National Park Service. They have, in David Lowenthal's term, become "landscapes of accretion." Each of these groups have stratified these landscapes in a very particular way, and a brief excavation is in order.

During the post-Reconstruction period, as the United States was developing into a world power, deep consciousness of nationalism pervaded much of the country. As Merle Curti notes, the roots of this sentiment were not so much derived from "the older legalistic concept of Union" as from "the organic theory of the nation" as a gradually evolving entity with a rich cultural tradition. Numerous patriotic

societies were founded, and more and more Americans sought to understand and give expression to feelings of national unity and patriotism.[15] Civil War battlefield sites became the scene of veritable ritual celebrations of national unity—especially rituals of reconciliation between Union and Confederate veterans. In 1875, Confederate veterans from Virginia and South Carolina took part in the Bunker Hill centennial celebration and were cordially received. By 1881, various veterans organizations were holding reunions on battlefields for the "sole reason of rejoicing that they were no longer enemies." This outpouring of national sentiment prompted Congress to appropriate funds to mark *Confederate* and U.S. Regular Army troop positions at Gettysburg. The twenty-fifth anniversary celebration at Gettysburg in 1881 was attended by large numbers of Union and Confederate veterans.[16]

In the wake of this flurry of veterans' activity and intense interest in battlefields, Congress moved in 1890 to authorize the first National Military Park, Chickamauga-Chattanooga. The dedication ceremony, held September 18–20, 1890, was presided over by the Vice-President of the United States. Fourteen governors were in attendance as were 40,000 veterans. As historian Paul Buck remarks:

> The sentiment everywhere expressed was pride in the fact that after thirty years the survivors of the two armies could meet again on the field of conflict under one flag, all lovers of one country . . . they welcomed the mellowed recollection of their quarrel as a bond of union, where once they feared it might divide. . . . Something remarkable in history had occurred.[17]

By 1899, three other parks had been added to the system: Shiloh (1894), Gettysburg (1895), and Vicksburg (1899). In each case, preservation efforts of private citizens' groups were taken over by the federal government and placed under the jurisdiction of the War Department. The veterans' rituals of reconciliation continued in the new parks. The last great reunion of Union and Confederate veterans was at Gettysburg in 1938.

The reason given by Congress for the federal government assuming ownership of the sites is interesting, for it adds yet another dimension to the rationale for battlefield preservation: the bill signed by President Benjamin Harrison for Chickamauga-Chattanooga on August 18, 1890, states that the purpose of the park is "preserving and suitably marking for historical and professional military study the fields of some of the most remarkable maneuvers and most brilliant fighting in the war of the rebellion."[18] The bill thus emphasizes the battlefields as a didactic tool to teach military strategy. Chickamauga was placed under a three-man commission that was to preserve the battlefield in its state at the time of battle and lease land to farmers to keep it in an agricultural use. It was also to mark troop positions and erect towers for study of the field. States could erect memorials to their troops subject to the commission's approval. In 1896, Congress further defined the military park idea by declaring that all the national military parks and their approaches be national fields for military maneuvers for the Regular Army of the United States and the National Guards of the states. Representative John P. Tracy of Missouri, who supported the bill, said of Chickamauga-Chattanooga:

> As a theatre for military instruction, with its 10 square miles of battlefield and 40 miles of approaches, it can not be excelled. No other government owns such a theatre of notable engagements. A month's campaigning for practical study on such a field of maneuvers by the corps of West Point cadets, where the lines of battles and the movements in the engagement of nearly every organization of each side have been ascertained and . . . marked with historical tablets . . . would be worth an entire course in textbooks on the strategy of a campaign and battle tactics.[19]

Using the best tools and personnel of military historiography, especially the expertise of John B. Bachelder, and inspired by the exact standards of German military scholarship, the War Department meticulously mapped troop positions and marked them with cast-iron tablets (Fig. 4). These tablets today lend a certain remoteness to the battlefield landscape and seem to make it conform to a written historical text. One has the distinct impression reading these tablets that the battlefield one views beyond them is more the illustration of a history text than a living landscape.[20]

So the battlefields have had many uses: memorials of the valor and sacrifice of Union troops, places for rituals of reconciliation, laboratories for military tactics, and parks that preserve the site of important events pertaining to the preservation of national unity.

So important did the federal government deem battlefield preservation that it successfully challenged the attempt of private entrepreneurs to build a trolley line across the battlefield at Gettysburg. The entrepreneurs challenged the government's right of eminent domain, but the government's position was upheld by the Supreme Court in 1896.[21]

After this initial flurry of battlefield preservation activity in the 1890s, interest of Congress in such initiatives tended to wane until after the First World War. During the early twentieth century, four battlefield sites were brought into the system, including Antietam, which marked a different approach to the acquisition of land. Instead of buying large parcels of land, the federal government bought thin strips of land along the line of troop positions, fenced these off, and built roads where necessary for access. Outside these boundaries, the land was privately owned and continued to be used as farmland. The so-called "Antietam Plan" set a precedent for battlefield preservation and was quite popular with Congress since it required a much smaller appropriation for land acquisition (Fig. 5).

In 1926, in the heyday of the renewed sentiments of nationalism that occurred after the success of the First World War, Congress authorized the War Department to survey all the battlefields in the United States and to recommend which should be preserved or at least marked with commemorative tablets. Following the Department's recommendation, 12 national military parks were added to the system.[22]

In 1933, the battlefields were transferred from the jurisdiction of the War Department to that of the National Park Service. The War Department had built many roads, erected many tablets, and encouraged the further erection of monuments. The National Park Service has left its own distinct mark on the battlefields it received from the War Department and has added seven more battlefields to its holdings. The

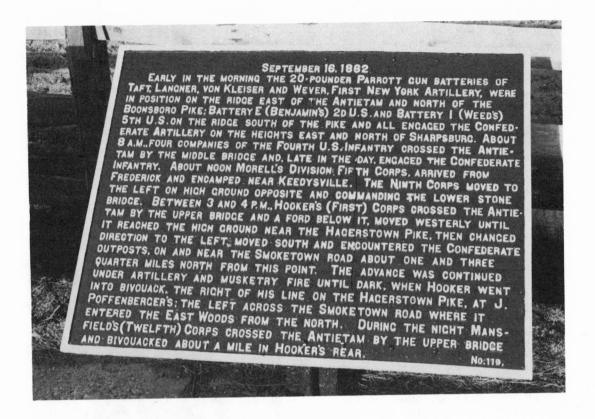

SEPTEMBER 16, 1862

EARLY IN THE MORNING THE 20-POUNDER PARROTT GUN BATTERIES OF TAFT, LANGNER, VON KLEISER AND WEVER, FIRST NEW YORK ARTILLERY, WERE IN POSITION ON THE RIDGE EAST OF THE ANTIETAM AND NORTH OF THE BOONSBORO PIKE; BATTERY E (BENJAMIN'S) 2D U.S. AND BATTERY I (WEED'S) 5TH U.S. ON THE RIDGE SOUTH OF THE PIKE AND ALL ENGAGED THE CONFEDERATE ARTILLERY ON THE HEIGHTS EAST AND NORTH OF SHARPSBURG. ABOUT 8 A.M., FOUR COMPANIES OF THE FOURTH U.S. INFANTRY CROSSED THE ANTIETAM BY THE MIDDLE BRIDGE AND, LATE IN THE DAY, ENGAGED THE CONFEDERATE INFANTRY. ABOUT NOON MORELL'S DIVISION, FIFTH CORPS, ARRIVED FROM FREDERICK AND ENCAMPED NEAR KEEDYSVILLE. THE NINTH CORPS MOVED TO THE LEFT ON HIGH GROUND OPPOSITE AND COMMANDING THE LOWER STONE BRIDGE. BETWEEN 3 AND 4 P.M., HOOKER'S (FIRST) CORPS CROSSED THE ANTIETAM BY THE UPPER BRIDGE AND A FORD BELOW IT, MOVED WESTERLY UNTIL IT REACHED THE HIGH GROUND NEAR THE HAGERSTOWN PIKE, THEN CHANGED DIRECTION TO THE LEFT, MOVED SOUTH AND ENCOUNTERED THE CONFEDERATE OUTPOSTS, ON AND NEAR THE SMOKETOWN ROAD ABOUT ONE AND THREE QUARTER MILES NORTH FROM THIS POINT. THE ADVANCE WAS CONTINUED UNDER ARTILLERY AND MUSKETRY FIRE UNTIL DARK, WHEN HOOKER WENT INTO BIVOUACK, THE RIGHT OF HIS LINE ON THE HAGERSTOWN PIKE, AT J. POFFENBERGER'S; THE LEFT ACROSS THE SMOKETOWN ROAD WHERE IT ENTERED THE EAST WOODS FROM THE NORTH. DURING THE NIGHT MANSFIELD'S (TWELFTH) CORPS CROSSED THE ANTIETAM BY THE UPPER BRIDGE AND BIVOUACKED ABOUT A MILE IN HOOKER'S REAR.

NO: 119.

Fig. 4. A typical example of battlefield interpretation by the Department of War. Such cast-iron tablets tend to encourage the perception of the battlefield landscape as an illustration in a military history textbook.

Fig. 5. A classic example of the Antietam Plan of battlefield preservation initiated by the Department of War at Antietam. Land beyond the fence on either side of the road is privately owned and presently under cultivation. Only the road and its shoulders to the fence are owned by the federal government.

passage of the Historic Sites Act in 1935 increased the activity of the Park Service in battlefield preservation. During the early New Deal, several units of the Civilian Conservation Corps were put to work clearing forests of undergrowth, building roads, and stabilizing fortifications—the fields of commemoration became fields of employment for sufferers of the Depression.

After the Second World War, the Mission 66 program of the Park Service built many new visitor centers on the battlefields, commissioning in some cases prominent architects, such as Richard Neutra, who designed the new center at Gettysburg. The new visitor centers, often imposing structures equipped with sophisticated audiovisual presentations and elaborate museum displays of artifacts, became the new guides to the battlefields, replacing the oral tradition of the now-dead veterans and the old guide books to the monuments. The new visitor centers also supplemented the primarily military-historical interpretations of the War Department with a much wider range of information. The interpretive content of these centers varies, but they have a tendency to recall the sufferings of war and the life of the common soldier, as well as to provide detailed information about tactics and technology. The battles are also placed in their broader historical contexts, although little tends to be said about the basic issues for which the Civil War was fought.[23]

Monuments continued to be added to the battlefields, but certainly not in the number of the 1880s. Most of them were by Southern states and commemorate the deeds of the troops of an entire state, rather than specific military units; as time distances us from events, our monuments become more general (Fig. 6). During the 1970s so-called "living history" demonstrations were introduced, and visitors were instructed (often more entertained) by personnel in authentic uniforms, firing muskets and cannon and explaining the battle. Perhaps we can view these personnel as thespian replacements for the living presence of the old veterans.

Thus these memorial landscapes have many accretions, knowledge of which is necessary if one is to address the question of why preserve them (Fig. 7). With this rather lengthy but necessary historical prolegomena behind us, let us turn to the task. Clearly, certain reasons for the preservation of battlefields in the past are no longer relevant today. In an age of thermonuclear weapons, their value as classrooms for the study of strategy and tactics is clearly limited, although they are still of great value to military historians. The Civil War veterans who used them for reconciliations with their former foes are long deceased, and the nation's need to heal the wounds of

Fig. 6. The North Carolina monument at Gettysburg by Gutzon Borglum, dedicated July 3, 1929. While erected on the spot where North Carolina troops began their participation in Pickett's famous charge, the monument is to the troops of the entire state, not just a particular unit.

civil strife and reaffirm national unity has long since vanished.

Are these landscapes then wasted space? Are they bombastic glorifications of war (a critique often heard at the height of the Viet-Nam protests in the early 1970s), which do not merit the funds necessary to maintain them? Could they, through adaptive reuse, such as for more intensive recreation, better serve the needs of the regions where they are located? Do they usurp funds from other more worthy projects of preservation?

In 1979 no less a person than William Whalen, the Director of the National Park Service, confided to a *Philadelphia Inquirer* reporter that he had "had it up to here" with battlefields and that we knew more about "the genealogy of every Civil War general's horse" than about some of the distinguished artists in American history, such as Richard Rodgers and Ernest Hemingway, who "should be enshrined." On another

Fig. 7. A juxtaposition of mid-twentieth-century modes of battlefield interpretation with the older mode at the site of the Crater at Petersburg. In the foreground is a National Park Service audiovisual exhibit, complete with recording device in the brick box, which provides a narration of the battle. The tablets contain a reproduction of John Elder's nineteenth-century painting of the Crater episode and a diagram of the troop movements at the Crater. The obelisk in the background is an early-twentieth-century memorial to Brigadier General Mahone, who led the Confederate counterattack at this site.

occasion, Whalen suggested the Park Service consider retaining jurisdiction only over Fort Sumter, Gettysburg, and Appomattox Courthouse, and turn all other battlefields back to the states, presumably freeing funds for uses he thought more pressing.[24] (Whalen's remarks evoked a storm of protest both from within the Park Service and from private citizens' groups and never even came close to implemention.)

Our historical investigation should have made it clear that there is no substance to the charge that the battlefields glorify war. To be sure, landscape perception is in the eye of the beholder,[25] but if one takes the trouble to observe present preservation efforts of the Park Service, the stress is upon historical context, technology, and the experience of the ordinary frontline soldier, especially the suffering of war. At the Antietam visitor center, one is confronted with lucite panels etched with quotations from letters of the battle participants, who speak of their fears of battle and their grief for fallen comrades. One quote describes what it feels like to be wounded by a musket ball. Indeed, such realism causes some visitors to remark that the Park Service display is "anti-war." The visitor

centers at Fredericksburg, Chancellorsville, the Wilderness, Spotsylvania Courthouse, Gettysburg, Petersburg, and Manassas contain similar material. From the very outset, these landscapes were set aside to function as memorials to remind one of obligations to the Constitution and the sacrifice that may be required to honor that obligation. The profuse use of monuments may offend current canons of artistic taste and appear to some to be bombastic, but this says more about those who make the judgments than about the original understandings of those who erected the monuments. Our current canons of taste will no doubt chagrin, amaze, and amuse critics of future generations.

One can also understand the need of local communities for expanded recreational facilities. The spring-time automobile *passeggiáta* at Petersburg referred to above is primarily composed of local teenagers who view the park as a suitable place to celebrate the rites of spring—and after all, the battlefield does resemble a landscape park. Cross-country skiers recently filled the visitor center parking lot at Manassas, making it very difficult to visit the center

77

itself. The undulating terrain of the field could not be better for an exhilarating ski outing. The need for recreational space in some regions creates pressure on the Park Service to condone such uses. To date, the policy has been to prohibit active team sports or other forms of recreation that might interfere with the interpretation of the battlefield or damage the preserved fortifications. Passive recreation is usually confined to special areas away from the major portions of the field.

One can also understand the need to cut costs by the Park Service as well as the beginning of efforts to preserve cultural landscapes that honor great artists and musicians.

Yet to convert a preserved battlefield into yet another pleasant park for little league baseball, soccer, or whatever lawn sport may be in fashion (regardless of how worthwhile the pursuits are in themselves) would be to deprive the nation of some of its most valuable memorials. To turn most of them over to state control would, in many cases, be sure to bring this about, because many of them, especially those like Manassas, Fredericksburg, or Petersburg, which are encircled by rapidly expanding urban areas, would be much more vulnerable to local pressures for extensive adaptive reuse for recreation.

Why are these landscapes such valuable memorials that their continued preservation is mandatory? Stated quite generally, these landscapes preserve tangible evidence of some of the most significant events in American history. They merit preservation for the same reason any artifact, building, or landscape merits preservation: they help maintain a consciousness of the past that is essential for the development of a coherent cultural identity. As David Lowenthal aptly remarks: "Awareness of the past is essential to maintenance of purpose in life. Without it we would lack all sense of continuity, all apprehension of causality, all knowledge of our own identity."[26] Cultural traditions are transmitted, reevaluated, and renewed in a number of ways, and effective memorials are surely an important part of that process. Battlefields are especially significant memorial landscapes, for they challenge us to recall basic realities of historical experience, especially those of death, suffering and sacrifice—realities often ignored. The battlefield landscape itself, combined with sensitive interpretation, can concretize the experience of war and evoke reflection on its role in American cultural history in a way no literary text, photograph, or film can. Landscape is, as Lowenthal observes, "memory's most serviceable reminder"; we may not understand the reason for this, but the reality of our own experience attests to it. A visit to Dachau brands one's consciousness with the unfathomable horror of the Holocaust in a way no narration or photograph can.

There is something about the experience of the physical reality of the place, of being there, of walking over the grounds; it internalizes the immediate sensations in a way that admits no substitute. Of course, one brings knowledge and memory to such places—photography, art, and literature contribute greatly to this; these things always act in concert.

The reflections evoked by battlefields will, of course, vary from individual to individual and from generation to generation; memorials are as protean as culture. When General Daniel E. Sickles introduced legislation to preserve Gettysburg, he remarked that war is a necessary reality of culture and that future generations will be prepared to face the inevitable if they are conscious of how suffering and sacrifice have been valued and celebrated by previous generations.[27] Today, when the threat of thermonuclear war renders Sickles' reflections on the inevitability of war questionable, the very battlefield he helped to preserve provokes new thought in an altered context.

The potential power of a battlefield to evoke thought is illustrated by Matthew Stevenson's recent article in Harper's, "The Bloody Angle: Reagan and the Civil War." Stevenson contrasts "the romantic view of war" of President Reagan and Secretary of State Haig with his own perception of the grim reality of war mediated by a visit to the Bloody Angle portion of the Spotsylvania Courthouse Battlefield, where Union and Confederate troops fought hand-to-hand for almost 20 hours. Stevenson remarks that "the romantic picture of war is so much easier to project than the actual landscape of the battle," and notes that "no battlefield I have seen, with the possible exception of Verdun, is a stronger reminder of the tragedy of war than Spotsylvania."[28] Stevenson's critique of President Reagan may or may not be just—for us that is not the immediate issue. The point is the power of the battlefield landscape to evoke reflection and counter a tendency to romanticize war. (One recalls that civilians rode out from Washington in carriages to enjoy the romantic spectacle of the battle at Manassas and were rudely awakened by what they witnessed.) For Stevenson, he "who is ignorant of the past is condemned to repeat it" (Santayana). For someone else, the response could well be different; it could perhaps evoke an awakening of pride in the courage of American soldiers, or a reflection on the broader issues for which the battles were waged—slavery and the preservation of the union. Let us not deprive ourselves of the occasion for such reflections by converting these monuments to pleasant greenswards for lawn sports or whatever other use one might envision.

J. B. Jackson suggests that the traditional role of memorials in our culture, to provoke thought and to renew obligations, has declined, having been replaced in large part by ritual reenactments of the past, colored by nostalgia and a lack of interest in particular historical personages or events—whether in re-creations of seventeenth-century Spanish villages or eighteenth-century New England farms:

> The past is brought back in all its richness. There is no lesson to learn, no covenant to honor; we are charmed into a state of innocence and become part of the environment. History ceases to exist.[29]

There is much to support this view. However, in our opinion, memorials in the classic sense are essential to the health of a culture, and the experience recounted in Stevenson's article suggests that they are still capable of functioning and need to be preserved. Well over a million people journey to Gettysburg each year, and other battlefields receive heavy visitation. No doubt this continuing interest is attributable to many factors. But the fact that the National Park Service's interpretation treats these sites as memorials in the classic sense, and that visitors often return, suggests the concept of memorial is not dead.

There is yet another reason to continue the preservation of these landscapes. In a sense, when one preserves the battlefields of the Revolution or the Civil War, one is dealing with the preservation of a preservation. Especially with the older battlefields—Gettysburg, Shiloh, and Antietam—one has to consider the way our forefathers commemorated war. Those monuments, which were intended to honor sacrifice and heroic deeds, have become historic artifacts in themselves, even though that was not the original intention. It would be worthwhile to preserve many of the battlefields for this reason alone, quite apart from their power to evoke reflection on the issue of war.

Visual Appearance

If battlefields are worth preserving both to function as memorials in the classic sense and to bear witness to the way past generations commemorated war, what should be their visual appearance? This issue is a difficult one for many reasons. The oft-overheard remark by visitors at preserved battlefields, "It certainly doesn't look like a battlefield," leads us to the core of the problem.[30]

Battlefields are landscapes extraordinarily difficult to either preserve or restore to a condition that even closely resembles their original state (Fig. 8). Of course, much hinges on what we mean by "original state." This refers primarily to the condition at the time of battle and includes traces of the battle itself upon the landscape: trenches, forts, etc., and in some cases actual alterations of the terrain itself by the power of explosives. Most other types of landscapes singled out for preservation bear the mark of routin-

ized human behavior, such as the seed time and harvest of the farm, or the orchestrated rhythms of the factory. Such routinization produces relatively stable, orderly, and well-defined landscapes, which ease the task of preservation. Battles are unique, complex, ephemeral events; they mark a landscape with fortifications and debris, which quickly disappear. Indeed, many battles fought on American soil occurred on agricultural land, which the owners wished to return to tillage as soon as possible. Hence artifacts were rapidly removed and fortifications destroyed (this is why the Gettysburg Battlefield Memorial Association moved so quickly in their preservation efforts). What human initiative does not transform, soil erosion and plant succession quickly erase, especially the lush vegetative growth of the Southern and Mid-Atlantic states, where so many of the battlefields are located.

In cases where battlefield lands have been acquired piecemeal, the mark of later generations is much in evidence, especially in the form of farms or dwellings. At Petersburg a major portion of the battlefield long remained in private hands, and a golf course, complete with clubhouse, was erected on the site of the "Crater," one of the most significant landmarks of the battlefield.[31] In other cases, many important landmark structures existing at the time of battle have disappeared, such as the original Dunkard Church at Antietam, which fell victim to fire. In almost all cases, residential and commercial development have obtruded on the borders of battlefields, destroying many historic vistas (Fig. 9). The most blatant example of this is the 300-foot "National Tower" at Gettysburg, whose pseudo-patriotic name scarcely atones for the fact that its Flash Gordon Revival space needle peers over the field, destroying virtually every historic vista and providing an absurd counterpoint to the monuments (Fig. 10).

In our preservation efforts what visual appearance should we strive for? Older battlefields marked with numerous monuments erected in the late nineteenth and early twentieth centuries should be preserved as they are now. They should also be interpreted. While much National Park Service interpretation is quite comprehensive, visitors to Gettysburg or Antietam might understand these places in more depth if some material on the history of their preservation, especially on nineteenth-century ideas of battlefield preservation, were included in the interpretation.

In the case of both the more recent battlefields, which have comparatively few monuments, and the older ones, the battlefield itself should be restored to look as much as possible as it did at the time of battle. Such restoration can only be an approximation. Vistas to and from the battlefield need to be protected, preferably by land acquisition, which is the surest

Fig. 8.   Fort Mahone, a major bulwark of the Confederate line at Petersburg shortly after its capture in 1865. This wasteland of treeless, compacted earth is typical of the original condition of the battlefield, which is quite impossible to preserve. (Courtesy of the National Archives)

Fig. 9.   Strip development at Petersburg has covered a portion of the original battlefield that the federal government failed to purchase. The granite monument at the corner of the building marks the position of a Confederate artillery piece.

Fig. 10. Henry Kirke Bush-Brown's equestrian statue of General Meade shadowed by the 300-foot space needle of the "National Tower" at Gettysburg. This is a classic example of what can occur if there is no visual protection for the perimeters of battlefields.

means to achieve this. Obtrusive development on the perimeters of battlefields should be controlled by effective zoning and land-use planning, although this is exceedingly difficult. Scenic easements are a viable but less desirable alternative, since they can create extensive legal problems and are not as iron-clad as ownership of land in fee simple. Since most of the battles were fought on agricultural land, the fields themselves should be returned to this condition. Literal replication of crops and fields is usually impossible and, even if it were, creates great problems of maintenance. Leasing the land to farmers who will keep it in crop land that is financially feasible should suffice to suggest the nineteenth-century agrarian landscape. In this fashion, much prime agricultural land could continue to remain in production, and maintenance costs would be quite meager. This is the present policy of the Park Service and it is an excellent one.

The open spaces of the landscape should be maintained to approximate their appearance at the time of battle, for they are important to understanding the strategy of any battle. Again, given the dynamic quality of vegetation, this can only be an approximation. As Robert Utley, of the Park Service, remarks:

At Gettysburg . . . we can insure that there will always be a copse of trees at Bloody Angle, although the trees may not

always be the exact size of those that were there in 1863. . . . We can see that the forest does not advance into what at the historic moment were open meadows and interfere with vistas crucial to an understanding of the Gettysburg battle.[32]

The clearing of such vistas is expensive work. In an era of austerity, park directors have to single out the most important vistas for such treatment.[33]

Fortifications pose a particular problem, especially those constructed of such impermanent materials as earth and logs. Most have already eroded badly—trenches are filled and forts appear as smooth earth berms. Such marks of the battle should be stabilized, yet they need not be fully restored. They provide a subtle sign of decay and aging which suggests the antiquity of the battle. They are marks of the authenticity of the field. As Lowenthal aptly remarks, "Total restoration subverts historical awareness. The newly-minted completeness of Williamsburg and Old Sturbridge Village makes it difficult to imagine oneself back in the past."[34]

This certainly applies to remains of fortifications, quite apart from the exorbitant expense of total restoration. However, as an aid to memory, partial restoration of fortifications may be warranted. At Petersburg a small fragment of the trenches and bomb proofs has been restored, which effectively suggests the whole. Such efforts, when guided by meticulous historical accuracy and marked by restraint, are quite warranted, for they surely aid our understanding of the site. However, the re-creation of battlescars on the landscape is unwarranted gimmickry lacking the true ring of history—like false wormholes in furniture. The Crater at Petersburg is a case in point. It was originally a hole, 170 feet long, 60–80 feet wide, and 30 feet deep, blown in the Confederate line by Union troops who tunneled underneath and planted a charge. Today the Crater has been filled in by erosion and hardly resembles its former self. Some have suggested the Park Service dig it or, better yet, blast it out again and then stabilize the sides to create a dramatic experience for visitors. The Petersburg authorities have quite rightly refused to resort to such restoration theatrics.

Yet, as Kevin Lynch has pointed out, our interest in the past frequently causes us to alter it markedly.[35] Fortifications are a case in point. The parklike ambience of Petersburg is caused in large part by the turf used to stabilize large areas of ground that was originally the bare, compacted earth characteristic of trench warfare. The same is true of Yorktown. Again, some interpretive information provided in the visitor centers might explain the parklike appearance of the field in terms of preservation technology.

The question of structures that existed on the site at the time of the battle but that have long since disappeared poses special problems. If one refuses to blow open the Crater again, why reconstruct a long-vanished structure? In our opinion, it is warranted when a landmark critical to an understanding of the battle has disappeared. Hence portions of the wall along the Sunken Road at Fredericksburg have been reconstructed, as has the Dunkard Church at Antietam—both are important landmarks and such work is justified. In most cases, a marking of foundations and a photograph or rendering of the original structure or an interpretive plaque will suffice. The problem with such reconstructions, besides expense, is that the general public will often regard them as the real thing despite all efforts to the contrary.

Whether or not to remove structures erected on the site at a later time is also problematic. If later structures are of historic significance and interest in their own right, it would be an error to destroy them. Perhaps they can be moved if they obtrude on a central position of the field. Each case must be judged in its own right. If subsequent structures are of no particular distinction, they should be removed. The old golf clubhouse at the Crater was used for a while as a visitor center, then dismantled to make room for the new center. It was a structure of no particular architectural merit or historical importance, so this was warranted.

Ironically, some of the most obtrusive structures on the battlefields are the Park Service visitor centers (Fig. 12). Robert Utley is correct when he remarks, "The first question to ask is not where to place the visitor center but whether one is needed at all."[36] The same is true of roads, parking lots, maintenance facilities, and other visitor accommodations.

In our opinion, the visitor centers at Gettysburg, Antietam, Yorktown, and Manassas obtrude on their sites. They occupy important troop positions and become the visual focal point of the battlefield itself. Much more successful sitings, which subordinate the building to the landscape, occur at Petersburg and Chancellorsville. The small interpretive shelters at the Wilderness and Spotsylvania Courthouse are outstanding. They provide succinct and relevant information yet are unobtrusive.

Thus, battlefield preservation demands compromise and the judicious use of the power of suggestion. One can only allude to the original conditions, not re-create them. The trend at present in the National Park Service is away from the symbolic landscape of memorials and to the realism of re-creating the condition of the land at the exact time of battle. Like Capability Brown in the eighteenth century, who turned from the profuse use of temples and follies in site plans to a simple palette of forest, lake, and greensward, present work tends toward a realism that pays particular attention to suggesting original patterns of vegetation, limiting automobile access, and dispensing with elaborate visitor centers. Much of this has to do with waning enthusiasm for the erection of monuments. In the projected plans for Monocacy National Battlefield (the site where Jubal Early's raid on Washington was temporarily halted in July 1864), the small visitor center is on the perimeter of the site, and access to the main portion of the battlefield is solely by foot trails.[37] In what is one of the most thoughtful treatments of battlefield preservation in recent literature, Robert W. Meinhard, chairman of battlefield preservation of the National Congress of Civil War Roundtables, strongly defends what we call the realistic approach, stating that the battlefield park "should resemble as closely as possible its appearance at the time of the Civil War" and calling for as little development along park boundaries or construction within the park as possible, including roads, monuments, and visitor centers.[38] Robert Z. Melnick's proposed standards for the preservation of "historic landscapes," while not specifically geared to battlefield preservation, reflect a similar position and offer many valuable insights for battlefield preservation per se.[39] This "realistic" treatment, which we also espouse, bespeaks a sensitivity to the historic integrity of the site. Also, the tabula rasa of the more realistic treatment seems to free us from the bombardment by

Fig. 11. A portion of the Petersburg battlefield today. The cannon are pointed toward the site of the "Crater," which is on the horizon in the middle of the photograph. This parklike appearance results from the use of turf to stabilize ground that was originally without vegetation and subject to rapid erosion. Forests had overgrown much of the site, necessitating a clearing of the vista to the Crater at considerable expense.

Fig. 12. Architect Richard Neutra's visitor center at Gettysburg. The cylindrical portion on the left houses Philippoteaux's cyclorama. This is one of the more elaborate visitor centers erected by the National Park Service during its Mission 66 program of expansion. While Neutra's building is a striking work of architecture, it obtrudes on the battlefield, occupying a major portion of Cemetery Ridge, an important landmark.

monuments and cast-iron tablets to reflect on the meaning of the place. Spotsylvania Courthouse is preserved very much in this way, and this is the landscape that so moved Matthew Stevenson in his *Harper's* article.

On one level, this treatment is economical, well-serving an era of tight budgets: maintenance costs are lower and construction of expensive facilities is avoided. Yet it requires in many cases the protection of the site by land purchase or problematic scenic easements, which can incur considerable costs. Yet the integrity of the landscape is well worth the expense.

Interpretation

The manner in which a battlefield is interpreted is crucial to its ability to function as a memorial. In the remaining part of this essay, let us examine some issues of battlefield interpretation.

The first has to do with "living history," which began to be employed by the National Park Service in the early 1970s and perhaps reached its peak in mid-decade. At present, budgetary cutbacks have reduced it considerably. At Petersburg, a brochure distributed to visitors during the summer, when the living history program functions, describes it in part as follows:

> Stop 3—Union Camp: Walk back to 1864. Visit the camp of the 200th Pennsylvania Volunteer Infantry. A soldier or campfollower will escort you through the reconstructed living quarters and earthworks. . . . (Fig. 13).

> Stop 5—Fort Stedman: Confederate and Union private soldiers will talk with you about the Battle of Fort Stedman, March 25, 1865, General Robert E. Lee's last offensive.

> Stop 5—Artillery Demonstration: Representatives of Louisiana's Washington Artillery gallop into the area with cannon and limber drawn by a 6 horse team. Using the authentic Civil War drill, the 12 pounder Napoleon field gun is fired at 11:00, 2:30, and 4:30.[40]

The potential value of such demonstrations is that they can sharpen our understanding of the battle itself, thus provoking significant reflection on the meaning of the events that occurred there. The problem with such activities is that they become ends in themselves—a celebration of military technology, or a charming demonstration colored with nostalgia, which may instill a superficial romanticism about war. Often visitors leave the park with little else in their memories than the performances of the living history personnel.

Whether the origin of such activity lies in an emulation of Walt Disney's living history at Disneyland, or the hucksterism of the Civil War Centennial, or deeper shifts in our historical consciousness is not for us to decide. Certainly such "living history" can quite easily become precisely the kind of "historical, theatrical, make-believe" that J.B. Jackson speaks of, which blots out the lessons of the past and charms us into a state of innocence, where history as the precise memory of personages and events ceases to exist.

It is no surprise that historians in the National Park Service have become very wary of it. Robert Utley reminds park supervisors of the propensity of living history to "blur our understanding." He notes it is of "utmost importance" for park officers to "critically examine the appropriateness of their living history programs," which, far from being "harmless diversions," can become "unusually distractive." Utley does not call for the outright abolishment of such programs, but his remarks, if heeded, would certainly lead to their curtailment.[41]

However, the National Park Service has forbidden outright one form of living history—namely, battle reenactment. The policy stems in large part from problems arising from enactments permitted by the Park Service on battlefield sites during the Civil War Centennial. In the heat of the reenactment of the First Battle of Manassas, some participants were bayoneted and accidentally shot by ramrods, and some even attempted to sue the Park Service for failure to ensure adequate safety. (Litigation may indeed be an unexplored deterrent to war.) Regardless of the fact that some reenactment groups have strict safety standards and serious didactic purposes (The North-South Brigade, which participates in Civil War reenactments in the Washington, D.C. area, notes that "by these presentations we hope to educate the public and rekindle the flames of patriotism and encourage the study of our nation's heritage and history,"[42] indicating that the group clearly considers itself a memorial in the classic sense), we can only agree with the present policy of the Park Service. The issue is not so much that of public safety as that such reenactments inevitably distort historical events and often damage the battlefields themselves. More importantly, they turn what is essentially a human tragedy into the occasion for recreation. Ben Levy, Acting Chief Historian of the National Park Service, states the case most decisively when he says that "people seek enjoyment out of what was literally a human tragedy. I am appalled. . . . I would hope we would be emerging from this form of cowboys and Indians."[43] Edwin C. Bearss, National Park Service Supervisory Historian and combat veteran of the Second World War, shares Levy's perspective, calling such reenacts "historically inaccurate," "demeaning," and a "charade of the combat soldier."[44] We quite agree; such actions performed on preserved battlefields can only distort their function as memorials. If reenactment groups wish to engage in these activities elsewhere, that is, of course, their prerogative. In our opinion, the last legitimate reenactments were those of the veterans themselves,

Fig. 13. Living history at Petersburg, a reconstruction of a portion of the camp of the 200th Pennsylvania Volunteer Infantry. Such demonstrations, when carefully supervised by a qualified historian and done on a limited scale, can contribute to the visitor's understanding of the battle. If not, they become gross distortions of historical events and an end in themselves. (Courtesy of the National Park Service; photograph by Walter H. Miller)

who often replaced the mimicry of combat with rituals of reconciliation. At Gettysburg, on July 13, 1913, survivors of Pickett's Charge dressed ranks 100 feet from their former adversaries and rushed forward to embrace them, while a huge crowd of spectators cheered.

Is it advisable to allow the judiciously supervised living history "demonstrations" (as opposed to reenactments) that Utley suggests? Or should such activity be discontinued altogether as tending toward "total restoration that subverts historical awareness"? In the particular case of battlefields, so great is the danger of distortion that such activity should be severely curtailed. Much depends on the supervision of personnel by a trained park historian. Well-instructed individuals in uniform on specific battle sites can obviously serve as extremely valuable guides. Too much pageantry and demonstration of the technology of war can overpower other themes in the interpretation and become an end in itself. Each case must be judged in the total context of a battlefield park's entire facilities of interpretation by a competent historian. In cases of budgetary restraint, preservation and maintenance of the landscape itself is a far greater priority than such living history programs.

While many issues in battlefield interpretation revolve around the distortion or embellishment of history, a central problem is the omission of certain events embodying modes of behavior that are shock-ing or repugnant. Traditionally, historic preservation has been primarily motivated by patriotism or the desire to celebrate the positive attributes of a given culture. The motto of Colonial Williamsburg is "That the future may learn from the past," and the official guidebook states that the visitor should "see Williamsburg as an affirmation of the spiritual vigor which must underlie any strong democratic society."[45] To seek encouragement and inspiration from one's cultural past is certainly a worthy endeavor, but it often leads to an outright repression of the less savory dimensions of the past, which also have their pedagogical value. A humorous example is the dismantling of a memorial to Gold Rush prostitutes by the irate city fathers of Kern County, California, who regarded such individuals unworthy of commemoration.[46] A more serious one is the frequent omission of slave cabins from eighteenth- and nineteenth-century Southern plantation reconstructions, which present a nostalgic image of luxury and elegance divorced from the perverse social system that supported it.

Battlefield interpretation presents a similar problem. It is often said that battle brings out the best and the worst in its participants, yet it is usually only the best that is recounted in battlefield interpretation. There is indeed much to celebrate: the courage and sacrifice of innumerable combat troops, who in the Civil War suffered staggering casualties in large part because tactics and strategy had not caught up with advances in weaponry; heroic deeds of compassion, like those of Richard R. Kirkland, the "Angel of Marye's Heights," who risked his life to minister to the wounded of both sides at Fredericksburg (Fig. 14); General Gordon's chivalric care for General Barlow, his wounded adversary, in the heat of the Battle of Gettysburg, which has been commemorated in a diorama at the visitor center; the brilliant tactics of Stonewall Jackson at the Battle of Chancellorsville. The examples are legion.

Yet there were often darker sides to many battles, the knowledge of which is essential to a serious reflection on the issues involved. Omission of such events in battlefield interpretation deprives these landscapes of much of their efficacy as memorials. We are not speaking here of self-destructive, masochistic reveling in the negative aspects of one's cultural past. It is a question of developing a mature cultural memory that is able to acknowledge past mistakes — even barbarisms — as errors that have been transcended or as potential reoccurrences to be avoided in the present.

Certain events in the seige of Petersburg and their interpretation at the Petersburg visitor center and by on-site guides and recordings will serve to illustrate the point. At one time in the ten-month seige of Petersburg, some members of the 48th Pennsylvania Volunteers, many of whom were former coal miners, devised a daring plan to tunnel underneath the Confederate earthworks and blow a gap in the line, which could then be taken by direct assault. Under the supervision of Lieutenant Colonel Henry Pleasants, a 585-foot shaft was dug and about four tons of black powder set for detonation. The explosion was planned for July 30, 1864, and Union troops were made ready to assault the line. Originally a division of black troops (the Fourth Division under the command of General Edward Ferrero) were to lead the assault and had undergone special training for the task. Following the suggestion of General George G. Meade, General Ulysses S. Grant decided at the last minute to replace these troops with white troops, for political reasons, lest it appear the black troops were being sacrificed if the venture should fail. The black troops were relegated to a support role in the assault.

The full details of the debacle known as the Battle of the Crater need not concern us.[47] The black powder charge blew an enormous hole in the Confederate lines, henceforth known as "the Crater." In the ensuing battle, the Union assault force was poorly led and poorly coordinated and lost what should have been an almost certain opportunity to take the town of Petersburg and end the seige. The black support division remained committed to the action even when the chances for success had been all but lost, and they suffered heavy casualties. In the fierce and successful

counterattack led by Confederate Brigadier General William Mahone, many Confederate troops refused to take the black soldiers prisoner and killed them outright. In some instances, black troops were even bayoneted by white Union soldiers when they retreated to the rim of the Crater, since the whites feared the Confederates might kill them also if they were captured fighting alongside blacks. George L. Kilmer, of the 14th New York Heavy Artillery, provided the following eye-witness account of the Crater episode:

> White men [Union troops] bayoneted blacks who fell back into the Crater. This was in order to preserve the whites from Confederate vengeance. Men boasted in my presence that blacks had been thus disposed of, particularly when the Confederates came up.[48]

How is the episode of the Crater treated at Petersburg? In the visitor center, the audiovisual presentation recounts the digging of the tunnel by the former Pennsylvania miners, but makes no mention of the participation of the black troops in the assault. An entire display panel of the center's exhibit hall is devoted to the Crater episode, but, again, participation by the black troops is not mentioned, although a sketch by A. R. Waud, which depicts them going into action, is exhibited (Fig. 15). At the site of the Crater, a recording mentions their participation in the action but does not refer to the atrocities committed against them. However, a guide on duty at the Crater in the summer has been fully briefed on the details of the episode and is prepared to provide details about it if asked. A new panel specifically devoted to the contributions of black troops at Petersburg is being prepared for the visitor center, but there are no plans at present to mention the atrocities against them. Literature on sale at the visitor center, on the other hand, does document the episode.

One can well understand the hesitation of officials at Petersburg to bring such shocking atrocities to light. Yet, in our opinion, they should be included in the interpretation. Such events remind us that slavery was a major issue in the Civil War and of the suffering that the black minority has been subjected to in our nation's history. (One also notes that at present no mention is made of the fact that most of the elaborate Confederate earthworks defending Petersburg were dug by slaves — although the new panel will help correct this omission.)

How should such events be included? We suggest they be recounted in the recording at the Crater site and in the new panel on black troops. One need only recount the event; to moralize about it would be trivial. It speaks for itself. A quotation of George L. Kilmer's account would suffice. If, on other bat-

Fig. 14. The monument to Richard R. Kirkland, "The Angel of Marye's Heights," at Fredericksburg. It is a celebration of his compassion. The tendency in battlefield interpretation, however, has been to commemorate deeds of valor and sacrifice and to make no mention of atrocities or other negative modes of behavior.

tlefields, similar events occurred, they should be recorded, for they are part of the reality of the event. To repeat, the point is not to indulge in masochism, but to overcome nostalgia in order to develop a mature cultural memory that does not hestitate to acknowledge both error and evil in one's national tradition.[49]

Inevitably we renew our acquaintance with the past through the perspective of the present. Preservation is a never-ending process. Kafka remarked, "Books often work like a key to unknown rooms in one's own castle." Preserved battlefields can work the same way. They number among our most important historic landscapes.

NOTES

1. For an excellent discussion of European war memorials, see James S. Curl, *A Celebration of Death: An Introduction to Some of the Buildings, Monuments, and Settings of Funerary Architecture in the Western European Tradition* (New York: Charles Scribners Sons, 1980), Chap. 11.

2. As quoted in Kathleen R. Georg, "Gettysburg: A Happy and Patriotic Conception" (Unpublished ms.), pp. 2–3. Ms. Georg is Research Historian, Gettysburg National Military Park. This manuscript contains much valuable information on the preservation work at Gettysburg.

3. *The Complete Guide to America's National Parks: The Official Visitors Guide of the National Park Foundation* (The National Park Foundation, 1979), p. 292.

4. See Robert W. Meinhard, "Battlefields under Fire," *National Parks and Conservation Magazine* (October 1979): 9–11; and Paul B. Beers, "This Ground Hallowed?" *Civil War Times Illustrated* (February 1972): 37–47.

5. A brief, but excellent, discussion of some basic issues confronting those who engage in historic preservation can be found in Pierce F. Lewis, "The Future of the Past: Our Clouded Vision of Historic Preservation," *Pioneer America, The Journal of the Pioneer America Society,* VII, 2 (July 1975): 1–20.

6. A consideration of battlefield preservation efforts by various state governments is beyond the scope of this study, although it is certainly an interesting and important area for investigation.

7. The most thorough treatment of the history of battlefield preservation is Ronald F. Lee, *The Origin and Evolution of the National Military Park Idea* (United

Fig. 15.   Alfred R. Waud's sketch of the black Fourth Division going into action at the Battle of the Crater. In the present interpretive displays at Petersburg, no mention is made of the atrocities committed against this unit by both the Confederate and the Union troops in the heat of battle. (Courtesy of the National Park Service; drawing by Alfred R. Waud)

States Department of the Interior, National Park Service, Office of Park Historic Preservation, 1973).

8. As quoted in K. Georg, *op. cit.,* p. 3.

9. Robert M. Utley, "A Preservation Ideal," *Historic Preservation,* 28, 2 (April–June 1976): 40.

10. K. Georg, *op. cit.,* pp. 4–5.

11. "Minutes of the Gettysburg Battle-field Memorial Association," March 25, 1884, p. 98. Original is in the Visitor Center Library at Gettysburg National Military Park.

12. S. R. Koehler, "Our Public Monuments," *The Art Review,* I, 1 (November 1886): 9. An excellent study of the memorials at Gettysburg is Wayne Craven, *The Sculptures of Gettysburg,* scheduled for publication, Spring 1982, by the Eastern National Park and Monument Association.

13. As quoted in Lee, *op. cit.,* p. 19

14. J. Howard Wert, *A Complete Hand-Book of Monuments and Indications and Guide to the Positions of the Gettysburg Battle-field* (Harrisburg, Penn., 1886), p. 212.

15. Lee, *op. cit.,* p. 6.

16. *Ibid.,* p. 16.

17. As quoted in *ibid.,* p. 32.

18. As quoted in *ibid.,* p. 31.

19. As quoted in *ibid.,* p. 35.

20. I am indebted to David Lowenthal for this observation. See David Lowenthal, "Age and Artifact, Dilemmas of Appreciation," in *The Interpretation of Ordinary Landscapes,* ed. D.W. Meinig (New York: Oxford University Press, 1979), pp. 109–111.

21. Lee, *op. cit.,* pp. 14–15. The trolley line itself can be seen on the battlefield map included in L. W. Minnigh's *The Battle of Gettysburg, How to See and Understand It* (Mt. Holly Springs, Penn., 1888).

22. Lee, *op. cit.,* pp. 51–52.

23. These observations are based on a study of the present exhibits and audiovisual presentations at Manassas, Gettysburg, Antietam, Chancellorsville, Fredericksburg, and Petersburg.

24. As quoted by Susan Q. Stranahan, "From Coal Fields of Penna. Came a Keeper of Parks," *Philadelphia Inquirer,* Monday, November 12, 1979, Sec. B, pp. 1–2.

25. See D. W. Meinig, "The Beholding Eye, Ten Versions of the Same Scene," in *The Interpretation of Ordinary Landscapes* (New York: Oxford University Press, 1979), pp. 33–48. A perceptive exploration of the relativity of landscape preservation.

26. Lowenthal, *op. cit.,* p. 103.

27. As quoted in Craven, *op. cit.*, p. 5.

28. Matthew Stevenson, "The Bloody Angle, Reagan and the Civil War," *Harper's,* 263 (December 1981): 80–82.

29. J. B. Jackson, *The Necessity for Ruins* (Amherst, Mass.: University of Massachusetts Press, 1980), p. 102.

30. In the following discussion, we address the issue of the proper appearance of the preserved battlefield. The first step in any preservation work is to evaluate the resource and decide if it is significant enough to merit preservation. Our discussion presupposes this step has been taken. A development of criteria for evaluating the significance of particular battlefields and whether or not they merit preservation is beyond the scope of this essay.

31. Lee A. Wallace, Jr., "A History of Petersburg National Military Park, Virgina" (Unpublished ms., 1957), p. 19 (see also App. XI). In the Petersburg Visitor Center Library.

32. Utley, *op. cit.*, pp. 42–43.

33. Utley, *op. cit.*, p. 43–44. Utley points out that individuals with backgrounds in natural or scenic parks maintenance often find it difficult to cut down trees or otherwise modify a natural process of plant succession to restore a battlefield to its original appearance. Rather, they prefer to let nature take its course and find it difficult to regard vegetation patterns as historic.

34. Lowenthal, *op. cit.*, p. 117.

35. Kevin Lynch, *What Time Is This Place?* (Cambridge, Mass.: MIT Press, 1972), p. 237.

36. Utley, *op. cit.*, p. 44.

37. "General Development Plan, Monocacy National Battlefield" (National Park Service, U. S. Department of the Interior, no date).

38. See note 4.

39. Robert Z. Melnick, "Preserving Cultural and Historic Landscapes," *Cultural Resources Management Bulletin,* 3, 1 (March 1980): 1–2, 6–7.

40. "Petersburg National Battlefield 1981 Summer Schedule," brochure (National Park Service). The special effects of living history can be quite ingenious. At Manassas, the smell of chloroform is simulated in a restored farmhouse that served as a field hospital.

41. Utley, *op. cit.*, p. 44.

42. As quoted in Betty Doak Elder, "War Games: Recruits and Their Critics Draw Battle Lines over Authenticity," *History News, American Association for State and Local History,* 36, 8 (August 1981): 9–10. This is an excellent investigation of the issue of battle reenactment.

43. As quoted in *ibid.*, p. 11.

44. As quoted in *ibid.*, p. 11.

45. *Colonial Williamsburg: Official Guide Book,* 3rd. edition (Williamsburg, Virginia 1957), p. X. I am indebted to David Lowenthal for this example.

46. Lowenthal, *op. cit.*, pp. 117–118.

47. See Richard Wayne Lykes, *Campaign for Petersburg,* National Park Service History Series (National Park Service, 1970), pp. 24ff; and Bruce Catton, *A Stillness at Appomattox* (New York: Washington Square Press, 1953), Chap. IV.

48. George S. Bernard, *War Talks of Confederate Veterans* (Dayton, Ohio: Press of Morningside Bookshop, 1981; Facsimile of 1892 ed.), p. 169. See also Catton, *op. cit.,* pp. 283–84; and J. T. Wilson, *The Black Phalanx, A History of the Negro Soldier in the United States in the Wars of 1775–1812, 1861–1865* (Hartford, Conn.: American Publishing Co., 1892), pp. 415–420.

49. On the difficulty of developing a mature cultural memory, see David Lowenthal, "Past Time, Present Place: Landscape and Memory," *Geographical Review,* 65 (1976): 1–36.

The author wishes to thank the following National Park Service personnel for their assistance on the project: Pettersburg National Battlefield, John R. Davis, Jr., and Christopher Calkins; Fredericksburg and Spotsylvania County Battlefields National Military Park, Robert Krick; Gettysburg National Military Park, Kathleen R. Georg, Thomas Harrison, and John Heiser; Antietam National Battlefield, William R. Orlando and Paul Chiles; Manassas National Battlefield Park, Stuart G. Vogt.

Common Sense: Guidelines for Greens

Thomas Paine, ASLA

To design professionals, the New England green is hallowed ground. It has inspired village-scaled development since the mid-nineteenth century,[1] most recently condominium-shared open space. The green itself, however, is taken for granted.

Dominating its turf is a granite Civil War monument; above its canopy of trees soars the spire of a white clapboarded church; and among the tree trunks is spread, on a fine October day, the largess of a country fair. But go look at the green itself. Over time, imperceptibly, clutter, abuse, and confusion have accumulated. Before long, the green will have shrunk to a mere median strip, telephone poles and signposts outnumbering tree trunks, and memorials aligned as in a military cemetery. We are not preserving our legacy very well, and that should disturb design professionals.

The great problem facing landscape architects concerned with historic preservation is that no one else is going to carry out their mission for them, or if they do, then not as well. Come close as it might, the preservation movement that has come of age has heretofore embraced an immature view of landscape.

There are now over 500 local historic districts nationwide. Of the 150 in Massachusetts and New Hampshire alone, many surround greens but, in a sense, do not include them. Greens are publicly[2] owned ground amidst privately owned lots, and the Board of Architectural Review is preoccupied with regulating changes proposed by homeowners and businesses, not changes proposed by the Park Department, the Public Works Department, or the Lions Club for the green.

Design review criteria rarely include landscape issues and even then only in a way parenthetical to architecture. But rob a historic street of its fences, shade trees, brick sidewalks, and cast-iron lampposts and the architecture would stand brutalized. The integrity of the ensemble requires the joint custodianship of the private-property owner (for the fence) and local government (for the shade tree, sidewalk, and lamppost). And for the green, virtually all change is in the hands of local government, with the attendant conflicts between various jurisdictions or the utility companies.

Lessons learned in formulating and implementing an action plan for Litchfield Green[3] in Connecticut suggest that the public has difficulty recognizing a problem so long in the making. However, once this difficulty has been dispelled, it is essential that comprehensive decision-making criteria — guidelines — be officially adopted by the community so as to require that due deference be accorded them on the part of all actors, whether municipal departments, service clubs, volunteers, or utility companies. In litigation, courts appreciate explicit guidelines.

A powerful tool in winning both initial adoption of the guidelines and then in guiding implementation is the private, nonprofit charitable organization with a broad membership, whose purpose is to safeguard the green.[4] It would have the advantage of long-term continuity, and it would review design, use, and management issues. Early in its life, it would research the history of the green, important not only for general historical significance, but for understanding existing problems, the rate of deterioration, for example. Clearly, without this record, the guidelines are less useful.

GUIDELINES

The guidelines that follow are experimental and general. Each green requires a more specific analog. Appropriate here are general stylistic considerations that distinguish greens as a group from parks or public gardens.

Townscape Enclosure

Important as the landscape of the green is in its own right, it is inseparable from the backdrop of open space and architecture. The local historic district[5] provides the best framework for assuring compatible architecural change, whether infill or addition. In urban areas the paramount issue is highrise, although scale concerns even small communities.[6] Because landscape features are so important to townscape, design-review criteria should include fences, walls, gates, steps, hitching posts, paving, shade trees, signs, and lighting fixtures, and it should address off-street parking.[7] (Many of the following guidelines concerning the green per se are also applicable to townscape.)

Focus

Proposed embellishments should be located so as not to compete with the traditional focus. The typical green is dominated by a Civil War monument, ornamental fountain, bandstand, flagpole, or even a church. Such a focus deserves first-priority protection, restoration, or repair. Proposed embellishments—a new fountain, bandstand, or flagpole—should be neither located too near the traditional focus nor randomly scattered. Vista sight-lines, balance, and appropriate terrain should all be taken into consideration. In cases where the green lacks a monumental focus, typical choices for location are the center of the space, the center of one side, an apex, or a corner.

Proposed embellishments should also be designed of the best traditional materials. Because embellishments assume focal importance in their own right, quality of materials and execution will reflect on the whole space. Compatibility with the traditional focus can be achieved by the use of either identical materials (a granite fountain to match a granite statue) or different materials of comparable quality and execution. An all-wood bandstand is far more traditional and appropriate than a brick one: wood ornament is festive, but brick piers seem heavy-handed. A white aluminum flagpole, on the other hand, may be a good substitute for a traditional white wooden one. What is suitable for a park may not do for a ceremonial, symbolic space: the green is no place for avant-garde design statements.

Landscape

Maintain characteristic simple planting of indigenous deciduous trees and turf and preserve traditional vistas. Tree species should be chosen according to historical precedent and in other respects follow best landscape architectural practice by taking into account soils, hardiness, and special topographical, hydrological, or geological considerations, and by avoiding species prone to litter, disease, or vandalism. An exception is the inimitable American elm, but this is recommended only with a vigorous Dutch elm disease/elm bark beetle control program.[8] Salt-vulnerable species such as sugar maple should not be located near roads or paths likely to be salted. Common choices include maples, oaks, and ashes; unusual choices include tulip tree, tupelo, and sweetgum. Conifers should be used sparingly; many greens do use one as a Christmas Tree.

Shrubs and vines are inappropriate except as a sparingly used foundation planting for embellishments; English ivy, mountain laurel, yew, and juniper are traditional. Annuals and perennials are too gardenesque unless confined to a planter, such as a recycled watering trough. Therefore picturesque effects such as dramatic contrasts of form and texture (a spruce next to a beech, blanket planting of purple wintercreeper) belong elsewhere. Exotic species belong elsewhere. And overplanting belongs nowhere. On the other hand, a loose tree canopy should not be confused with the original design intent: sparseness may well be attributable to storm damage, road-deicing chemicals, disease, and road widening. Traditional design tended to planting in perimeter rows around a central greensward and to framing vistas such as of a church facade, but tree clumps in groves were not unusual.

Enclosure

Strengthen the perimeter with a fence and/or trees as needed. Decline most likely begins at the periphery. Typically, surrounding roads are widened for parking; the original row of street trees is felled, the fence removed, and utility poles perhaps installed. The first consideration is to explore the possibility of reclaiming lost ground.[9] Sound arguments address the issues of vehicular and pedestrian safety and the burden on highway maintenance of unneeded paving.

Once the perimeter line has been established, curbing is recommended, not because it is traditional, but because it is an unobtrusive concession to changing needs for controlling vehicles and runoff. Behind this line of defense, the fence can follow historic precedent or can even be upgraded in quality to accommodate increased levels of wear and tear. Therefore, instead of the traditional all-wood post-and-crossrail fence, the equally traditional split-granite posts with chain or wood crossrail, or again the cast-iron post-and-crossbar or post-and-chain types may be more appropriate. Traditional colors are black, white, grey, brown, or green.

Traditional tree planting in a row monoculture is often impractical: staggering several species will better hide inevitable gaps left by removed trees.

Paving

Maintain the characteristic simple circulation system of straight, narrow walks. The curving path is another trademark of park or garden design that does not belong on the typical green; however, for greens transformed into Victorian or Edwardian parks, the dictates of the latter may well prevail. Appropriate for most greens is the system of straight crosswalks and paths to embellishments. Just as new paving should only be introduced when turf-wear becomes irreversible, conversely, underused paths should be removed. Path clutter should be controlled; it should be reduced, if possible, either by outright removal or by depressing paths slightly below grade so that they vanish, at least when viewed obliquely from another path. This may not be traditional, but it does further traditional goals. Lastly, paths should not exceed a width of four to five feet, even for most urban contexts, except around the perimeter. Few abuses on a green can match the overengineering of paths.[10]

Pave unuseable or unsightly off-path areas where turf cannot survive. This departure from tradition must be carefully considered, and it should be undertaken only after best efforts to save the turf, such as irrigation, aeration, and use-management, have failed. Because use of the green by the general public is as desirable as the green's symbolic or pictorial role, paving may well be a justifiable concession to heavy use. Given sensitive and unobtrusive design, the result need not rob the green of its simple, heroic character as the community's downtown landscape monument. Spot-paving should also be considered for such areas as beneath benches or around the base of a popular embellishment.

Choose traditional materials of the highest quality. Gravel, brick, and stone are preferred. If bituminous or regular concrete is unavoidable, a top coat of peastone should be considered. If two materials are to be used together—and this is a departure from tradition—avoid weak contrasts (grey granite paving dividers between grey concrete paving squares). Lastly, consider the no-masonry option: pavers laid dry to aid groundwater recharge, or stone dust.[11]

Furniture

Minimize clutter and coordinate styles. Benches, litter receptacles, drinking fountains, bicycle racks, bus shelters, information booths, markers, signs, and lighting fixtures should be compatible with traditional historic features and with each other. Some greens have more posts than trees: if one is good, then ten must be better. This must be countered with the dictum that underfurnishing is preferable to overfurnishing. Where supply-and-demand are in balance, clustering is preferable to scattering. Most users prefer to be in the throng, contrary to conventional wisdom.[12] Therefore, consider combining a bench, litter receptacle and drinking fountain in a coordinated grouping that defines a small space, in relation to existing or proposed walks. The threat, of course, is a hodgepodge of mixed metaphors—high-tech lighting, a cast-iron Victorian bench, and a 55-gallon oil drum side by side. But another threat is the overdesigned system that seems too instantaneous, too lacking in a sense of slow evolution over generations. Urban commons may even be large or busy enough to accommodate several distinct styles of bench, for example.[13] The key is a coordinated system according to best professional practice.[14]

High-tech may be appropriate for bus shelters or information booths, but these do not belong on the green and, if they must be there, look absurd in mock Colonial or Victorian style. On the other hand, separate signs should more appropriately be low-tech, displaying serif typefaces and traditional colors; this may well apply even to highway signs.[15] Lighting, too, should be low-tech. Accent lighting of the focus should be soft. Where perimeter street lighting does not suffice, on-green fixtures should be low-level, pedestrian-scaled, and traditional; many styles are available.

Choose traditional materials of the highest quality. Except for high-tech furniture—limited to bus shelters, information booths, and markers—wood, granite, and painted metal are preferred to concrete or even brick. Wood can be either painted or preservative-stained to match the treatment of focal features. Among stones, granite is the superior choice for fenceposts, markers, bench supports, or drinking fountains, although regional variants include marble, limestone, and brownstone. Unlike these last three choices, granite should not be cut but split because, traditionally, cut granite was a luxury reserved for the focus, such as the Civil War monument. Glacial boulders or granite fieldstone masonry are not unknown.

For cast-iron, the traditional paint colors are black, green, or brown. Earth-toned extruded steel or aluminum is unobtrusive for poles, posts, or signs. Cast bronze is traditional for plaques mounted on stone. Concrete is appropriate where invisible, particularly for footings.

Overhead Utility Lines

Relocate electric, telephone, and cable-television lines off the green or underground. For the visual degradation that they inflict and the maintenance and safety problems that they cause, overhead wires and poles ideally belong nowhere. The cost of relocating the lines can be met through political leverage or comprehensive downtown infrastructure improvement funding.[16]

Accessibility

Provide adequate crosswalks with curbcuts. A signalized crosswalk with special paving (brick or granite) is preferred for each corner, but no more than 200 feet apart. If the encircling roads are more than two lanes wide, consider a traffic island at the crosswalk midpoint. Curbcuts, mandated for the handicapped, more frequently serve infant strollers and cyclists. Improved access will save the green from its status as a median strip.

Expropriation

Defend the green from conversion to permanent facilities serving special interest groups. Parking lots, basketball courts, even tot-lots all have their place, but that place is elsewhere. Substantial paved areas rob the green of its primary role: a unified landscape serving the general public for strolling, picnicking, sitting, and other unstructured uses occurring daily.

Special Events

Encourage community events that do not require permanent facilities. Structured uses, such as turf sports, are appropriate on large greens, where the required field does not cover more than half of the area. Even then, formal sport competition better belongs on the playground. Backstops and goal posts overwhelm all but the largest greens and, if used, should be consistent with the standard of other furniture. Play must not exceed the carrying capacity of the turf.

Events such as fairs, parades, reenactments, and dances should be encouraged. The green should provide the setting for not just official ceremony—Memorial Day observances, for example—but also for any responsible activity, including political protest. In this same tradition, it can be expected that Nativity displays will soon share ground with the Star of David.

Busy greens may require an events coordinator to provide a liaison between user groups and municipal agencies, to schedule events, to supervise installation and clean-up, and to encourage high standards for temporary structures and signs.

Maintenance

Follow best professional practice. A specific priority plan balancing routine expenses with capital improvement should include furniture, paving, electrical and irrigation systems, as well as plant materials. In this regard, the green, the park, and the garden are equivalent.

Irrigation and Drainage

Where turf wear is excessive, consider improving surface drainage and installing an underground irrigation system. Poor drainage inhibits turf performance and can be locally controlled by minor regrading and dry wells, which should also be used to intercept runoff along footings and paths. A subsurface drainage system should be avoided unless it assists local recharge. Clearly, most greens are of sufficiently mild gradient to have no need of drain inlets. On the other hand, an underground irrigation system will assist turf and tree performance, particularly in urban areas where turf receives heavy use and tree root systems are constricted.

Interpretation

Provide the visitor with substantive information on the evolution of form, use, and significance of the green. Interpretive markers using a metal-photo process can convey graphic as well as textual information, and this is an improvement over the lifeless plaque or tree label. A favorite vintage view can be reproduced on a marker placed at the same vantage point. Public education begins on the green, but can move off the green as well in the form of fliers or media coverage. Obviously, an informed public is the best safeguard for the long-term integrity of the green.

The green or common has made an enduring contribution to the landscape in the Northeast and continues to inspire design across the country. If the metaphor has seemed more durable than the artifact, the guidelines suggested here can form the basis for guiding change so that competing goals of wide use and pristine appearance are reconciled and that the essential artifact will continue to endure. The guidelines are general enough to encourage creativity, but creativity of a kind muted out of reverence to the special tradition of the green. Each particular green will require custom-fitting. Specifics may vary, but the issues remain the same. And this applies, in the wider sense, to other historic landscape types, such as parks, gardens, and courthouse squares, that deserve equally rigorous treatment.

NOTES

1. Examples are Llewellyn Park, Orange, New Jersey (1859), Oak Bluffs, Massachusetts (1866), Greenbelt, Maryland (1935), and Baldwin Hills Village, California (1941).
2. In Massachusetts, for example, commons explicitly conveyed in public trust forever cannot be expropriated for other public uses. However, some greens are privately owned, such as the New Haven Green, owned by the Committee of the Proprietors of the Common and Undivided Lands, a group that effectively stopped the installation of an underground garage.
3. Thomas Paine, *Action Plan, Litchfield Green, Litchfield, Connecticut,* prepared for the Litchfield Garden Club, 1978.
4. Under Internal Revenue Code, S. 501 c.3, donations are tax-deductible and the organization is tax-exempt. This is in the tradition of the Village Improvement Society movement whose origins hark back to the Laurel Hill Society, Stockbridge, Massachusetts, 1852. An alter-

native is the Committee such as was formed in Litchfield following adoption of the Action Plan in 1978.

5. Massachusetts Historical Commission, *Establishing Local Historic Districts,* Boston, ca. 1975, available from MHC, gives enabling legislation, M.G.L. Ch. 40c, which may serve as a model.

6. Deering, New Hampshire, passed a bylaw limiting the height of structures around its common.

7. Boston Landmarks Commission, Ch 3, St.8 s.101, May review "exterior architectural features," which include off-street parking open to view.

8. The annual cost per tree of the systemic fungicide Lignasan^(TM), which has a 95 percent success rate, is $400; the rate for the insecticide Methoxyclor^(TM) is lower.

9. Dawes Park, Cambridge, Massachusetts, was reclaimed in time for the Bicentennial.

10. In 1976, Boston Common was subjected to unecessary overengineering: brown strips of dead turf along the sides of a major walk were attributed to overuse and the path duly widened by 50 percent when the real culprit was the use of deicing chemicals.

11. Lexington Green, Massachusetts, has paths of stone dust renewed once annually.

12. William Whyte, *The Social Life of Small Urban Spaces,* Conservation Foundation, New York, 1980, p. 16 ff.

13. On Cambridge Common, Massachusetts, granite block benches define a new paved area around the Civil War Monument, and slatback benches line the paths.

14. For examples, see Center for Design Planning, *Steetscape Equipment Sourcebook 2,* Urban Land Institute, Washington, D.C., 1979.

15. Highway signs in the historic district of Annapolis, Maryland, are reduced in scale and display off-white serif type on a bronze background.

16. Bedford and Sudbury, Massachusetts, both won the undergrounding of utilities on the common in exchange for permitting new transmission lines elsewhere in town.

"Magic Markers"

Kenneth I. Helphand

Historic markers are typically plaques or relics denoting the significance of places, artifacts, persons, or events. As purveyors of historical information, they have a role in our environment. However, the concept of the historic marker has been limited in effectiveness, scope, and design. Just as the possibilities of historic preservation have been enriched in recent years, so too our concept of the marker needs to be enriched. Why not "magic markers"?

What are magic markers, and what are their implications for landscape design? The idea begins with the concept of historic markers as physical indicators of the significance of places, people, and events. This may be expanded beyond its current, conventional connotation to the realm of "magic," implying that which has a surprising, involving, and even enchanting aspect. Magic Markers is also the brand name of felt-tip pen, implying yet another meaning: something bold, visual, graphic, and colorful. In combination, the idea is to explore the possibilities of magical, involving, activist-oriented, beautiful, historical information systems, i.e. magic markers.

What should be the information presented, the "content," of these historic magic markers? The answer lies in a broader humanistic perspective of landscape history. Magic markers can help add to what D.W. Meinig calls the "life-enriching" aspects of environment. The historic marker can become more immediate and accessible, as opposed to state highway roadside markers glimpsed it a turn of the head at 60-miles-per-hour. The marker should reflect a more popular and personal concern in its historical information. The marker should have an environmental presence and immediacy. An emphasis on local and personal history is imperative. As Meinig has noted:

It is "place" or "locality" which may be taken to refer to areas and their contents defined at a human scale, areas we can directly experience. Logically, the locality most of us know best is that of our home area, yet inevitably that which is so familiar, so routinely part of our lives, tends to be taken for granted until something unusual happens to jar us into seeing more clearly through the daily blur.[5]

Markers can and do jar us out of our daily blur. The preservation effort is directed not only toward the continued existence and transformation of sites. The place must be experienced—individuals need to encounter the place and its meaning. Of course the site's inherent character and our associations with it are primary, but that experience can be enhanced. A marker, first of all, is a "sign"—it identifies and signifies. It can orient and direct us, focus our attention and observations—make us aware. Sometimes the effect can be a "shock of recognition," the spontaneous consciousness of a new way of seeing—"I'm now standing where it happened"—the sudden wonder of beginning to sense what the childhood of one's grandparents was like, what 200 years means, or even 2000. A few examples serve to illustrate this "shock of recognition."

In 1980, the original pre-Dutch settlement shoreline of lower Manhattan was marked on the New York landscape by a blue and green painted stripe crossing streets, structures, fences, cars, and grass, often hundreds of yards from the modern shoreline. The landscape had been temporarily transformed into a life-size historical atlas. The pedestrian could imagine the layers of transformation the shoreline had undergone in successive filling for fortification, port facilities, parks, and highways (Fig. 1).

Another New York artist, Alan Sonfist, has designed "Time Landscape." On a site in lower Manhattan, a forest was planted based on what the site had been like "before"—before the freeway, the buildings, the settlers, or the oaks. In a similar vein, there have been many outdoor wall mural projects which have depicted landscape transformations. These are often in *trompe l'oiel*-fashion, giving the illusion of what a site had looked like at a particular date in its past. Significantly, these are located on or near the actual historic site. The viewer can make his or her own visual comparison and personal evaluation of the landscape transformation, an instant recognition of before and after. These walls increase the visibility of historical information by placing it in a public setting, and perhaps broaden the historical awareness of landscape change. At the very least these projects contribute to an enriched and often surprising environmental encounter (Fig. 2).

The goal of magic markers is to expand the limited conception of the historic marker: to design markers to

Fig. 1. Nieuw Amsterdam Shoreline by Eric Arctander, 1980. Signs along the 7000 foot line note: This line demarks the original contour of Manhattan when settled by the Dutch in the 17th century.

increase historical awareness, time awareness, and landscape awareness. The physical environment is an educational resource. It is a multilayered collage of the physical relics of our collective past. For scholars in environmental history, the physical environment is primary source material. It is a grand library, the "literature" of the history of places—the historical "record." This history must be seen, "read," and its meaning revealed. To do this necessitates an interest and training in reading the environment. Secondary sources have been developed as aids in this reading process: guides, indicators, interpreters, markers. In the landscape, the historic marker is an explicit indicator. However, most literature of this landscape library remains uncataloged, unresearched, and "invisible." Magic markers are methods of making that invisible information visible in the revelation of pattern, place, people, and pace. Richard Saul Wurman, who has been a key figure in placing environmental education in a central position in design, has written of making environments both observable and accessible. He

has catalogued and designed material for revealing environmental information.

We continually use historical information for orientation and wayfinding in the environment, and, in the deepest sense, for knowing where we are in time and in space. Markers can intensify and enrich our sense of relatedness to place and of our connectedness in time. They can add a richness of information and detail to the physical environment, enhancing our appreciation of the complexity and experience of place. Markers can indicate our position in space. Mapping is one method of communicating spatial location. Maps can be on the ground—a landscape atlas at one-to-one scale. These lines on the land can show all that a map does. They can mark modern or ancient boundaries between settlements, watersheds, soil types, habitats, armies, or the continental divide. They can show routes of traders, wagon trains, trollies, road racers, or migrating animals. We can mark the habitat of the buffalo, the route of Lewis and Clark, or archaic walls now visible only on aerial photographs. Seattle has produced manhole covers with downtown maps cast on the surface. As part of the 1979 Jubilee Project in England, concrete relief maps of London have been installed; Bicentennial legacy maps are located at significant locales in Boston. These maps are all on-site and invite participation—not just visual, but tactile. Telling us where we are can be both educational and surprising. The road to the Dead Sea or to Death Valley demarcates sea level. A sign on Interstate 5 in Oregon advises you that you are at 45°N—half-way between the equator and the north pole. A similar sign is found on Nova Scotia highways (Fig. 3). Vy's Pies is a roadside cafe of local renown near Vida, Oregon, with a map of the United States and a world map on the ceiling studded with hundreds of colored pins; these locate the hometowns of visitors. It is a wonderful marker: surprising, dynamic, personalized, and site specific.

Markers can indicate events and the gradual passage of landscape time. George Kubler, the art historian, has noted that "the aim of the historian, regardless of his specialty in erudition, is to portray time. He is committed to detection and description of the *shape of time.*" The designer can work with this fourth dimension, bringing it to the level of consciousness.

The section is a particularly effective method because it inherently reveals the historical dimension, showing growth by natural accretion. Think of the Grand Canyon, soil horizons, tree rings, archaeological excavations, buildings under demolition, or the butcher shop. Designers use sections in their work to show relationships.

Making the invisible visible is a particularly appropriate way to describe the process of designing

Fig. 2.   A concrete "Please Touch" relief map on the south bank promenade, London.

Fig. 3.   The forty-fifth parallel. Falmouth, Nova Scotia.

visual evidence of the ephemeral. In areas that have suffered the vicissitudes of floods, one can often see markers that show high-water marks on telephone poles or high on trees (Figs. 4 and 5) Statistics begin to take on life as you imagine yourself floating high or 20 feet underwater. Again the on-site location is an essential aspect of the experience. Why not markers indicating glacial depth, underground rivers, or depth to a water table? Singular events may be objectified, sometimes literally made concrete. This occurs on sidewalks inscribed with names and dates by concrete , graffitists and masons. Montreal's sidewalks are imprinted with brass maple-leaf plaques noting the construction date. Outside the Children's Museum in Mun-

Fig. 4. Flood marker, Connecticut River Valley, Massachusetts. Floods 1927, 1936, 1938.

Fig. 5. Flood marker, Old Town, Portland, Oregon.

cie, Indiana, the sidewalk is stamped with footprints, handprints, names, dates and symbols — a permanent reminder of the museum's dedication day (Fig. 6). In 1715, the Thames River froze and Londoners transformed the frozen surface into a fete. Broadsides were printed on the ice in commemoration of this rare climatic event (Fig. 7). These types of markers have another potential. Ronald Fleming of Vision Inc., Cambridge, Massachusetts, has written of the need for "lovable objects." These are environmental elements that transcend any practical or educational function and appeal directly to our emotions. They are physical objects which become symbols of a collective memory. Their appeal spans the emotions from surprise to poignancy to humor. Witness Mag Harries' sculpture of bronze newspapers and cabbage embedded in the sidewalk of Boston's Haymarket or manhole covers in New Orleans with a text of *Dept des Flambeaux et du Gumbo*.

Telling time is an age-old civic function; it includes town criers, sundials, and bell and clock towers. Historic markers indicate time as well. This is most commonly done by dating construction on cor-

nerstones, lintels, plaques, and pediments. The curious discover this information on sidewalks, manhole covers, mailboxes, fire hydrants, and street furniture, as well. Organized dates can be made into chronologies, time lines, and synchronologies. The text of a painted wooden marker on the Locust Grove Church (which is now a barn) is truely instructive (Fig. 8.) Why don't we make more use of such graphic depictions of time and change in chronologies of structures and of sites?

We mark our personal histories in the landscape as well. Our environmental autobiographies are celebrated in the tree planted when a child is born, in gravestones, and in the relics of personal significance with which we adorn our homes. However, in a mobile society, we may be assuming nomadic traits, investing more of our wealth in goods and more meaning in movable possessions; these may transform places, but are uprooted in periodic migrations. In many Islamic countries it is customary to paint doorways and walls when an individual makes *hajj*, the sacred pilgrimage to Mecca and one of the five Pillars of the Faith. Here a most personal article of belief is given public land-

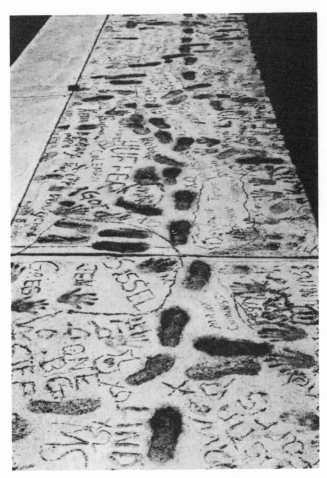

Fig. 6. Commemorative sidewalk, Children's Museum, Muncie, Indiana.

scape expression. Doorways are adorned with Kaaba in Mecca, the local mosque, and the mode of transportation, with paintings of planes, boats, and camels.

There is another kind of history: an act of imagination and speculation that enters the realm of "What if. . .?" A wall mural in Venice, California, by Terry Schoonhoven, imagines "Venice in the Snow." What would Texas look like if it had remained independent, Arizona if it was still Mexico, or your town if it had been settled by Swedes or bypassed by the Interstate?

The location of markers is critical. There are places we expect to find them: museums, historic sites, national parks, and observation points. But what is essential is that the locale provide a reference point for the experience. Information should ideally be on-site or en route. The walls of the South Street Seaport area in New York are affixed with broadside posters (Figs. 11 and 12). This imaginative series describes activities no longer in that area, structures now demolished, the "writing on the wall" (explaining brick patterns), and publicized preservation activities. Why not markers most anywhere? They could be at bus stops and in buses; in subways, schools, and lobbies; or on doorways, ceilings, sidewalks, menus, place-mats, telephone booths, marquees, and video games; or even on television (remember Bicentennial minutes?).

Preservation activity cannot be separated from landscape design nor can it be separated from environmental and cultural education. One of its goals is to increase our awareness and consciousness of our connections to landscape and place. Yi-Fu Tuan has noted that we transform space to place by imbuing it

Fig. 7.   Frost Fair on the Thames, London.

Fig. 8. Locust Grove Church Chronology, near Wasco, Oregon. Church building is now used as a hay barn.

Fig. 9. Trompe l'oeil mural of downtown Arcata, California, as it was.

Fig. 10

Figs. 10 and 11.   Broadside posters: Sidewalk history project, South Street Seaport Museum, New York City.

with meanings constructed by experience. Magic Markers are one way of helping infuse meaning to that experience. They can reveal the invisible and conjure up the shape of time.

Kevin Lynch has noted the richness of an environment that is a "temporal collage," a dynamic layering of the physical manifestations of time. "Magic markers directs themselves toward the explicit recognition of elements of this "temporal collage." They, themselves, add to the collage. It is the designer's response making time and history visible and vivid.

NOTES

1. Fleming, Ronald Lee. "Loveable Objects Challenge the Modern Movement," *Landscape Architecture,* vol. 71, no. 1, January 1981, pp. 88–92.
   _____. "Recapturing History: A Plan for Gritty Cities," *Landscape,* vol, 25, no. 1, 1981, pp. 20–27.
2. Fleming, Ronald Lee and Renata von Tscharner. *Place Markers,* (Cambridge: The Townscape Institute), 1981.
3. Kubler, George. *The Shape of Time.* (New Haven: Yale Univ. Press, 1962).
4. Lynch, Kevin. *What Time Is This Place?.* (Cambridge, Mass.: MIT Press, 1972).
5. Meinig, D. W. "Environmental Appreciation: Localities as a Humane Art," *Western Humanities Review,* vol. XXV, no. 1, Winter 1971.
6. Robertson, James (ed.), *Old Glory: A Report on the Grass Roots History Movement and the First Hometown History Primer.* (New York: Warner Books, 1973).
7. Tuan, Yi-Fu. *Space and Place.* (Minneapolis: University of Minnesota Press, 1977).
8. Wurman, Richard Saul. *Making the City Observable.* (Cambridge, Mass.: MIT Press, 1971).

Part Two:
The Implementation

Conservation Planning Along an Historic Corridor

Kerry J. Dawson

Long before the technological revolution bypassed the historic travel routes of early America, transportation centers were closely tied to the natural landscape by necessity. Valleys, gaps through the mountains, and rivers were corridors that dictated development, while massive mountains, remoteness, and nonnavigable wetlands acted as impediments.

In the exploration and settlement of the southeastern Atlantic Coast of the United States, rivers afforded the best and most direct access to the Appalachian Plateau. Hundreds of square miles of coastal plain were interlaced with massive wetlands and travel overland proved very difficult.

With the most fresh-water flow of any Atlantic river system south of Chesapeake Bay, the Altamaha River served for over a thousand years as the primary transportation route for movement through central Georgia. So important was the lower Altamaha, historically, that along the lower 100 miles of the river alone, 125 identifiable historical and archaeological sites exist.

The following article is a summary of a plan begun in 1977 by the Georgia Department of Natural Resources to inventory historic sites along the lower Altamaha and to offer a reasonable solution to conservation and interpretation of the Altamaha heritage. The study format was for scenic and recreational status along the river where natural and cultural history are balanced to emphasize heritage conservation.

In all, the plan calls for the creation of a management complex covering over 150,000 acres: 18,570 acres in the existing Altamaha State Waterfowl Management Area; 30,000 acres in the existing Brunswick Pulp and Paper Company Public Hunting Area; 5,126 acres in the existing Wolf Island National Wildlife Refuge; 1,271 acres at the existing Hofwyl-Broadfield Plantation and Fort King George State Historic Sites; 10,000 acres in proposed state and private recreation areas, historic sites, natural areas, river buffers and easements, and additions to the Altamaha State Waterfowl Management Area; 66,000 acres in proposed privately held public hunting areas; and 21,000 acres in existing public domain marshes and waterways.

To briefly summarize the historical background, man first appeared in the Altamaha basin eleven to fifteen thousand years ago. The lives of these early people (Paleo-Indian period) closely followed the natural cycles and physiography of the land. A predominantly hunting and plant-gathering group, they undoubtedly were attracted by the large concentrations of wildlife and fishery resources along the Altamaha.

The early Spanish explorers called the coastal Indians in Georgia "Guale." They were a Muskogean-speaking people related to the Creek tribes of the interior parts of Georgia. Old Spanish maps show the Altamaha as "Rio de Talaja" and mark the Indian towns of "Talaxe" on the south bank of the Altamaha and "Tolomato" near Darien.

When England's Charles II granted all American lands south of the 29th parallel to Carolina in 1663, the Altamaha became the focal point in a four-power struggle (Indian-French-Spanish-English) that was not resolved for 150 years. English and pirate ship attacks led to the final retreat of Spanish missionaries from Georgia to Florida in 1686. By this time, the lives of the coastal Indians had been completely disrupted and few settlements remained.

Early in the eighteenth century, rumors began to spread through the Carolina settlements that the French, well-established in the Mississippi Valley, were planning to start colonies on the banks of the Altamaha. The English were aware of the French "Grand Design of Encirclement" to crush the English colonies, and already the French had connected colonies in Canada with the Mississippi Valley holdings. Settlements on the west-east flowing Altamaha would complete the circle. Colonel John Barnwell ("Tuscorora Jack") and Joseph Boone were sent to England to present to the Board of Trade a plan for a line of forts designed to stop French expansion. Funds permitted only one fort at the onset, and on July 13, 1721, Barnwell, Indian guides, sawyers, and a band of province scouts landed at Lower Bluff near the north branch of the Altamaha and began construction of Fort King George.

The Treaty of 1763 set the Indian-White border about 50 miles west from Fort King George (later the town of Darien). By the late 1760s, this boundary line

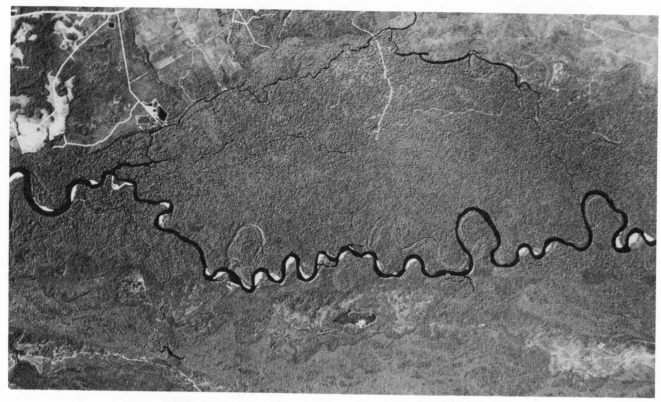

Fig. 1.   Infrared photograph showing the extensive concentrations of resources along the lower Altamaha. (Courtesy of Georgia Department of Natural Resources)

was firmly established. English settlements along the lower Altamaha then began in earnest, and from 1760 to 1775, 72,000 acres of land along the Altamaha were deeded in 143 separate grants.

Military concerns became dominant in the lower Altamaha region during the American Revolution. The strategic importance of the upper delta area was recognized, and an old fort at Barrington Ferry was refurbished under a new name, Fort Howe. For much of the war, this fort served as the military headquarters for the southern Department of Operations. Controlling the only sizable passage across the lower Altamaha, the fort was seen as indispensible in assuring the smooth northward flow of soldiers, foodstuffs, and artillery for the Continental Army.

Plantations, based on the production of rice, indigo, sugar, and, after Whitney's cotton gin in 1873, cotton, thrived in the Altamaha Delta after the revolution. While nearly all delta landowners cultivated rice, it was the South Carolinian grantees who established the most famous plantations. They came to the Altamaha River with the technology and experienced slave manpower required to build and run massive operations. The most important river-plantations were developed in the early 1800s and lasted through the Civil War.

The development of the Georgia Piedmont became

increasingly dependent on the Altamaha in the 1800s as riverboat pilots began to improve their knowledge of the area. The expanding tobacco and cotton plantations in the upper coastal plain and piedmont became totally dependent on the Altamaha and its tributaries for bringing their goods to market.

During this same early nineteenth-century period, timber in the Altamaha basin became a serious enterprise. Live oak forests growing extensively on the sea-islands and bluffs near the Altamaha were known as "the most durable wood in the world" and St. Simons live oak was used in the construction of the most famous American fighting ship, the *U. S. Frigate Constitution,* later called "Old Ironsides." However, it was not until steam sawmills were built that lumbering became substantial.

Life along the lower Altamaha and use of the river were altered by the Civil War. The delta rice and sea-island cotton plantations which flourished before were completely devastated. For many years of the late 1800s, some planters tried to refurbish and maintain their river plantations. For a while, it seemed like they might be successful, but willing and skilled labor needed for the difficult tasks of maintaining the dikes and canals and of nursing the crops through harvest could not be secured.

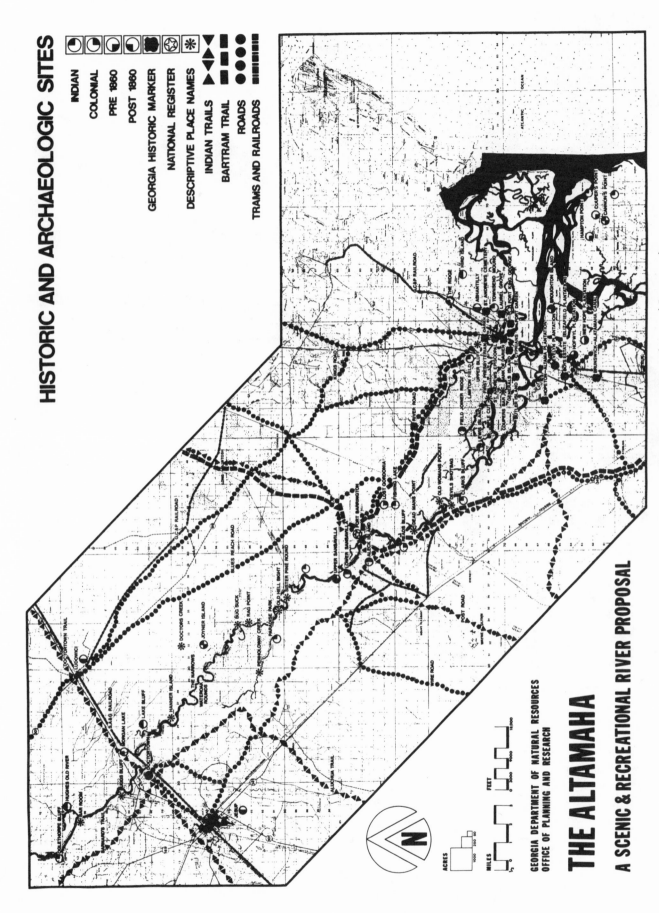

HISTORIC AND ARCHAEOLOGIC SITES

INDIAN

COLONIAL

PRE 1860

POST 1860

GEORGIA HISTORIC MARKER

NATIONAL REGISTER

DESCRIPTIVE PLACE NAMES

INDIAN TRAILS

BARTRAM TRAIL

ROADS

TRAMS AND RAILROADS

GEORGIA DEPARTMENT OF NATURAL RESOURCES
OFFICE OF PLANNING AND RESEARCH

THE ALTAMAHA
A SCENIC & RECREATIONAL RIVER PROPOSAL

Fig. 2. Historic sites map. (Courtesy of Georgia Department of Natural Resources)

Fig. 3. Dedication of a historic marker for the Old Post Road, which ran along lower Altamaha. (Courtesy of Georgia Department of Natural Resources)

It was during these years shortly after the Civil War that people turned to the Altamaha's natural resources with great intensity. The delta rebuilt itself rapidly and, with capital brought in by Altamaha lumber, it soon became more prosperous than ever before. By 1868, Darien timber exports topped 20 million board feet and, by 1874, they shipped out over 100 million board feet. Altamaha lumber again became known throughout the world, and Great Britain, Holland, Norway, Sweden, Italy, Germany, Portugal, and Brazil established consulates in the delta.

The 1890s brought the last of the boom years to the lower Altamaha. In 1900, the highest annual timber export was reached: 112 million board feet. Steamship freight and passenger cruises also peaked in the 1890s. The decline in river use did not occur until the twentieth century, although the inevitable decline had been predicted many years earlier.

In recent years, the inherent values of the lower Altamaha's natural and historic resources have begun to be appreciated more than ever before. Some areas of the river-delta have been set aside for wildlife management, natural area protection, and historic interpretation, and many are beginning to rediscover the aesthetic value associated with the Altamaha's wild beauty.

At present, over 80 percent of the river frontage along the lower Altamaha has been acquired by the Georgia Department of Natural Resources and the Nature Conservancy. This has led to the very successful preservation of the majority of the historic sites listed. In addition, the significance of the remaining sites has been well publicized by the study, and conservation efforts have progressed through the creative use of easements and access agreements. Most importantly, interpretive trips, following the historic Bartram Trail, are now possible along the lower Altamaha River. This allows a significant and guided overview of the role the Altamaha played in the development of America.

Fig. 4. Early steamboat era along the Altamaha. (Courtesy of Georgia Department of Natural Resources)

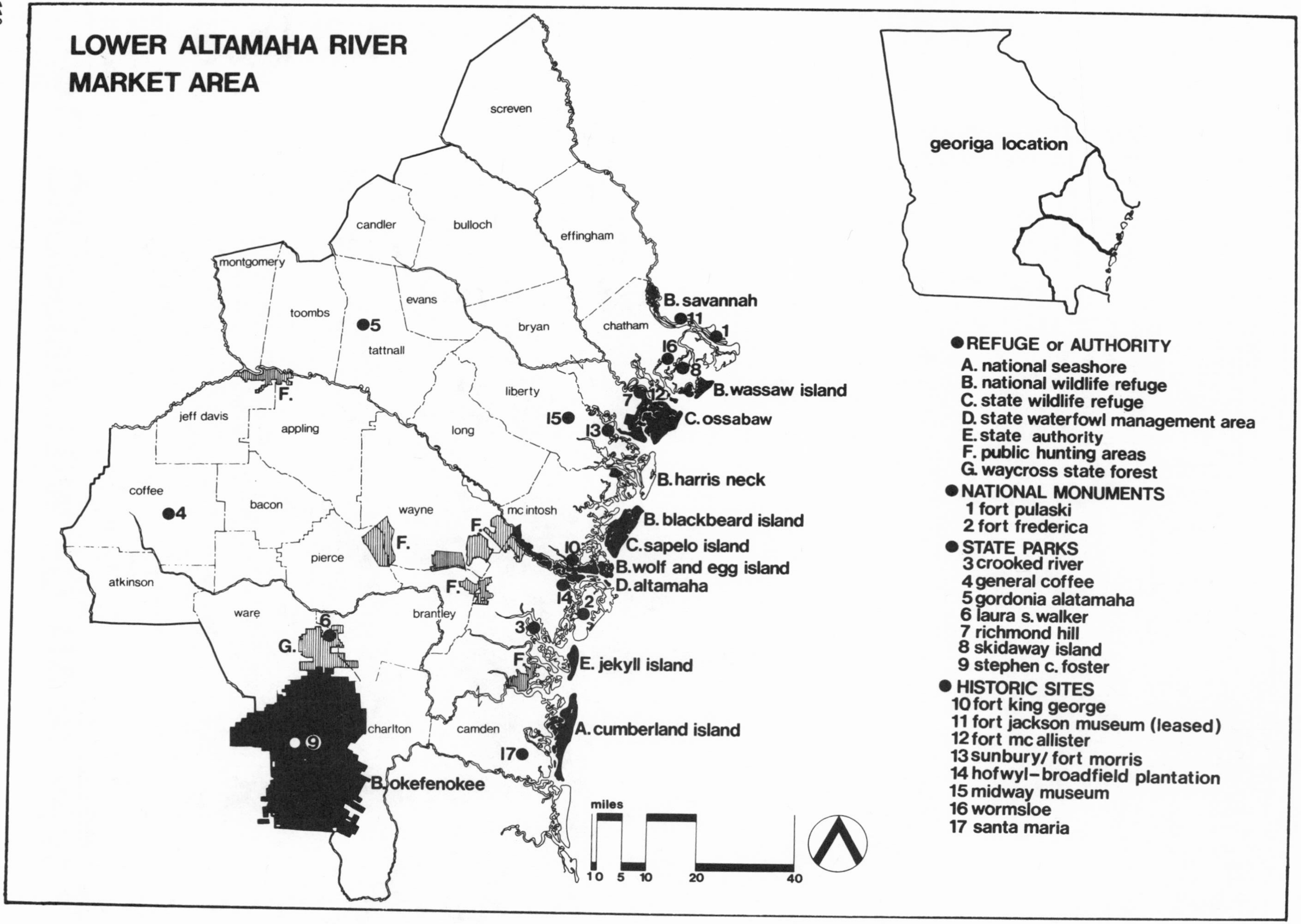

LOWER ALTAMAHA RIVER MARKET AREA

georiga location

● REFUGE or AUTHORITY
A. national seashore
B. national wildlife refuge
C. state wildlife refuge
D. state waterfowl management area
E. state authority
F. public hunting areas
G. waycross state forest

● NATIONAL MONUMENTS
1 fort pulaski
2 fort frederica

● STATE PARKS
3 crooked river
4 general coffee
5 gordonia alatamaha
6 laura s. walker
7 richmond hill
8 skidaway island
9 stephen c. foster

● HISTORIC SITES
10 fort king george
11 fort jackson museum (leased)
12 fort mc allister
13 sunbury/ fort morris
14 hofwyl–broadfield plantation
15 midway museum
16 wormsloe
17 santa maria

screven
effingham
chatham
B. savannah
B. wassaw island
C. ossabaw
B. harris neck
B. blackbeard island
B. sapelo island
B. wolf and egg island
D. altamaha
E. jekyll island
A. cumberland island
bulloch
bryan
liberty
mcintosh
candler
evans
tattnall
long
wayne
brantley
camden
toombs
montgomery
appling
pierce
ware
chariton
B. okefenokee
jeff davis
bacon
coffee
atkinson

miles
10 5 10 20 40

Fig. 5.   Market area map. (Courtesy of Georgia Department of Natural Resources)

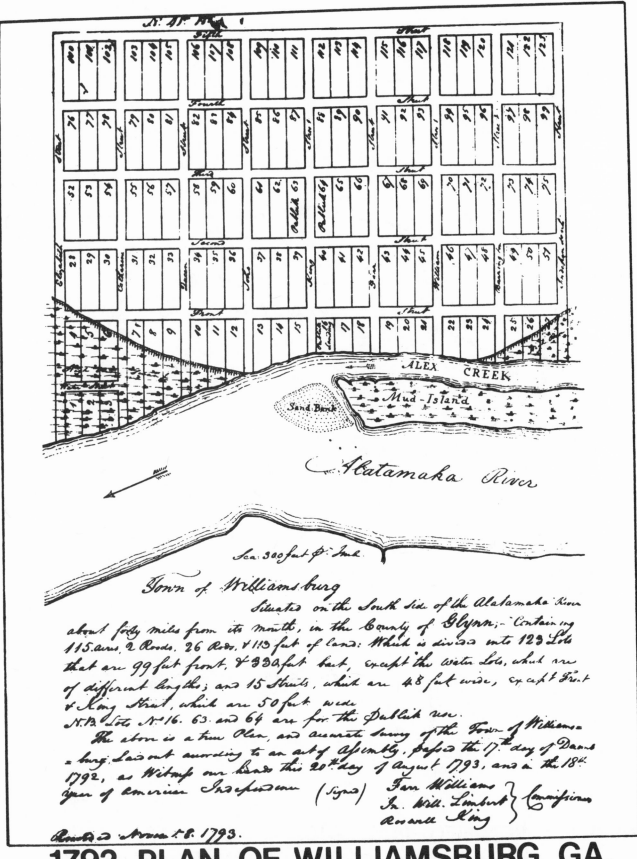

1792 PLAN OF WILLIAMSBURG, GA.

Fig. 6. Williamsburg was originally laid out on a bluff just above the delta. It was sparsely settled and ultimately abandoned. (Courtesy of Georgia Department of Natural Resources)

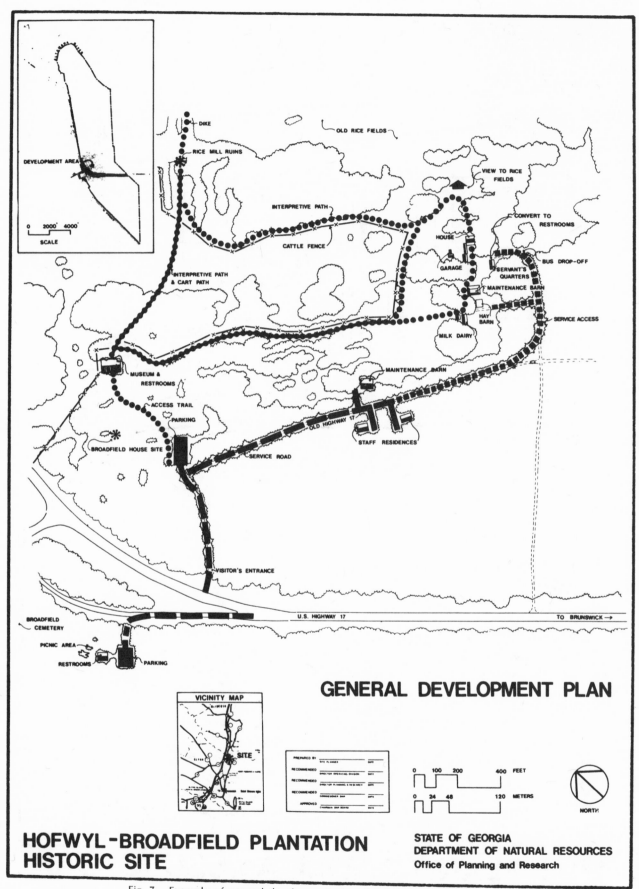

GENERAL DEVELOPMENT PLAN

DIKE
RICE MILL RUINS
OLD RICE FIELDS
INTERPRETIVE PATH
VIEW TO RICE FIELDS
CATTLE FENCE
CONVERT TO RESTROOMS
INTERPRETIVE PATH & CART PATH
HOUSE
GARAGE
SERVANT'S QUARTERS
BUS DROP-OFF
MAINTENANCE BARN
SERVICE ACCESS
HAY BARN
MILK DAIRY
MUSEUM & RESTROOMS
MAINTENANCE BARN
ACCESS TRAIL
PARKING
BROADFIELD HOUSE SITE
OLD HIGHWAY 17
STAFF RESIDENCES
SERVICE ROAD
VISITOR'S ENTRANCE
BROADFIELD CEMETERY
PICNIC AREA
RESTROOMS
PARKING
U.S. HIGHWAY 17
TO BRUNSWICK →

DEVELOPMENT AREA
0 2000' 4000'
SCALE

VICINITY MAP
SITE

PREPARED BY SITE PLANNER DATE
RECOMMENDED DIRECTOR OPERATING DIVISION DATE
RECOMMENDED DIRECTOR PLANNING & RESEARCH DATE
RECOMMENDED COMMISSIONER DNR DATE
APPROVED CHAIRMAN DNR BOARD DATE

0 100 200 400 FEET
0 24 48 120 METERS

NORTH

HOFWYL-BROADFIELD PLANTATION HISTORIC SITE

STATE OF GEORGIA
DEPARTMENT OF NATURAL RESOURCES
Office of Planning and Research

Fig. 7. Example of general development plans for State historic sites purchased along the lower Altamaha. (Courtesty of Georgia Department of Natural Resources)

HISTORIC SETTLEMENTS

Aleck Island
Ashintilly*
Cannon's Point
Carteret's Point
Clark's Bluff
Couper's Point
Darien Bluff
Doctortown
Fishing Lake
Hampton Point
Hird Island
Hughes Old River
Jesup
Joiners Island
Joiners Old Field
Lake Bluff
Lawton's Field
Lower & Upper Sansavilla
Ludowici
Morgan's Lake*
Oglethorpe's Bluff
Paradise Park
Reid's Bluff
The Ridge*

HISTORIC PLANTATIONS

Altama*
Broughton Island
Broadfield***
Butlers Island*
Elizafield*
Evelyn
Generals Island*
Grantly
Hofwyl***
New Hope

HISTORIC TRAVELWAYS

Aluchua Trail
Barnard's Trail
Barrington Ferry
Barrington Road
Bartram Trail*
Blue's Reach Road*
Doctortown Path
Fort Barrington Road
Ga. Coast and Piedmont RR
Grants Ferry Road
King's Road
Oglethorpe Bridge
Old Barrington Road
Old Post Road
River Road
Shell Road
Wire Road

HISTORIC RIVER LANDINGS

Brown's Lake
Clark's Bluff
Holland
Honeygall
Joiners
MacFishery
Oak
Old Still
Opossum
Ox Lot

HISTORIC STRUCTURES

Bank of Darien*
Bethlehem Church
Brunswick/Altamaha Canal*
Clayhole Church
Cox Cemetery
Darien Presbyterian*
Dixie School
Dixie School Church
Evelyn Mounds
Laurel Grove Site*
Little St. Simons Mounds
Lower-Bluff Mill*
McClendon School
Midway Church*
Mount Venture
Old Meeting House*
Penton Hill Church
Spanish Mission*
St. Andrews Cemetery*
St. Andrews Episcopal*
St. Cyprians Episcopal*
Townsend Mound
Union Church

HISTORIC FORTS

Fort Barrington**
Fort Darien*
Fort King George***

NOTE: * Georgia Historical Marker
       ** National Register of Historic Sites
      *** Georgia State Historic Site

HISTORIC RIVER PLACE NAMES

Alligator Congress
Bar Room
Blackbeard's Creek
Box Point
Boyles Island
Brian's Wood-yard Round
Bug Bluff, Suck & Island
Casino Ridge & Slough
Cathead Creek
Clark's Reach
Clayhole Creek
Couper's Bar
Deadman's Point
Doctor's Creek
General's Cut
Half-moon Bluff
Hannah Island
Harper Slough
Honeygall Creek
Kneebuckle Island
Johnson's Lake
Lewis Island & Creek
Mad-Dog Point
Miller Lake Cut-off
Old Hell Bight
Old Man's Shotbag
Old Woman's Pocket
Penholoway Creek
Pico Island
Rag Point
Rifle Cut
Sister Pine Round
Spill-over Bar
The Narrows
Wateroak Rounds (1st & 2nd)
Webb-Stump Bight
Westley Horn
Wreck-of-the-Louise

HISTORIC SITES OF THE LOWER ALTAMAHA RIVER

Fig. 9. Of the theme-needs identified in Georgia, many are possible for interpretations along the lower Altamaha. (Courtesy of Georgia Department of Natural Resources)

STATE HISTORIC SITE "THEME" NEEDS

Major Theme		Subtheme
1.	Agriculture	(Georgia at Work)
2.	Georgia Ways of Life	(Society and Social Conscience)
3.	Revolutionary War	(Major Georgia Wars)
4.	Development of the English Colony (Political)	(Development of the English Colony)
5.	Commerce and Industry	(Georgia at Work)
6.	Political and Military Affairs 1783-1830	(Political and Military Affairs)
7.	Literature, Drama, and Music	(The Contemplative Society)
8.	Political and Military Affairs 1830-1860	(Political and Military Affairs)
9.	Education	(The Contemplative Society)
10.	Political and Military Affairs 1865-1914	(Political and Military Affairs)
11.	Science and Invention	(Georgia at Work)
12.	Spanish Exploration and Settlement	(European Exploration and Settlement)
13.	Indian Meets European	(Original Inhabitants)
14.	Transportation and Communication	(Georgia at Work)
15.	Political and Military Affairs 1914-present	(Political and Military Affairs)
16.	Internal Expansion	(Georgia's Expansion)
17.	English Exploration and Settlement	(European Exploration and Settlement)
18.	Frontier Trade	(Georgia Expansion)
19.	War of 1812	(Major Georgia Wars)
20.	Intellectual Currents	(The Contemplative Society)
21.	Social and Humanitarian Movements	(Society and Social Conscience)
22.	World War I	(Major Georgia Wars)
23.	World War II	(Major Georgia Wars)
24.	Spanish-American War	(Major Georgia Wars)
25.	Explorers	(Georgia's Expansion)
26.	Engineering	(Georgia at Work)
27.	Painting and Sculpture	(The Contemplative Society)
28.	French Exploration and Settlement	(European Exploration and Settlement)
29.	Environmental Conservation	(Society and Social Conscience)

Source: Georgia Department of Natural Resources, State Parks and Historic Sites Systems Plan.

Fig. 8. Table of historic sites of the lower Altamaha (see map in Fig. 2). (Courtesy of Georgia Department of Natural Resources)

New Center Neighborhood Rehabilitation

Johnson, Johnson and Roy, Inc.

Three years ago, Pallister Avenue in Detroit, Michigan, was part of a deteriorating neighborhood in the shadow of the General Motors Building. Today, major renovation efforts are giving a sizable area around Pallister Street a new and attractive face. The street is the first in an 18-square-block area just north of GM's headquarters to be renovated as part of the New Center Neighborhood Revitalization Program.

The name New Center first appeared in the 1920s in connection with the construction along Grand Boulevard of the mammoth General Motors Building (1922), the Fisher Building (1928), and the New Center Building (1932), all designed by famed Detroit architect Albert Kahn. Located 2½ miles north of the old center of town, this was intended as a "new center" of commercial activity for the city of Detroit.

The residential neighborhood dates back to much earlier. Grand Boulevard was conceived in the 1880s as a grand beltway, lined with stately elms and palatial residences, that would define the city limits of Detroit. Frederick Law Olmsted was called on to advise on the layout of the boulevard, and his recommendations, specifically the width of the street, the double rows of elms arched over the roadway, and the separation of grades at railroad crossings, were implemented.

Detroit's tremendous industrial growth, however, created a housing demand that soon outgrew the Grand Boulevard bounds. The avenues of Lothrup and Bethune, just north of Grand Boulevard, were quickly built upon and soon annexed into the city; by the early 1900s, they included the stretch from Pallister up to Virginia Park. New home owners who moved in sought houses in the prevailing taste. Thus we can visually trace the development of the area from the early, almost "Victorian" houses on Bethune and Lothrup, through the turn-of-the-century styles on Pallister, and, finally, to larger, more elaborate homes on Virginia Park. The houses at New Center fall into three architectural styles: Queen Anne Revival, Colonial or Georgian Revival, and Composite.

New Center Commons, a multimillion dollar project, has been named by the force behind the improvements—General Motors Corporation. In addition, 14 other area business firms, civic and community organizations, and numerous governmental agencies at all levels, including the City of Detroit and the federal Department of Housing and Urban Development (HUD) are also involved. Now well underway, the rehabilitation project includes approximately 125 single-family and 175 multifamily units. In addition to buying and renovating area homes for sale, the project involves government-subsidized housing for families and senior citizens, improvement of roads, alleys, and courtyards, and a village center for neighborhood shopping.

The rehabilitation began with an economic feasibility study prepared by Gladstone, Associates and a Comprehensive Community Development Plan prepared by Johnson, Johnson & Roy, Inc. Following completion of the Plan, two separate organizations were formed to undertake the New Center Revitalization Program. The first, New Center Development Partnership (NCDP), is a privately funded organization responsible for the residential development. A GM subsidiary participates as the general partner in NCDP, and 14 other business firms are limited partners. The second, New Center Neighborhood Services Corporation (NCNSC), a nonprofit organization, coordinates various activities on behalf of the public sector, particularly the public improvements funded by an Urban Development Action Grant and Block Grants.

The plan for rehabilitating this neighborhood features closed and realigned streets and alleys to reduce traffic volume and to increase privacy and security. New garages and guest parking spaces have been built in widened alleys. Utility lines are placed underground and pedestrian-level lighting installed. New Center Commons features decorative entry gates and walls, some brick streets, neighborhood identification, and street furniture. Other special treatments include landscaped open spaces, historic lightposts, and globes. Pallister Street, at the core of the Commons area has been realigned to provide access to the Village Center as well as reduce traffic through the residential heart of the area.

Parklike areas, created from the now-closed brick-paved streets that run through the neighborhood, have been highlighted by historic light posts, ornamental street trees, and new turf. Pallister Commons and Delaware Commons have been closed to vehicular

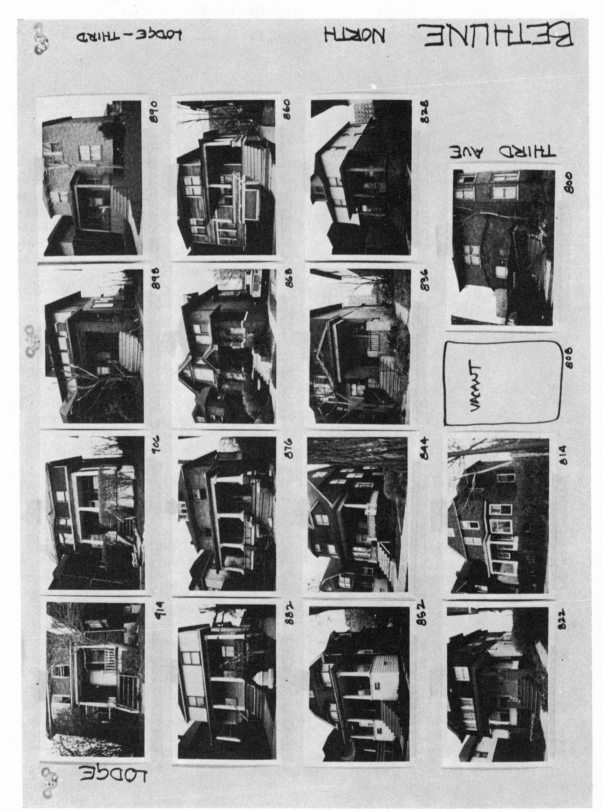

Fig. 1. Early in the planning process, planners catalogued each house by photo and videotape. They evaluated the potential for rehabilitation and the scale and styling that made up each streetscape. Here we see Bethune Avenue.

Fig. 2. Early aerial view of Pallister Avenue shows size and existing conditions of some of the homes.

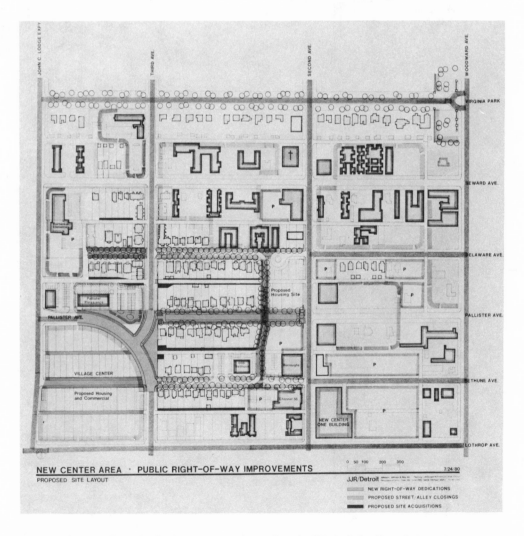

NEW CENTER AREA · PUBLIC RIGHT-OF-WAY IMPROVEMENTS
PROPOSED SITE LAYOUT

JJR/Detroit

NEW RIGHT-OF-WAY DEDICATIONS
PROPOSED STREET/ALLEY CLOSINGS
PROPOSED SITE ACQUISITIONS

Fig. 3. The immediate plan for improvements focused on the 125 single-family and 175 multifamily units.

117

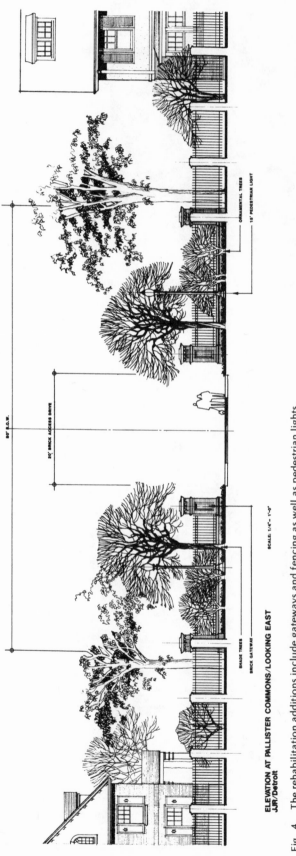

ELEVATION AT PALLISTER COMMONS/LOOKING EAST
JJR/Detroit

SCALE: 1/4" = 1'-0"

Fig. 4. The rehabilitation additions include gateways and fencing as well as pedestrian lights.

Fig. 5. Pallister Commons streetscape.

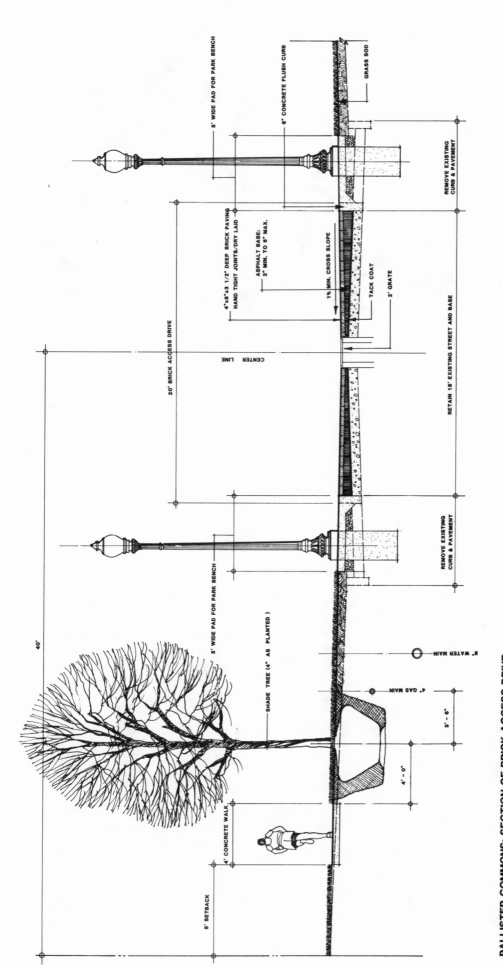

PALLISTER COMMONS: SECTION OF BRICK ACCESS DRIVE
JJR/Detroit

Fig. 6.

NEW CENTER AREA · ACCESS DRIVE
Proposed Service Court

JJR/Detroit

Fig. 7.

traffic except for emergency and maintenance vehicles. Owners have access to their homes via widened service drives along the old alleyways. Landscaped gateways, historic lightposts, and decorative fencing with brick support columns and walls follow along the side streets leading to the Commons.

The $3.4 million HUD Urban Development Action Grant (UDAG) provided for the relocation of tenants as well as for the physical improvements needed to complement rehabilitation; these include street changes, landscaping, roadway and pedestrian lighting, burying utility lines, and widening alleys. As an example of private expenditures, where garages were demolished to accommodate alley widening, parking pads and wood-frame garages with redwood siding are being built to match existing architectural character. Also, landscaping and wood picket fencing accent property lines. Property owners who remained in the neighborhood were directly involved in planning the alleyway improvements and gave more to the plan than verbal approval by agreeing to sell a portion of their property for widening the alleys.

The Development Partnership's rehabilitation of the

homes is aimed at attracting families, and prices had been set in the moderate range. Not all houses are single-family units. The two-family residence at 739–741 Delaware, for example, is ideal for a buyer seeking income property. This house is accented by three bay windows; each unit has two bedrooms, a full bath, a formal dining room, and a living room with fireplace. The deed restrictions for this house, which is priced at $72,500, require the owner to live in one of the units.

Owners of houses and businesses are also contributing to the improvements of the neighborhood with their own improvements, supplementing the work begun by the Development Partnership. Some concentrate on one room at a time while others have extensive remodeling plans, following the guidance provided by the Partnership Rehabilitation Manual.

Landscaping and street furniture are also planned for the major streets tying the neighborhood to the nearby concentration of major offices and attractions. A pedestrian circulation system will enable people to walk through the concourse or skywalks from Second Avenue to social, employment, and shopping ac-

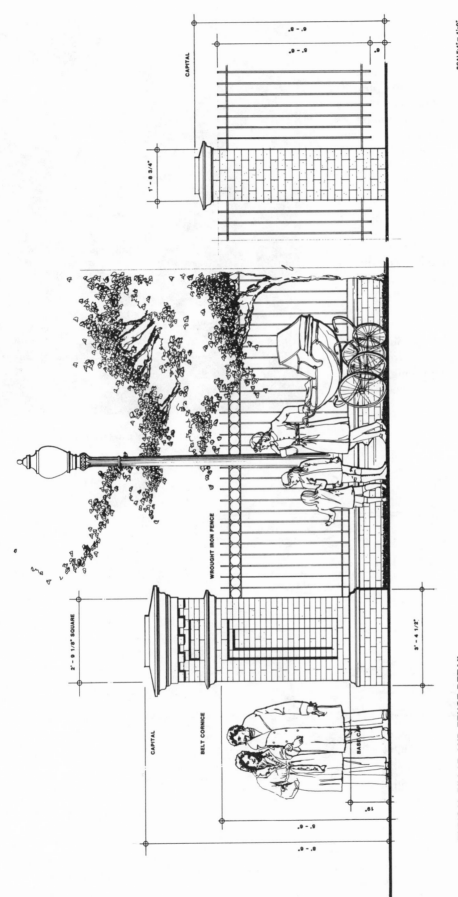

TYPICAL PILLAR AND FENCE DETAIL
JJR/Detroit

Fig. 8.

tivities in the New Center, Fisher, General Motors, and New Center One buildings and in the Hotel St. Regis.

New Center Commons represents the successful joining of hands between a major corporation and the public sector in order to breathe "new life" into its community. General Motors spearheaded the revitalization of the neighborhood surrounding its world headquarters, not only to provide for the security of its employees, but also to afford a sense of home and improved quality of life for the area. The significant improvements accomplished to date are recognized, by both public and private interests, as an important step toward achieving the goals of the overall development plan.

The standards of neighborhood revitalization set by this project have been high. They match the quality of the structures and neighborhood, and they reflect Detroit's feeling of the importance of the area.

A neighborhood of historic homes has been preserved and adapted to the needs of families. The opportunities for shopping in the area, previously gone, are returning. Property values have begun to rise, and adjacent streets and properties are improving, showing evidence that the spark of renewal has been established.

Fig. 9. One of the decorative entry gates under construction, with Pallister Commons in the background.

Fig. 10. The Partnership Rehabilitation Manual advised the use of foundation planting to provide a rich contrast to the lawn and a soft transition to the house foundation. Front yards should form continuous band of open green space that allows views to the "rhythm" of the architecture. The formal planting of street trees in the grass panel between the sidewalk and the curb has been re-established.

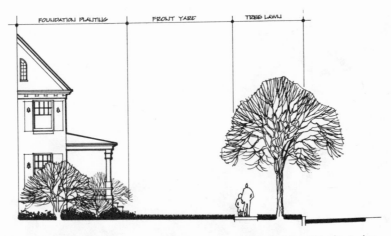

Fig. 11. The Manual also advised that foundation planting should be limited to the line of the front porch steps, and that owners should keep front yards open and free of hedges, fences, and statuary.

Fig. 12. The alleyways and backyards were cleared, and widened accesses, new garages, and security improvements were established.

Fig. 13. Rehabilitation, house by house, by contractors.

123

Fig. 14. Pallister Avenue, showing a mix of homes rehabilitated by the Development Partnership as well as some by private owners.

Fig. 15. A completed rehabilitated home, in use in 1981 as a sales model.

Fig. 16. The revitalization included new public spaces linking the Commons and the busy New Center office area.

Community-based Preservation in the Amana Colonies

Timothy and Genevieve Keller

Amana Colonies is a 26,000 acre National Historic Landmark and Iowa's leading tourist attraction; Land and Community Associates of Charlottesville, Virginia, have outlined a master plan for historic preservation (*Culture and Environment: A Challenge for the Amana Colonies* published in 1978) of this area. By living and working within the Amana Colonies for major periods since 1977, Land and Community Associates have become partners with local residents in developing and implementing preservation strategies sensitive to the physical and social needs of this unique community.

In the middle of the nineteenth century, the Amana Inspirationists, a pietistic, communal German sect, founded a network of seven villages in the midst of the agricultural lands and forests along the Iowa River. The seven autonomous but interrelated villages, known as the Amana Colonies, offered a spiritual alternative to the secular world. Unlike many other communal groups in America, the Amana Inspirationists were able to modify their system by reorganizing into two distinct groups: one spiritual and one secular. Although they abandoned communalism in the reorganization, or Great Change, of 1932, the Amana people still live on their Iowa lands within the physical boundaries of the original colonies and are a living, working rural community. The Amanites living in the seven historic villages make up a distinct cultural group that has maintained a substantial degree of its environmental and historic heritage in an ongoing and dynamic community. In the history of American communal groups, the Amana Colonies are a significant historic landscape that, although modified, still reflects the influence of 78 years of communal living.

The Amana plan was a response to the results of the 45 years of largely unrestricted, individual modifications in the physical environment since the Great Change of 1932 ended the communal era of total environmental control and architectural uniformity. Land and Community Associates developed a plan addressing the issues confronting the seven Amana villages and the total Amana community. These issues included unsightly use of the historic environment, inappropriate growth and development, inadequate interpretation of the historic environment, congested and confused circulation, and, finally, the lack of community awareness of these threats to the preservation of their culture and their environment.

Inappropriate land use, a major threat to the Colonies at the onset of the planning project in 1977, has become an issue of even greater significance since a January 22, 1982, Iowa Supreme Court ruling struck down the 50-year-old deed restrictions held by the Amana Society, secular and corporate successor to the original communal organization. For 50 years, the Amana Society exercised the right to control use of the individual properties that residents purchased for residential and commercial use when private property was sold during the 1932 reorganization. The recent court decision means that, although the Amana Society still controls the land in its possession—all of the agricultural lands and the forests as well as many village lots—the Amana villages, located in a rural county without zoning, are vulnerable to commercial exploitation until new controls can be established.

While the Amana Society will probably continue to preserve the essential rural character of the Amanas through practicing agriculture and forestry and avoiding strip development on the land between the densely settled villages within its boundaries, it is likely that private individuals and commercial interests will introduce inappropriate developments in the villages until one of the following occurs: Iowa County adopts a zoning policy protecting the historic and visual qualities of the Amana Colonies; the Amana community takes steps to incorporate as a separate municipality, with its own controls; or the village residents petition and vote to become historic districts as established by Iowa law.

The decision-making process necessary to take one of these essential actions depends upon an informed and educated Amana population. Realizing that these decisions might ultimately confront the community, the plan emphasizes community spirit and awareness as the primary component. With the possibility of the Amana Society losing much of its land-use control, community cooperation is necessary to develop strategies to implement the plan's other three components: enhanced visual quality and order, appropriate growth and development, and improved circulation and interpretation.

Citizen participation was an integral part of this pro-

126

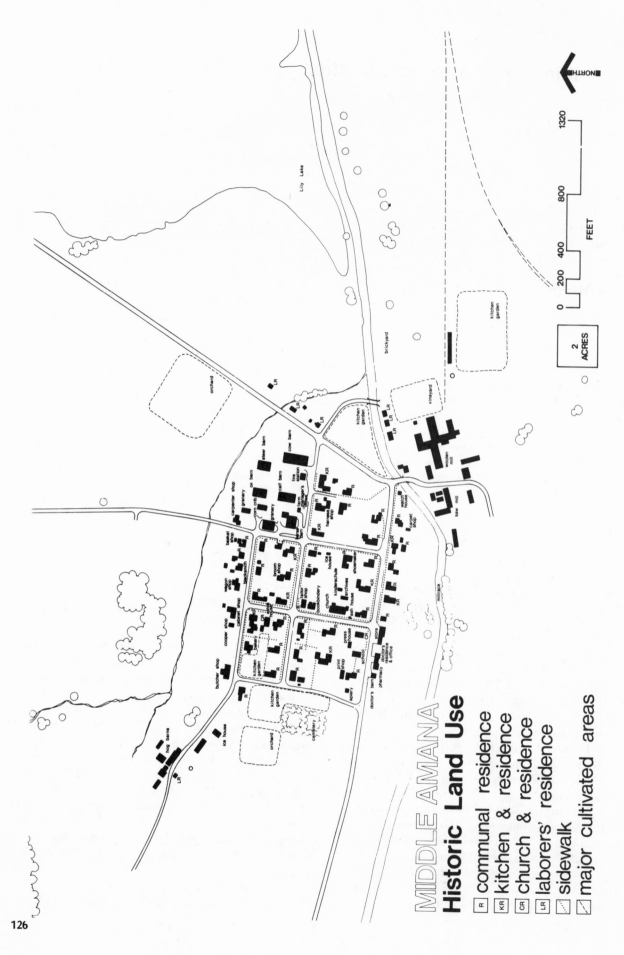

MIDDLE AMANA
Historic Land Use

R communal residence
KR kitchen & residence
CR church & residence
LR laborers' residence
sidewalk
major cultivated areas

Fig. 1.

Fig. 2. Historic photograph of High Amana, showing density of settlement and agriculture, c. 1900.

ject from the start. The Amana Landmark Committee, a representative community group set up to initiate historic preservation efforts in the Colonies, met weekly with Land and Community Associates principals while they were in residence in the community. A citizen liaison from each village worked with the team to complete the historic inventory of each village. These inventories provided necessary documentation and historical background information. To involve the total community in this documentation effort, Land and Community Associates presented its findings for verification and additions at a public meeting in each village. These meetings were the first step in initiating community awareness of historic resources and in stimulating residents to take an active role in planning for their community. The meetings produced additional information about Amana's environment—particularly historic landscape elements, such as orchards and vineyards, that had not been documented in the 1932 appraisal inventory identifying all financial assets, including all extant buildings and structures.

Each meeting concluded with residents discussing the issues affecting their village and the community as a whole. In each village, residents expressed a desire to return to the Amana of 1932 while retaining such post-1932 improvements as paved roads, water towers, and other features that provide the amenities of modern life. Residents regarded each village as threatened by excessive commercialism; uncontrolled tourism; disappearance of the traditional functional landscape of fruit trees, gardens, vineyards, and orchards; and deterioration and modification of historic Amana architecture. The village meetings played a

significant role in bringing residents together to use their collective memory in indentifying the past uses of historic buildings and the locations of landscape elements that had disappeared and to express their hopes and fears for their village and for the entire Amana community.

The village meetings also convinced the Landmark Committee and the project staff to develop the Plan at two scales, with proposals directed at the issues in each village and with recommendations for preservation of the Amana Colonies as a whole. Building on the Amana heritage of a concentrated environment in which there was no tradition of scattered buildings, fields, or services, Land and Community Associates developed the theme of concentration as the major concept of the plan at both scales: the components of the plan outline how concentrations of the traditionally uniform structures and landscapes, clearly defined and concentrated commercial areas, and concentrations of visitor-related services and facilities can improve both visual quality and quality of life in Amana Colonies. The plan recommended limited commercial and interpretive development in four villages and strict preservation of the predominantly residential character of the other three villages. Recommended historic district boundaries, new village sites, entry and scenic pull-offs, an open space system, and a bicycle trail were other integral aspects of the plan. The plan also identified the prominent visual corridor in which conspicuous new development would be inappropriate as well as areas where new development would not visually intrude into Amana's historic character.

As a supplement to the Plan, Land and Commun

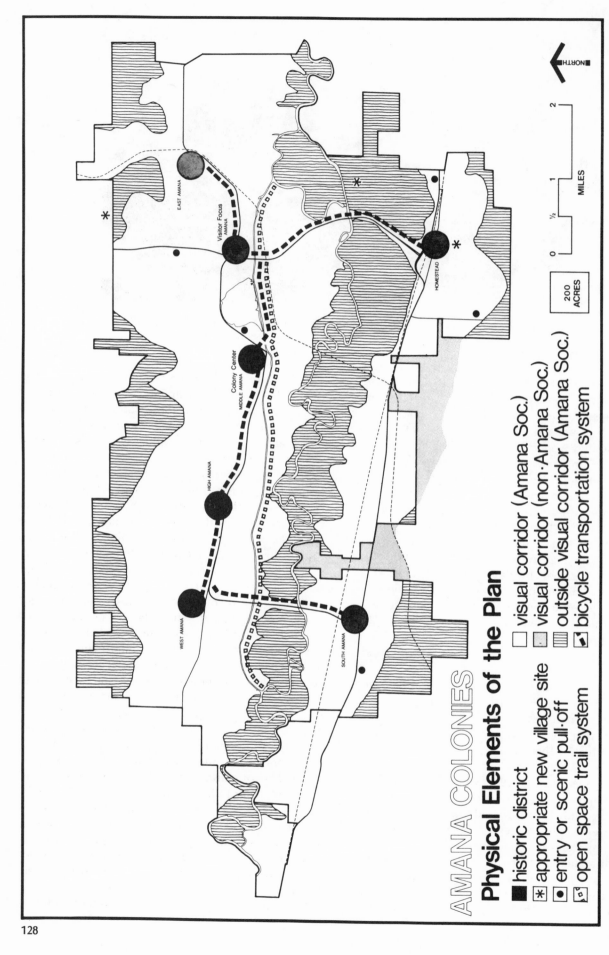

AMANA COLONIES

Physical Elements of the Plan

- ■ historic district
- ✳ appropriate new village site
- ● entry or scenic pull-off
- ░ open space trail system

- □ visual corridor (Amana Soc.)
- ▨ visual corridor (non-Amana Soc.)
- ▤ outside visual corridor (Amana Soc.)
- ◪ bicycle transportation system

Fig. 3.

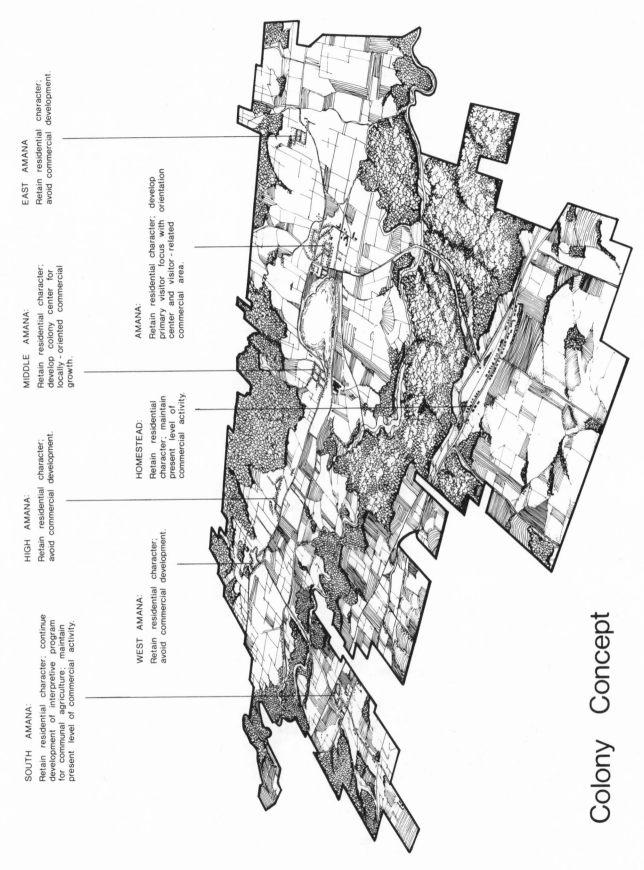

SOUTH AMANA:
Retain residential character; continue development of interpretive program for communal agriculture; maintain present level of commercial activity.

WEST AMANA:
Retain residential character; avoid commercial development.

HIGH AMANA:
Retain residential character; avoid commercial development.

HOMESTEAD:
Retain residential character; maintain present level of commercial activity.

MIDDLE AMANA:
Retain residential character; develop colony center for locally - oriented commercial growth.

AMANA:
Retain residential character; develop primary visitor focus with center and visitor - related commercial area.

EAST AMANA:
Retain residential character; avoid commercial development.

Colony Concept

Fig. 4.

129

Associates produced a *Conservation Handbook for Amana Villages* to assist villagers in making decisions about restoration, renovation, reconstruction, and new construction of both buildings and landscapes. The handbook's guidelines emphasize that the Amana village in its layout, function, density, and simple architectural character is the most basic unit of Amana's landscape and culture. The guidelines offer design and technical information to aid homeowners in renovating the simple, unornamented Amana buildings. The handbook also discusses techniques for preserving and enhancing Amana's traditional landscape of vegetable and flower gardens, fences and hedges, grape vineyards and trellises, blocks and paths, streets and roads, lanterns and birdhouses, and orchards and cemeteries.

In the spring of 1978, at the conclusion of the planning phase, Land and Community Associates presented the plan and a summary of the recommendations contained in the Conservation Handbook in a meeting in each village. These concluding meetings ensured that the citizenry that had assisted in the plan's development had an opportunity to become familiar with the plan's concept and the specific recommendations for their village, and to publicly support preservation efforts. Support for the plan's suggestions that the community establish a nonprofit preservation organization resulted in the founding of the Amana Preservation Foundation in 1979.

The Amana Preservation Foundation has taken a lead in promoting and implementing a community-based preservation program, emphasizing that preservation is, first and foremost, for the Amana people and not for the hundreds of thousands of visitors who tour Amana each year. With the assistance of the Amana Society, which endorsed the master plan for historic preservation, the Amana Preservation Foundation opened an office in the Amana Colonies late in 1979. In 1980, the Amana Preservation Foundation conducted a community preservation program that included technical assistance to property owners; the establishment of a "colony attic" where historic building elements such as bricks, doors, and windows, could be stored for use in restoration projects; and the initiation of Amana Heritage Days (an environmental awareness program for the Amana Community School).

In 1981 the community awareness program continued with an increased emphasis on landscape preservation and implementation. With the assistance of a grant from the Iowa Arts Council, Timothy and Genevieve Keller, principals of Land and Community Associates, were again in residence in the community during the spring of 1981 to develop landscape preservation projects that could be implemented locally. As a model project, Amana school children documented and developed guidelines for historic Amana fences and gates and reconstructed fences in front of three historic residences along the main street. The Amana Preservation Foundation, in its quarterly newsletter, *The Lantern,* published specifications for reconstructing fences. As a result, several Amana residents

Fig. 5. Characteristic Amana dwelling (c. 1900), with grape trellises, rabatt (flower bed), fence, gate, lantern, and milkstand, in Middle Amana.

reconstructed fences during the summer of 1981. The fences that historically protected vegetable gardens from livestock driven through village streets now separate private yards from sidewalks, inconspicuously preventing tourist trespassing.

The Amana Preservation Foundation also sponsored tinsmithing workshops for both adults and students to reproduce historic Amana lanterns. The lanterns produced in these workshops have been installed in several Amana villages. In a historic photography workshop, the Foundation stressed the importance of using photographs as a resource in planning a restoration of a building or its landscape. Community participants also replanted an apple orchard near its original historic location in the village of South Amana. The Amana Preservation Foundation, local Boy Scouts, and Y-Teens have joined together to undertake a long-range enhancement project for the historic Amana Lily Lake. This project includes definition of parking areas, planting, layout of paths, installation of a historic marker, and the construction of compatible picnic tables and trash containers.

As its major educational activity of 1981, the Amana Preservation Foundation, with the assistance of the Iowa Humanities Board, presented a weekend symposium on the culture and environment of the Amana Colonies. Session topics included an overview of other communal sites in America; preservation techniques for historic Amana buildings and landscapes; the origins and development of the Amana religion; preservation of oral traditions and written and photographic documents; and the development of Amana arts and crafts. The symposium benefitted from having as speakers, panelists, and participants several members of the Alliance for the Preservation of Historic Landscapes that had held its annual meeting in the Amanas immediately preceding the symposium. In conjunction with the symposium, Land and Community Associates produced an exhibit of the historic environment of the village of Homestead and walking tour brochures for the historic villages.

The symposium resulted in increased community awareness of the importance of Amana's historic environment as a physical reflection of Amana's culture and heritage. Amana residents continued to explore the interrelationship of their religious and ethnic heritage with their simple and frugal, but productive, landscape. This awareness provides the philosophical framework necessary for continued implementation of preservation projects. Such ongoing education is an integral aspect of a community preservation program in a community that has no permanent preservation staff and must rely, ultimately, on its own resources on a day-to-day basis.

The Amana community has accepted and met the challenge of the 1978 master plan to educate and inform its residents about the role of historic preservation in the wise use of its environment. This informed citizenry must now make critical decisions about how to control land use within its historic boundaries to ensure that visual quality and order are preserved and enhanced and that growth and development be compatible and appropriate. If the Amana community is successful in the preservation of both its culture and an environment that reflects the influence of its heritage, the Amana Colonies will be a model for other communities in initiating and implementing historic preservation programs locally.

The Magnolia Mound Plantation

Unicorn Studio

Magnolia Mound Plantation is an excellent illustration of early (1800–1830) plantation life and landscape in south Louisiana. Surrounded by magnificent live oaks and sited upon a high terrace that once overlooked the Mississippi River, the main house is typically French, both in architecture and in its unique construction technique. It is one of the few remaining examples of its kind to be restored and open to the public. Of the site, however, only 12 of the original 900 acres remain intact and these are surrounded by the city of Baton Rouge.

The purpose of the master plan is to recapture and relate to the visitor the essence of plantation days on this much-reduced site while also addressing the contemporary issues of parking and circulation.

The planning concept that guided this effort recognized that landscapes are unique in terms of preservation, i.e., unlike the interior of the plantation home, they cannot be frozen in time. The site, as it exists today, was seen to be a result of numerous landscape layers, imposed progressively through time. Following this philosophy, some of the more recent "landscape layers" were accepted, allowed to remain, and incorporated in the overall scheme of things.

Two of the most prominent landscape layers are the parking area and the Victorian residence, with its accompanying rose gardens, built but a few hundred yards to the rear of the main plantation house. The parking areas are obviously the most recent layer, necessitated by the property's function as a public facility. The Victorian house serves as the Administrative Center. The question of whether or not to restore the formal gardens surrounding the house was answered by returning to the guiding concept, which accepts its presence. However, some separation between layers was needed for the sake of clarity, i.e., not to confuse visitors as they passed through time into these various layers. To meet this end, orchards were proposed in key locations and viewed as time-separation zones one must pass through.

Of the other issues to be solved by the Master Plan, parking and circulation were of highest priority. As it existed, parking was directly to the side of the main house — in full view. A new road alignment and parking system having the least negative impact on the historic

surroundings were designed. Proposed parking is tucked into the natural landscape wherever possible. The main visitor parking area is to lie along the backslope of the "mound," below the sightlines of visitors in and around the main house. The "mound," or highest ground, thereby remains sacred and is untouchable by vehicular intrusion.

Another unique issue was how to provide for flexible, multiuse areas in which various fund-raising and public events could take place without disrupting the historical message of the site. Plantation Day alone attracted 4,500 people in 1982. The yard and pasture area are proposed to contain these events, while all parking at such times is to be handled off the site.

The Overseer's House is to become an educational facility to supplement the Louisiana history course taught to local school children. Thus a separate entrance, restrooms, and outdoor classrooms are proposed for this area. This part of the site is to relate a more functional, agricultural message to the visitor. Features in this area will be the stable, various farm implements, and demonstration crops of sugar cane, cotton, and indigo.

In terms of ornamental plants and gardens relating to the plantation home, landscape features were kept to a minimum. This follows the belief that early plantation life at Magnolia Mound was a struggle, as evidenced by records uncovered in research. For this reason, the only garden, as such, proposed in the master plan is the kitchen garden, again in an effort to relay the functional aspect of the landscape at that period. The formal rose garden associated with the Victorian residence is in direct contrast with the kitchen garden: as exemplified by its formal layout, lilly pond, and gazebo, this rose garden is an obvious pleasure garden, reflecting a later, much-changed life style.

All design decisions were supported by extensive research in the areas of Louisiana plantation life, landscape, and architecture. Research specific to Magnolia Mound had been previously compiled by the client. In addition, archaeological studies were conducted prior to design finalization in an effort to identify areas of high sensitivity to development. Several areas having a high concentration of artifacts were

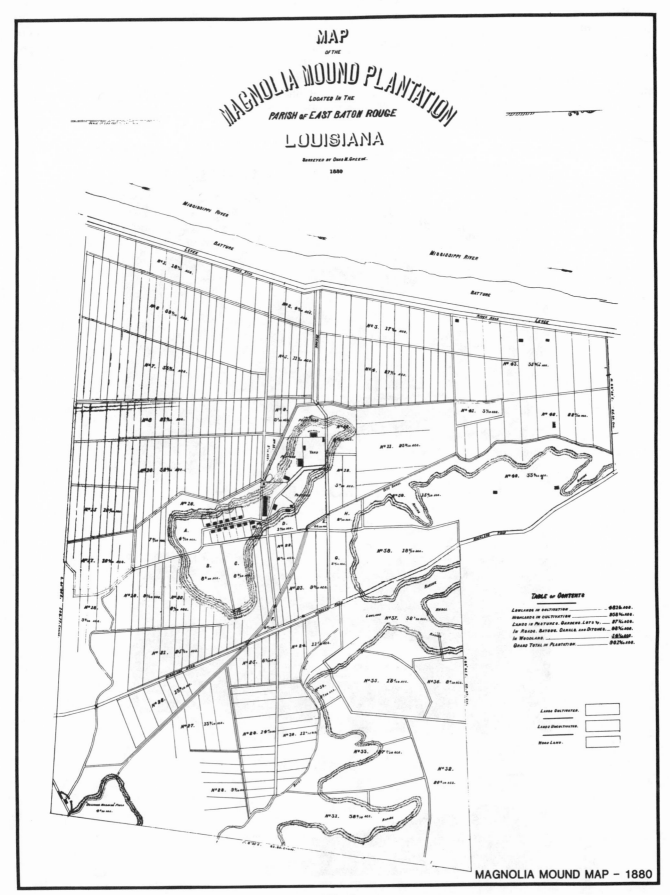

MAGNOLIA MOUND MAP – 1880

Fig. 1.

identified and as such were avoided in the proposed development.

In sum, by coupling the research and archaeological findings with the concept of "layering of the landscape," each element or area of the site is given a place in recapturing the essence of plantation days at Magnolia Mound. The agricultural aspects are stressed. Fences, orchards, and hedgerows structure the spaces and separate the "layers." The mound remains sacred and parking is limited to the backslopes. All this is done in an effort to correctly and clearly convey the message of Magnolia Mound to the visitor while accepting the site and all the various influences that have been imposed upon it through time.

MAGNOLIA MOUND PLANTATION

Fig. 2.

PROPOSED FENCING AROUND KITCHEN AND KITCHEN GARDEN

Fig. 3.

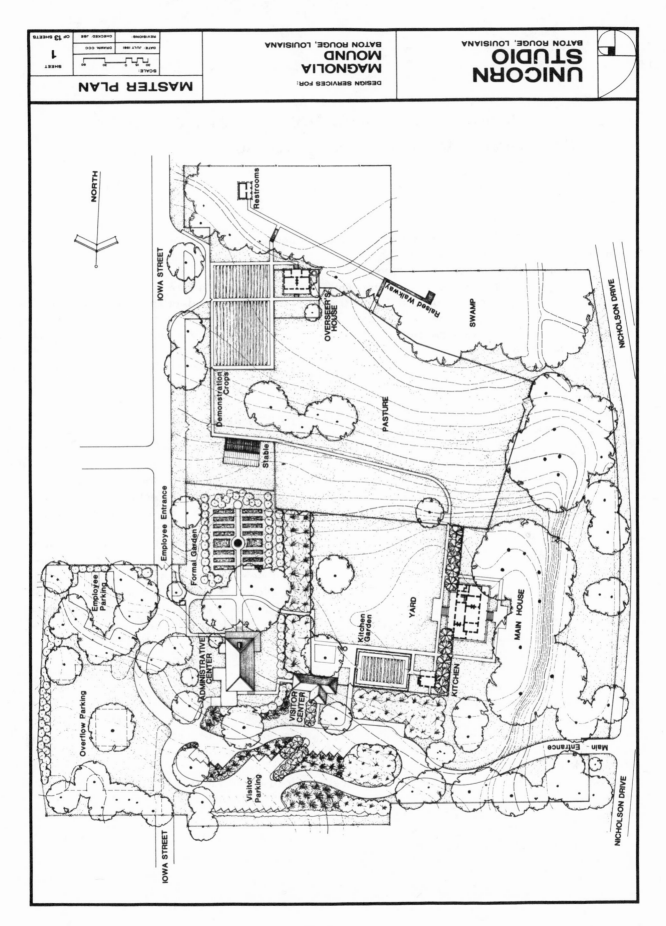

UNICORN STUDIO
BATON ROUGE, LOUISIANA

DESIGN SERVICES FOR:
MAGNOLIA
MOUND
BATON ROUGE, LOUISIANA

MASTER PLAN

SCALE:
0 15 30 60

SHEET
1
OF 13 SHEETS

DATE: JULY 1981 | DRAWN: CGC
CHECKED: JBE
REVISIONS:

NORTH

IOWA STREET

Restrooms

OVERSER'S HOUSE

Raised Walkway

SWAMP

NICHOLSON DRIVE

Demonstration Crops

PASTURE

Stable

Employee Entrance

Formal Garden

Employee Parking

Overflow Parking

IOWA STREET

ADMINISTRATIVE CENTER

VISITOR CENTER

Visitor Parking

Main Entrance

Kitchen Garden

YARD

KITCHEN

MAIN HOUSE

NICHOLSON DRIVE

Fig. 4.

A Living-history Farm: The Buckley Homestead

Charles F. Lehman ASLA and Janice A. Cervelli, Assoc. ASLA: LeRoy Troyer and Associates

The Buckley Homestead exists today as a 160-acre farmstead with existing farm buildings ranging in architecture from c. 1850 to 1920. Initial interest in the Buckley Homestead project began when the land became available for incorporation into the existing Lake County Parks system. Immediate community feedback suggested the development of the site as a community facility based on a farm theme. The Parks Department and staff began an initial investigation into development options and consulted LeRoy Troyer and Associates for assistance. The designer recommended a holistic master planning process, coordinating a wide range of resources for the stimulation of development alternatives and economic assessment.

Initial meetings of the Lake County Parks and Recreation Department and the designer involved the exchange of ideas regarding the purpose and potentials of the Buckley Homestead project. The goals and objectives that follow were jointly established to guide the development of the project.

PROJECT GOAL AND OBJECTIVES

The northwestern portion of Indiana has experienced a continual trend of urbanization and advanced agricultural mechanization over the past 25 years (this area represents the last portion of the state to be settled, due to the Kankakee Swampy Marsh). Development is posing an ever-increasing threat to the strong rural heritage of the area, characterized by the small family farm, a rural lifestyle (including self-sufficiency, independence, and resourcefulness), and the abundance of open and wooded wilderness. It is necessary, therefore, to conserve the historical resources of the area that illuminate the rural heritage of the past. It is also necessary to develop resources that explore the rural heritage of the future: the development of Buckley Homestead should be committed to the future while reflecting the past.

The objectives of the project are to provide: a project demonstrating stewardship of past resources for future generations; a historical representation of an agricultural community by depicting a series of time periods; an educational experience—for school children as well as for adults—of the agricultural heritage found in the northwest portion of Indiana during the time periods of 1850, 1880, and 1900, as well as of present and future techniques; a vehicle for an on-going cooperative effort between local public agencies and interest groups; and a unique leisure opportunity for residents of a large urban region to experience and participate in a natural rural setting.

DESIGN APPROACH

Upon the establishment of the goals and objectives, the designer took the lead. The Parks Department became responsible for the generation of interest and support within local community groups. The designer recommended a design approach that consisted of a series of cumulative steps leading to a master plan for the development of Buckley Homestead. The development of a program for the master plan required the initial steps of site inventory, team assembly, concept development, and analysis of economic feasibility in order to assess the historical and recreational potential of Buckley Homestead.

The most significant step in this process was the team assembly, which involved the organization of a wide range of disciplines and community backgrounds, coordinated by the designer. Such an assembly reflected the wide diversity of expertise required for the financial, promotional, educational, recreational, historical, and physical considerations in such a design problem. The role of the designer as coordinator/facilitator was most effective when focused on the management, communications, and human relations within the team.

SITE INVENTORY

The purpose of the site inventory was to gather material and data for use in the remaining steps of the design process and, in particular, the team assembly. The site was visited to gather information and to

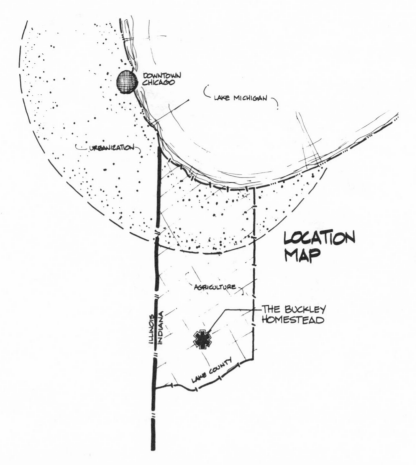

LOCATION MAP

DOWNTOWN CHICAGO

LAKE MICHIGAN

URBANIZATION

AGRICULTURE

THE BUCKLEY HOMESTEAD

ILLINOIS

INDIANA

LAKE COUNTY

Fig. 1. Buckley Homestead is located in southern Lake County, Indiana, approximately 60 miles from the Chicago metropolitan area. Lake County is contrasted by both intense urban development to the north and agriculture production to the south.

Fig. 2.

Fig. 3.

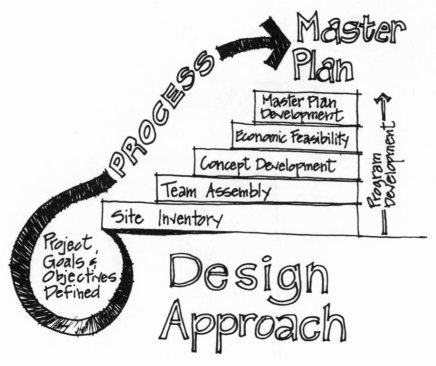

Fig. 4.

photographically document the site features and character of the surrounding community. State and local agencies were contacted regarding current site and development issues of concern to Buckley Homestead. From this data, an analysis report addressing the following elements was prepared:

1. topography and drainage
2. vegetation and natural features
3. soil limitations
4. existing structures
5. historical data on structures
6. utilities
7. land use and zoning of area
8. transportation and circulation
9. population
10. attendance in other park facilities in area

TEAM ASSEMBLY

In order to determine the most appropriate use for the farm site, the designer recommended the formulation of a "Planning Task Force." The purpose of the task force was to discuss, iterate, and evaluate the site and potential development programs and concepts. The designer assembled his consultants, including a market analyst, living-museum administrator, living-museum programmer, certified public accountant, and historical architect. The Park Department was instructed to select local community groups for

additional participation in the task force; it was recommended that this selection process focus on well-respected individuals representing a wide range of backgrounds and strongly committed to the planning effort. The list of community groups also served as a reviewing entity for the remaining steps in the process.

The planning task force, including consultants, community groups, the Park Department, and the designer, then assembled at the project site for a one-day work session. Invitations to the meeting also included the Park Board members. The following issues were addressed: historical interpretation; programs; staffing and personnel; promotion and market; funding; and land use. The data collected during the site inventory step served as background information in the discussion. A questionnaire was then distributed to the participants, requesting additional input regarding the above issues.

The final source of input came from written reports by the designer's consultants. Each report addressed the issues from a specific professional viewpoint. For example, the market analyst addressed comments and factual data from the standpoint of marketing and promotion. The task force recommended to the Park Board that the best potential use of Buckley Homestead be a living-history farm.

Background research during this step involved the review of ten other living-history farms across the Midwest. The designer collected data from each, including: season of use; activities; costs (admission,

138

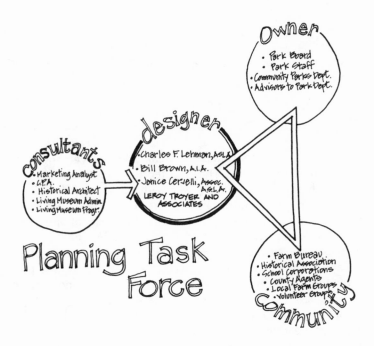

Fig. 5.

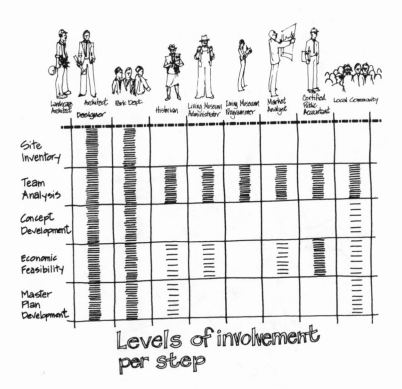

Fig. 6.

salaries, etc.); staffing and volunteerism; attendance; and capital improvements.

The information from the work session, questionnaire, consultants' reports, and background research was then compiled by the designer and the conclu-sions and recommendations were submitted to the Park Board. The Board approved the recommendation for the development of the Buckley Homestead as a living-history farm that would demonstrate a variety of farming eras.

ECONOMIC FEASIBILITY

Before an economic feasibility study could be prepared, development scenarios needed to be formulated. From the program development generated thus far in the design approach, functional relationships could be established and functional diagrams developed. In this process it became evident that several options or scenarios for development were available for short-term and long-term time tables. The various scenarios addressed such things as farming eras, their relationship to each other, land acquisition, circulation, etc. From this information a feasibility assessment of the options available was now in order.

The study of economic feasibility served several purposes for the Park Board and designer. First, it provided a management tool for the establishment of a development program. Secondly, it aided in the selection of one master plan concept from the various design scenarios of the concept development step. Such decisions were based on the information provided from the site inventory and team assembly steps. It was not the intent of this step to prioritize design components, options, or program issues that would occur in the master plan development step. The intent was to examine and select the optimum development scenario to use in the generation of the master plan.

The feasibility study utilized quantified factual data collected from similar facilities and national, state, and county agencies, and from demographics, etc., to make reasonable assumptions concerning the feasibility of the various development scenarios. Assumptions used in the study were classified into the following categories: operating periods and programs; staffing; operating expenses; admission; attendance; capital improvement costs; and itemized income projections. These assumptions were used in conjunction with the various development scenarios to generate a pro forma statement of income and cash flow for the first five years of operation. Assistance in this area was provided by the C.P.A. consultant members of the planning task force. It was the designer's role and responsibility, at this point, to be cognizant of the "wants, needs, and desires" on one hand and to weigh them against the "economic constraints, facts, historical research" on the other.

From the conclusions and recommendations submitted by the designer, the Park Board adopted the "optimum" development scenario, which contained a good balance of visitor appeal, utilization of existing resources, educational value, and economic ramifications. The scenario selected represented 5 periods of farming history in northwest Indiana: 1850s, 1880s, 1910s, contemporary, and future farms.

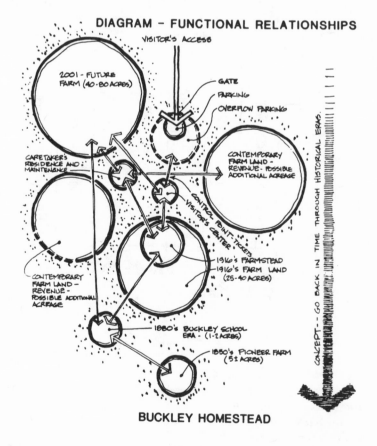

Fig. 7.

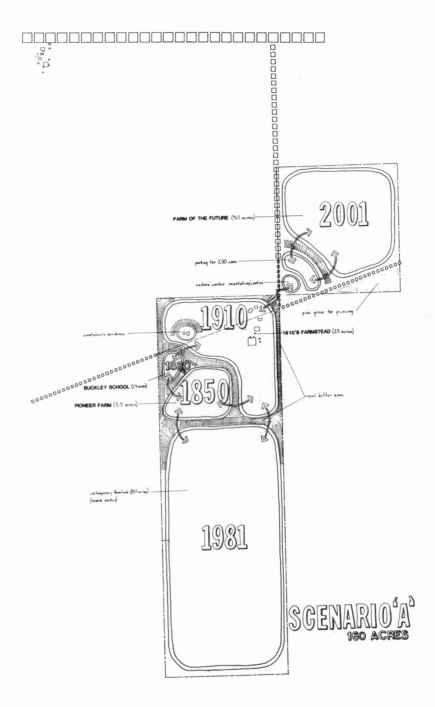

FARM OF THE FUTURE (30 acres)

2001

parking for 200 cars

visitors center orientation/control

pine grove for picnicing

1910

caretaker's residence

1910'S FARMSTEAD (25 acres)

1880

BUCKLEY SCHOOL (15 acres)

1850

PIONEER FARM (5.5 acres)

visual buffer zone

contemporary farmland (80 acres)
(revenue source)

1981

SCENARIO 'A'
160 ACRES

Fig. 8.

MASTER PLAN DEVELOPMENT

From the scenario adopted by the Park Board, a single approach to land development was now able to be addressed. From the many items and possibilities covered in the economic feasibility and the concept development steps, a solidified, prioritized, phased land-development program and master plan was developed. The program and master plan remained constant in objective and purpose while allowing flexibility for future growth potential in its design. From all the data, criteria, etc., established in the previous steps, a master plan was developed and reviewed by the community planning task force. The designer, with the support of the community groups, recommended the master plan to the Park Board, which they ap-

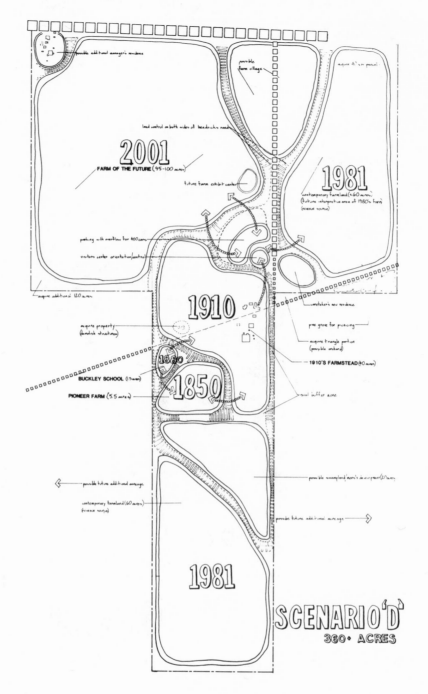

Fig. 8A.

proved and adopted. The intent of the development program prepared during this step is to provide a framework from which the implementation of the master plan can be carried out. It should be stated here that while historical inventory and investigation was done in the various steps it was preliminary in nature. Various details of historic dating, information, and construction will require research. This detailed historical research must be done during the schematic design phase of the construction documents, after the master plan is completed. Historical research can be collected from a variety of different resources, including "oldtimers" of the community, past records of the site, and historical documents.

The land use and land development of the various elements of the living-history farms master plan must be closely orchestrated to work in harmony with each other while still providing distinction and transition between historical periods and modern intrusions.

142

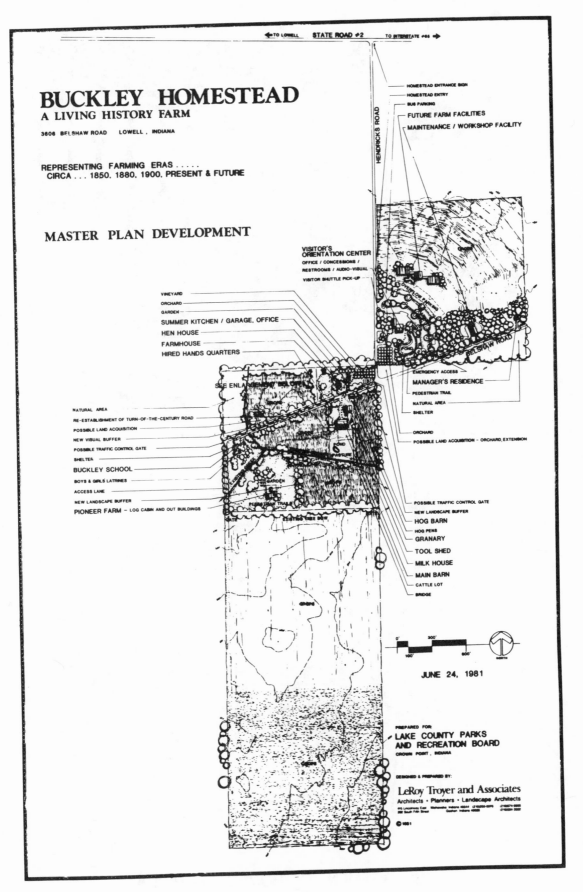

Fig. 9.

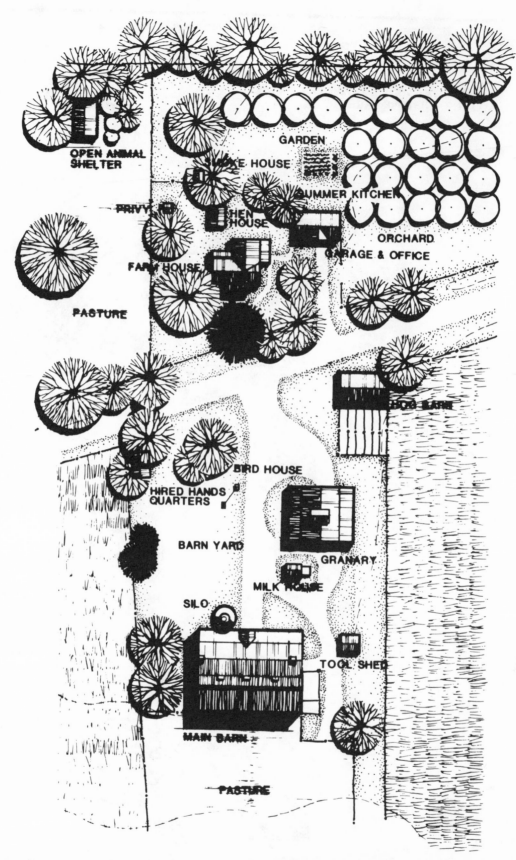

OPEN ANIMAL SHELTER

GARDEN

SMOKE HOUSE

SUMMER KITCHEN

PRIVY

HEN HOUSE

ORCHARD

FARM HOUSE

GARAGE & OFFICE

PASTURE

HOG BARN

BIRD HOUSE

HIRED HANDS QUARTERS

BARN YARD

GRANARY

MILK HOUSE

SILO

TOOL SHED

MAIN BARN

PASTURE

ENLARGEMENT OF HOMESTEAD AREA

Fig. 10.

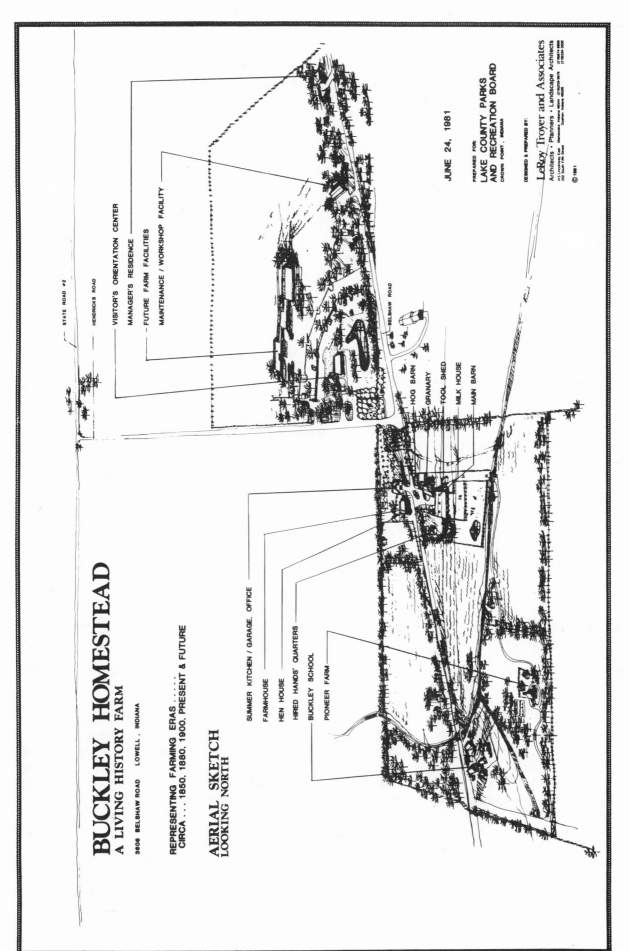

BUCKLEY HOMESTEAD
A LIVING HISTORY FARM

3908 BELSHAW ROAD   LOWELL, INDIANA

REPRESENTING FARMING ERAS . . . . . .
CIRCA . . . 1850. 1880. 1900. PRESENT & FUTURE

AERIAL SKETCH
LOOKING NORTH

STATE ROAD #2

HENDRICK'S ROAD

VISITOR'S ORIENTATION CENTER
MANAGER'S RESIDENCE
FUTURE FARM FACILITIES
MAINTENANCE / WORKSHOP FACILITY

BELSHAW ROAD

HOG BARN
GRANARY
TOOL SHED
MILK HOUSE
MAIN BARN

SUMMER KITCHEN / GARAGE, OFFICE
FARMHOUSE
HEN HOUSE
HIRED HANDS' QUARTERS
BUCKLEY SCHOOL
PIONEER FARM

JUNE 24, 1981

PREPARED FOR:
LAKE COUNTY PARKS
AND RECREATION BOARD
CROWN POINT, INDIANA

DESIGNED & PREPARED BY:
LeRoy Troyer and Associates
Architects · Planners · Landscape Architects
415 Lincolnway East   Mishawaka, Indiana 46544   (219)234-9999
202 South Fifth Street   Goshen, Indiana 46526 (219)534-3600
© 1981

Fig. 11.

145

Landscape Preservation of our Agricultural Heritage

Joseph S.R. Volpe

Efforts in preservation can deal more easily with objects and artifacts of history than with the historical environment. It is easier to preserve a single structure than a whole street, a neighborhood, or a district. When dealing with preservation in these urban environments, the emphasis has focused on the building facade. This has allowed changes in land use and the recycling of interior spaces while preserving the outer shell. The preservation of an agricultural landscape is more problematic because farming is a dynamic activity tied to the economics of production and distribution of the farm product: no agricultural product, no farming landscape. It is also subject to changing values of land use, usually moving toward urbanization or, in some areas, abandonment. If farming is abandoned, the dynamics of plant succession begin their inevitable sequence of spontaneous growth, which obliterates the farm. Nonetheless, our agrarian history is important to many communities, and efforts have been made to actively deal with this challenge in historic preservation. This paper looks at the proposal and the issues that arose when the town of Windsor, Connecticut, acquired a piece of disappearing farmland to be preserved through the mechanism of a municipal park.

NEW ENGLAND LANDSCAPE—AGRICULTURE, FOREST, AND URBANIZATION

The most persistently productive landscape in New England exists in the valley of the Connecticut River. The practice of farming has gone on uninterupted on this rich fertile land since the 1500s. At the time of the Revolutionary War, over 90 percent of New England was open farmland. It is a very different landscape today. Only the great river valley has continued to remain in agricultural production to any significant degree. Beyond the flood plains of the Connecticut Valley, however, on the very difficult glacial soils that cover most of New England, there emerged the dominant tree-covered landscape that characterizes the region. On these clayey and rocky soils, farming steadily declined after the opening of the more productive western prairie in Ohio and the Erie Canal in 1825. The soils of the prairie made farming much

easier and the new canals made it cheaper to distribute the agricultural products. New England, as an agricultural force, was in recession. What were once open, cleared fields as far as the eye could see now gave way to the spontaneous spread of plant succession. One successive vegetative community followed another, until the climax deciduous forest covered the abandoned farms. It was different, despite the growth of western farming, on the rich soils along the open fields of the Connecticut River, which continued to remain economically viable and competitive. Down into the twentieth century, agriculture not only thrived in the valley but contributed to the shaping of a unique landscape: the vast acres of shade-grown tobacco, with their grid pattern of post, wire, and cheesecloth. This cloth-covered landscape looks as if the minimalist artists Sol LeWit and Christo collaborated to create a great environmental art work. And a great cultural landscape it is!

But the farms along the river are nonetheless diminished by a new force on the landscape: the recent expansion of suburbs, office parks, and commercial developments. This is particularly true of the southern part of the river, which is within the orbit of the Boston-New York megalopolis, and includes virtually all of the valley in the state of Connecticut and the southern part of Massachusetts. It is within this ecological dynamic—this context—that this project was developed.

The town of Windsor requested a planning and design proposal for about 600 acres of forest and agricultural land it had assembled in a series of land acquisitions between 1971 and 1981. Windsor was once considered the capital of "tobacco valley," a name often used to describe the southern part of the valley at the height of the tobacco-growing era. As late as the 1960s, Windsor was still considered a rural tobacco-growing community, although the town was undergoing the effects of rapid development (Figs. 1 and 2). The community decided to preserve some semblance of its rural character by acquiring a relatively large piece of countryside made up of tobacco fields and forest land along a tributary of the Connecticut, the Farmington River. Besides serving as a physical symbol of Windsor's recent rural past, it

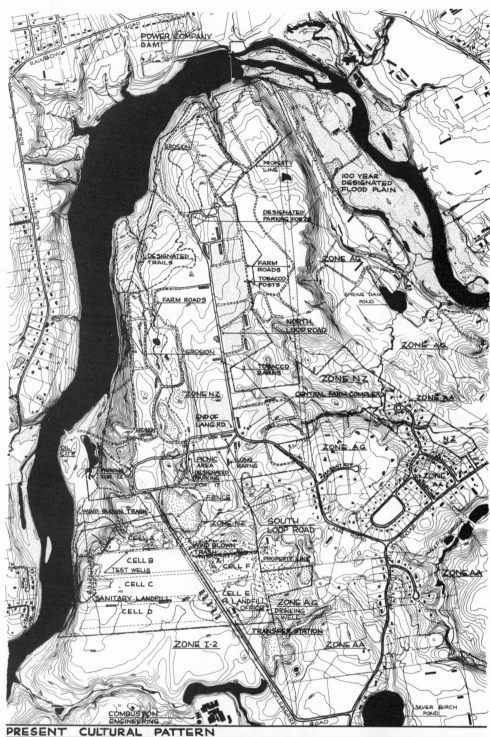

PRESENT CULTURAL PATTERN

SOURCE: MDC MAPS 1977 --- TOWN ZONING MAP --- TOWN FLOOD INSURANCE MAP --- PUBLIC WORKS MAP --- ASSESSOR'S MAP --- TREE WARDEN'S MAP --- LANDFILL PRELIM. PLAN --- SITE VISITS | SPRING 1981 | 5' CONTOUR INTERVAL | 0 100' 500' 1000'

NEW LAND USES OF RECREATION, HOUSING, AND INDUSTRY HAVE BEEN LAID OVER THE TRADITIONAL FARM LANDSCAPE TO FORM THE PRESENT CULTURAL PATTERN INSIDE AND SURROUNDING NWP. THE MAJOR DEVELOPMENTS IN NWP ARE 2 LOOP ROADS WHICH BRING CARS INTO THE MEADOWS AND A PEDESTRIAN TRAIL SYSTEM THROUGH THE WESTERN FOREST AND WETLANDS (SEE CIRCULATION PATTERN MAP FOR MORE DETAIL). THE WINDSOR SANITARY LANDFILL OCCUPIES THE SOUTHERN PART OF THE PARK. THE FARMINGTON RIVER POWER COMPANY OWNS A LONG STRIP OF LAND BETWEEN THE RIVER AND THE WESTERN BOUNDARY OF NWP. THIS INCLUDES THE HISTORIC DAM ABUTMENTS AT THE SITE CALLED OIL CITY. THE ONLY FLAT LAND ADJOINING THE RIVER. OUTSIDE THE PARK, ACTIVE FARMING STILL OCCUPIES THE FLOODPLAIN TO THE EAST. NEW HOUSING DEVELOPMENTS AND A ROAD SYSTEM SERVING THEM HAVE BRANCHED OUT FROM PROSPECT HILL ROAD AND THERE IS AN INDUSTRIAL COMPLEX SOUTH OF THE PARK. THIS AREA HAS BEEN MARKED BY RAPID CHANGE IN THE LAST 3 YEARS.

NWP IS DESIGNATED NZ (NO ZONING). THE LAND AROUND IT IS ZONED I-2 (INDUSTRIAL), AG (AGRICULTURAL), OR AA (RESIDENTIAL). AG ALLOWS 3ACRE LOT HOUSING, WHILE AA ALLOWS ½ ACRE LOT HOUSING. ZONING REGULATIONS SIGNIFICANTLY AFFECT THE DENSITY OF FUTURE DEVELOPMENT SURROUNDING NWP (SEE POTENTIAL DEVELOPMENT MAP).

NORTHWEST PARK — WINDSOR, CONNECTICUT

JOSEPH S. R. VOLPE AND ASSOCIATES
EDWARD M. MAHONEY
LANDSCAPE ARCHITECTS AND PLANNERS

320 PINE STREET
AMHERST, MASSACHUSETTS 01002
(413) 548-5961

Fig. 1.

ZONE AG
UP TO 2 HOUSES
EVERY 3 ACRES
IF 1 ACRE IS DED-
ICATED TO THE
TOWN AS OPEN
SPACE

DESIGNATED
100 YEAR
FLOOD PLAIN

ZONE AG

SPRING DAM
POND

ZONE AG

ZONE AG

ZONE AG

ZONE
AA

ZONE AA
1 HOUSE
EVERY ½ ACRE

ZONE AG

ZONE AA

ZONE I-2
INDUSTRIAL

SILVER BIRCH
POND

POTENTIAL DEVELOPMENT UNDER EXISTING ZONING LIMITS

| SOURCES: TOWN OF WINDSOR ZONING REGULATIONS | SPRING 1981 | 5' CONTOUR INTERVAL | 0 100'   500'   1000' | N |

UNDER EXISTING ZONING REGULATIONS, THIS MAP PROJECTS THE POTENTIAL DEVELOPMENT OF HOUSES AND INDUS-
TRY THAT COULD HAPPEN NEAR NWP. IT IS ESTIMATED THAT WITHIN THE AREA SHOWN ABOUT 250
COULD BE BUILT ON LAND ZONED AA AND UP TO 200 HOUSES ADDED TO THE LAND ZONED AG. EVEN MORE
HOUSES COULD BE BUILT IN ZONE AG IF ACRES IN THE DESIGNATED 100 YEAR FLOOD PLAIN WERE INCLUDED
IN THE ACREAGE COMPUTATION. INDUSTRIAL USE OF ZONE I-2 COULD BE INCREASED TO A MUCH GREATER
DENSITY. THIS MAP SHOWS ONLY THE DISTRIBUTION OF BUILDINGS, NOT THE ADDITIONAL IMPACT OF SUPPORT
ROADS THAT WOULD BE REQUIRED.

UNDER EXISTING ZONING REGULATIONS AND LAND OWNERSHIP, HOUSING DEVELOPMENT COULD PRESS AGAINST NWP'S EAST-
ERN AND SOUTHERN BOUNDARIES, INCLUDING THE BROAD CENTRAL TERRACE ABOVE THE EASTERN ESCARPMENT.

NORTHWEST PARK — WINDSOR, CONNECTICUT

JOSEPH S. R. VOLPE AND ASSOCIATES
EDWARD M. MAHONEY
LANDSCAPE ARCHITECTS AND PLANNERS

320 PINE STREET
AMHERST, MASSACHUSETTS 01002
(413) 548-5361

Fig. 2.

would also serve some of the growing recreation needs and provide a site for a landfill to handle the waste of its growing population. How does a town transform the land-use from private agriculture to public recreation and preserve some vestige of its agricultural past?

PRESERVATION OF ENVIRONMENTAL HISTORY

History surrounds us. It is in the many objects we handle every day. It is in the architecture of our homes, schools, and factories; in the environment of the city, town, neighborhood, and street; in the fields and woods that envelop us. With our growing interest in the many ways to preserve our heritage, we must continue to explore and to develop theory about the process of environmental history. We desire to look back imaginatively at the dynamic forces of history that we still see active today. Agricultural processes have created one such historical environment. The technology of agriculture works in concert with the natural processes of the land.

This paper explores four areas of historic preservation relevant to the proposal *(Plan for Northwest Park)* adopted by the town of Windsor, Connecticut, in January 1982. First, there is the description of the spatial characteristics of the historical imprint upon the landscape. Second, there is an exploration of the interaction between the decline of agriculture and the advance of plant succession. Third, there is the structuring of a new design based upon the order and dynamics of the agricultural imprint upon the land. Fourth, there is the proposal concerning the management and maintenance of the remaining vestige of historic agriculture—the meadows.

SPATIAL CHARACTERISTICS

Upon exploring the Windsor site through walking the land and studying ground and aerial photographs, one becomes aware of the past effects of agriculture. Actions of both recent and long-past farming have impressed a relief upon the land (Fig. 3). Through meadow and under forest, it takes the form of furrowed ripples in the surface of the soil; in the grid pattern of dirt roads overgrown with plants to various degrees; in the layout of the many long barns along north-south and east-west axes; in the grid layout of tobacco poles and wire; and in the strongest, yet most vulnerable, impression of all—the contrast of open meadow to surrounding forest. This imprint of historic agricultural practice is a response to the natural processes of the site and to the changing needs of agriculture from the sixteenth century until today (Fig. 4). The site was at first stripped and burned of its original trees to make way for farming, for fuel, and for a cash crop from the ashes of the burnt trees. Today all farming has come to

an end. The few remaining meadows are rapidly giving way to woody shrubs and to the advance of the forest that is once more reclaiming the land.

DECLINE OF AGRICULTURE AND ADVANCE OF SPONTANEOUS PLANT SUCCESSION

One of the most remarkable aspects of the landscape form at Northwest Park is the present pattern of meadow and forest. This rich complex currently contains all the plants in the whole sequence of plant succession (Fig. 5). This begins with grasses and herbaceous plants, advances toward woody shrubs, then pines and culminates in the mixed deciduous forest. Naturalists tend to study only individual plants or plant communities in the succession sequence, rich and varied as it is. But it is also a biological record marking the decline and withdrawl of past agricultural activities. There is a vigorous dynamic between the advance and decline of farming and the removal and return of plant communities; it is not only important as a record of the past but portends the future character and management of Northwest Park. It is not adequate to see the plants of meadow and forest as static individuals, missing completely the role that agriculture has played in this dynamic. The most mature deciduous forests are located on the steepest slopes, on the wettest soils, and on some of the more difficult soils derived from glacial till (Fig. 6). These are the areas most unsuitable for farming.

As farming tended to decline, the farmer abandoned the least suitable soils but kept in production the prime agricultural soils, particularly the fertile, well-drained sandy loams. Now even these meadows are rapidly moving through the stages of plant succession because there has been no farming or haying in Northwest Park since the summer of 1979. Unless some form of agriculture returns to claim the meadows or they are mechanically cut and mowed, the open fields will be lost to the forest. This would be a loss to plant diversity, which supports an equally diverse wildlife; for example, the birds and insects associated with the open space and grass would lose their habitat. Not to mention the complete loss of the historic agricultural character of field and meadow itself.

STRUCTURING A NEW DESIGN

One needs to understand the physical, biological, and cultural actions that shape a site. Historical process has been only one of many factors in the understanding of Northwest Park. An Ecology Model (Fig. 7) developed by the author is used to guide the design process. Analysis is the intellectual taking apart for the purpose of understanding things as they are. Synthesis is the imaginative putting together to create new

HISTORIC AGRICULTURAL IMPRINT

SOURCES: MDC MAPS 1961, 1973 --- TOWN AERIAL PHOTOGRAPHS 4-17-73

| SPRING 1981 | 5' CONTOUR INTERVAL | 0 100' 500' 1000' | N |

THE AGRICULTURAL ACTIVITIES OF THE PAST GENERATIONS HAVE IMPRINTED A GEOMETRIC PATTERN OF OPEN FIELDS CARVED OUT OF THE SURROUNDING FOREST. THE RECTANGULAR MEADOWS OCCUPY THE FLAT TO GENTLY ROLLING LAND. THE PRIME AGRICULTURAL LAND. THE FOREST COVER OCCUPIES THAT VERY STEEP OR WET LAND THAT WAS NEVER FARMED AND THOSE AREAS WHERE THE FOREST COVER WAS ALLOWED TO RETURN AS THE MORE EXTENSIVE AREAS OF CULTIVATION WERE ABANDONED. CAREFULLY ALIGNED FARM ROADS, TOBACCO BARNS, AND FARM HOUSES ANCHOR THE AGRICULTURAL FRAMEWORK.

NWP'S "NATURAL" DRAMATIC BEAUTY IS LARGELY DUE TO THE HUMAN INTERVENTION OF FARM LAYOUT AND AGRI-CULTURAL MANAGEMENT OF THE LAND.

NORTHWEST PARK — WINDSOR, CONNECTICUT

JOSEPH S. R. VOLPE AND ASSOCIATES
EDWARD M. MAHONEY
LANDSCAPE ARCHITECTS AND PLANNERS

320 PINE STREET
AMHERST, MASSACHUSETTS 01002
(413) 548-5961

Fig. 3.

150

LANDFORM AND SURFACE WATER

SOURCES: MDC MAPS 1977 --- TOWN FLOOD INSURANCE MAPS 9/28/79 --- LANDFILL PRELIMINARY PLAN 4/1/80 --- SITE VISITS	SPRING 1981	5' CONTOUR INTERVAL	0 100' 500' 1000'	↑N

NWP COVERS MUCH OF A TERRACED PLATEAU WHICH RISES ON A STEEP ESCARPMENT ABOVE THE FARMINGTON RIVER. BETWEEN THE BROAD CENTRAL TERRACE AND THE ROLLING UPPER TERRACE RUNS A COMPLEX SERIES OF RIDGES AND WETLANDS. A FEW FLOWING STREAMS HAVE CARVED RAVINES DOWN TO THE RIVER. THE RIVER IS DAMMED NORTH OF THE PARK FORMING RAINBOW RESERVOIR.

NWP IS A CONTRAST OF FLAT LANDS, GENTLY ROLLING HILLS, AND STEEP ESCARPMENTS. KETTLE HOLES DOT THE PLATEAU TO FORM BOWLS AND WETLANDS. THE DRAINAGE CHANNELS RUN MOSTLY DRY WITH A FEW WET, STEEP RAVINES THAT DRAIN INTO THE RIVER.

NORTHWEST PARK — WINDSOR, CONNECTICUT

JOSEPH & R. VOLPE AND ASSOCIATES
EDWARD M. MAHONEY
LANDSCAPE ARCHITECTS AND PLANNERS

320 PINE STREET
AMHERST, MASSACHUSETTS 01002
(413) 549-5361

Fig. 4.

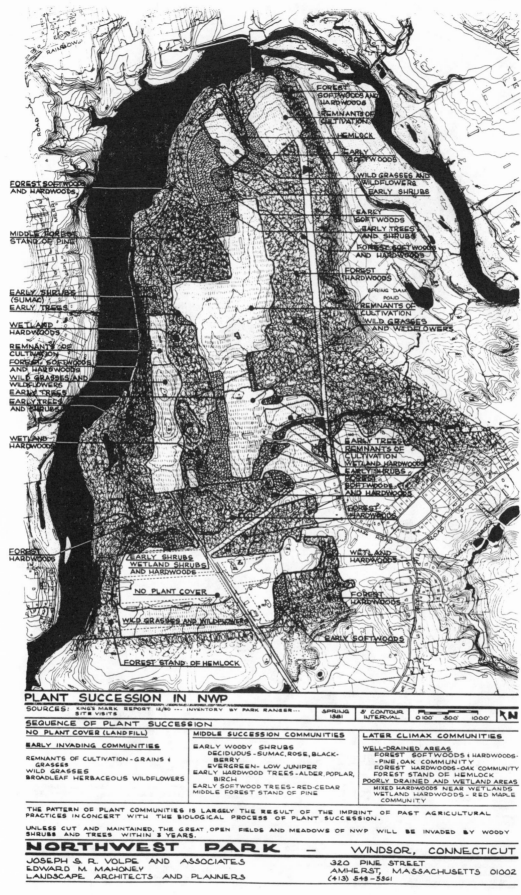

FOREST SOFTWOODS AND HARDWOODS,

MIDDLE FOREST STAND OF PINE

EARLY SHRUBS (SUMAC) EARLY TREES

WETLAND HARDWOODS

REMNANTS OF CULTIVATION
FOREST SOFTWOODS AND HARDWOODS
WILD GRASSES AND WILDFLOWERS
EARLY TREES
EARLY TREES AND SHRUBS

WETLAND HARDWOODS

FOREST HARDWOODS

FOREST SOFTWOODS AND HARDWOODS
REMNANTS OF CULTIVATION
HEMLOCK
EARLY SOFTWOODS
WILD GRASSES AND WILDFLOWERS
EARLY SHRUBS
EARLY SOFTWOODS
EARLY TREES AND SHRUBS
FOREST SOFTWOODS AND HARDWOODS
FOREST HARDWOODS
SPRING DAM POND
REMNANTS OF CULTIVATION
WILD GRASSES AND WILDFLOWERS

EARLY TREES
REMNANTS OF CULTIVATION
WETLAND HARDWOODS
EARLY SHRUBS
FOREST SOFTWOODS AND HARDWOODS
FOREST HARDWOODS

WETLAND HARDWOODS

EARLY SHRUBS
WETLAND SHRUBS AND HARDWOODS

NO PLANT COVER

WILD GRASSES AND WILDFLOWERS

FOREST STAND OF HEMLOCK

FOREST HARDWOODS

EARLY SOFTWOODS

PLANT SUCCESSION IN NWP

SOURCES: KING'S MARK REPORT 12/80 --- INVENTORY BY PARK RANGER... SITE VISITS | SPRING 1981 | 5' CONTOUR INTERVAL | 0 100' 500' 1000' | N

SEQUENCE OF PLANT SUCCESSION

NO PLANT COVER (LANDFILL)	MIDDLE SUCCESSION COMMUNITIES	LATER CLIMAX COMMUNITIES

EARLY INVADING COMMUNITIES	EARLY WOODY SHRUBS
	  DECIDUOUS - SUMAC, ROSE, BLACK-
	  BERRY
	  EVERGREEN - LOW JUNIPER
		WELL-DRAINED AREAS
		  FOREST SOFTWOODS & HARDWOODS
		  - PINE, OAK COMMUNITY

REMNANTS OF CULTIVATION - GRAINS &
  GRASSES
WILD GRASSES
BROADLEAF HERBACEOUS WILDFLOWERS
	EARLY HARDWOOD TREES - ALDER, POPLAR,
	  BIRCH
	EARLY SOFTWOOD TREES - RED-CEDAR
	MIDDLE FOREST STAND OF PINE
		FOREST HARDWOODS-OAK COMMUNITY
		  FOREST STAND OF HEMLOCK
		POORLY DRAINED AND WETLAND AREAS
		  MIXED HARDWOODS NEAR WETLANDS
		  WETLAND HARDWOODS - RED MAPLE
		  COMMUNITY

THE PATTERN OF PLANT COMMUNITIES IS LARGELY THE RESULT OF THE IMPRINT OF PAST AGRICULTURAL PRACTICES IN CONCERT WITH THE BIOLOGICAL PROCESS OF PLANT SUCCESSION.

UNLESS CUT AND MAINTAINED, THE GREAT OPEN FIELDS AND MEADOWS OF NWP WILL BE INVADED BY WOODY SHRUBS AND TREES WITHIN 3 YEARS.

NORTHWEST PARK — WINDSOR, CONNECTICUT

JOSEPH S. R. VOLPE AND ASSOCIATES
EDWARD M. MAHONEY
LANDSCAPE ARCHITECTS AND PLANNERS

320 PINE STREET
AMHERST, MASSACHUSETTS 01002
(413) 549-5361

Fig. 5.

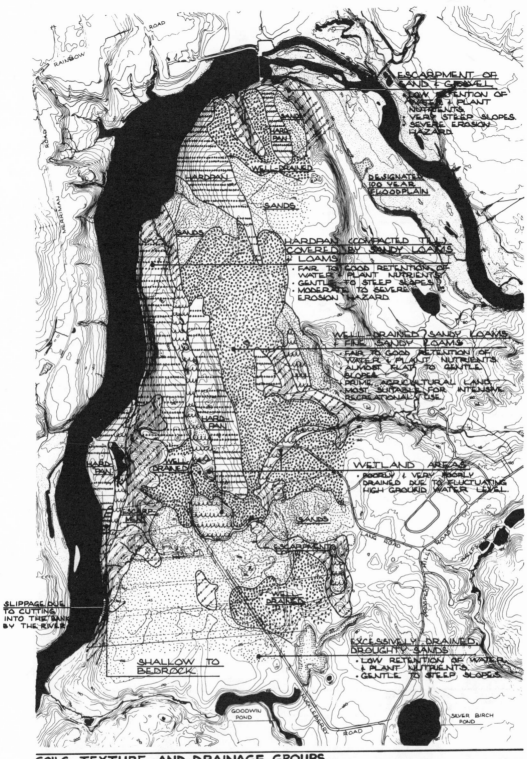

ESCARPMENT OF
SAND & GRAVEL
· LOW RETENTION OF
WATER & PLANT
NUTRIENTS.
· VERY STEEP SLOPES.
· SEVERE EROSION
HAZARD

DESIGNATED
100 YEAR
FLOODPLAIN

HARDPAN (COMPACTED TILL)
COVERED BY SANDY LOAMS &
LOAMS)
· FAIR TO GOOD RETENTION OF
WATER & PLANT NUTRIENTS.
· GENTLE TO STEEP SLOPES.
· MODERATE TO SEVERE
EROSION HAZARD

WELL-DRAINED SANDY LOAMS &
FINE SANDY LOAMS
· FAIR TO GOOD RETENTION OF
WATER & PLANT NUTRIENTS.
· ALMOST FLAT TO GENTLE
SLOPES.
· PRIME AGRICULTURAL LAND.
MOST SUITABLE FOR INTENSIVE
RECREATIONAL USE.

WETLAND AREAS
· POORLY & VERY POORLY
DRAINED DUE TO FLUCTUATING
HIGH GROUND WATER LEVEL.

SLIPPAGE DUE
TO CUTTING
INTO THE BANK
BY THE RIVER.

EXCESSIVELY DRAINED,
DROUGHTY SANDS
· LOW RETENTION OF WATER
& PLANT NUTRIENTS.
· GENTLE TO STEEP SLOPES.

SHALLOW TO
BEDROCK

GOODWIN
POND

SILVER BIRCH
POND

SOILS TEXTURE AND DRAINAGE GROUPS

| SOURCES: SCS MAPS FOR COUNTY --- KING'S MARK REPORT 12/80 --- SITE VISITS | SPRING 1981 | 5' CONTOUR INTERVAL | 0 100'   500'   1000' | N |

THE DOMINANT SOILS OF NWP ARE WELL-DRAINED SANDY LOAMS AND FINE SANDY LOAMS, AND EXCESSIVELY DRAINED, DROUGHTY SAND. THE WELL-DRAINED SANDY LOAMS ARE PRIME AGRICULTURAL SOILS. IN SOME AREAS COMPACTED GLACIAL TILL UNDER SOME OF THE SANDY LOAMS CREATES AN EROSION HAZARD EVEN ON GENTLE SLOPES. THERE IS A SEVERE EROSION HAZARD ON THE STEEP ESCARPMENTS. ORGANIC, SATURATED SOILS OCCUR WHERE A SEASONALLY HIGH WATER TABLE FORMS WETLANDS. EROSION POINTS ARE SHOWN ON THE PRESENT CULTURAL PATTERNS MAP.

THE MANY AND VARIED SOILS OF NWP CONTRIBUTE TO THE DIVERSITY OF THE LAND-SCAPE BY SUPPORTING A WIDE SPECTRUM OF NEW ENGLAND PLANTS.

NORTHWEST PARK — WINDSOR, CONNECTICUT

JOSEPH & R. VOLPE AND ASSOCIATES
EDWARD M. MAHONEY
LANDSCAPE ARCHITECTS AND PLANNERS

320 PINE STREET
AMHERST, MASSACHUSETTS 01002
(413) 549-5361

Fig. 6.

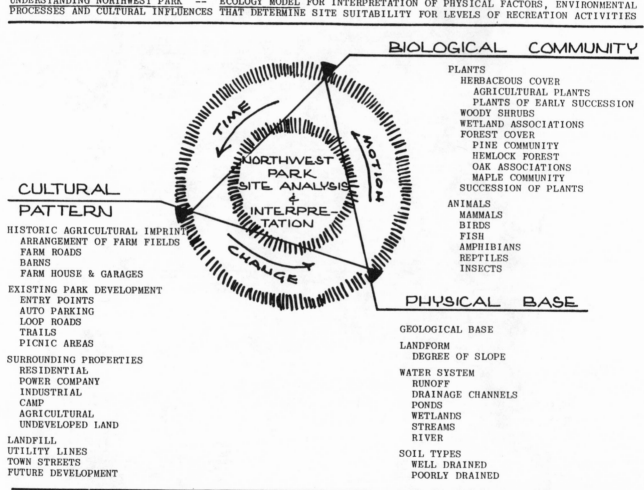

BIOLOGICAL COMMUNITY

PLANTS
  HERBACEOUS COVER
    AGRICULTURAL PLANTS
    PLANTS OF EARLY SUCCESSION
  WOODY SHRUBS
  WETLAND ASSOCIATIONS
  FOREST COVER
    PINE COMMUNITY
    HEMLOCK FOREST
    OAK ASSOCIATIONS
    MAPLE COMMUNITY
  SUCCESSION OF PLANTS

ANIMALS
  MAMMALS
  BIRDS
  FISH
  AMPHIBIANS
  REPTILES
  INSECTS

CULTURAL PATTERN

HISTORIC AGRICULTURAL IMPRINT
  ARRANGEMENT OF FARM FIELDS
  FARM ROADS
  BARNS
  FARM HOUSE & GARAGES

EXISTING PARK DEVELOPMENT
  ENTRY POINTS
  AUTO PARKING
  LOOP ROADS
  TRAILS
  PICNIC AREAS

SURROUNDING PROPERTIES
  RESIDENTIAL
  POWER COMPANY
  INDUSTRIAL
  CAMP
  AGRICULTURAL
  UNDEVELOPED LAND

LANDFILL
UTILITY LINES
TOWN STREETS
FUTURE DEVELOPMENT

PHYSICAL BASE

GEOLOGICAL BASE

LANDFORM
  DEGREE OF SLOPE

WATER SYSTEM
  RUNOFF
  DRAINAGE CHANNELS
  PONDS
  WETLANDS
  STREAMS
  RIVER

SOIL TYPES
  WELL DRAINED
  POORLY DRAINED

JOSEPH S. R. VOLPE AND ASSOCIATES
EDWARD M. MAHONEY
LANDSCAPE ARCHITECTS AND PLANNERS

320 PINE STREET
AMHERST, MASSACHUSETTS 01002
(413) 549-5961

spatial structures as they might be. For the purpose of this chapter, the focus is on the role of the historic agricultural imprint as it helped shape the physical design proposal for Northwest Park.

It was necessary to establish the recreation goals for Windsor's new park. The primary goal was that people should be able to be involved with the landscape elements—land, plants, water, and animals—and appreciate the rich imprint of the historic agricultural landscape of old farms, barns, and open meadows. The second goal was recreation for family groups, and the third for people to participate in competitive team sports.

It was necessary to determine which parts of Northwest Park were suitable for supporting various intensity levels of recreation. This study demonstrated that the more stable areas able to support more intensive recreation activities tend to be the more recently farmed land of the meadows, while the more fragile areas, least suitable for intensive recreation, tend to be the land long-abandoned by farming (see Fig. 8, "Black and White" Decisions). But this proved to be a simple cut of the information considering the need to preserve, in some semblance, the farm landscape (see Fig. 8, "Shades of Gray" Decisions). By synthesizing the recreation goals with an understanding of the suitability of the sites to support recreation, a concept proposal was developed. This established a purposeful location of recreation activities and a design concept for the circulation system (Fig. 9). The circulation system has a series of paths structured upon the old farm roads as they move through the open meadow. The siting of the three activity areas was largely shaped by the central barn complex and the location of the entry point into the park (Fig. 10). Since walking is the primary activity in Northwest Park that links the three recreation goals together, the spatial structure of the circulation system is critical. At the core it is built upon the Central Meadows Loop, the heart of the path system. At the outer edge is the River Boundary Trail. The Meadow Loop Connectors link the heart of the park with the edge. Between the River Boundary Trail and Central Meadows Loop is the great surround of the forest where the Forest Meander Trail makes its way through the dense woods (Fig. 11). The alignment of the path system was structured upon the historic relation between the barn layouts and the dirt roadways of the farm (Figs. 12 and 13). The final proposal of the path system is a network of quadruple tree-lined alleys radiating out from the Central Barn Complex. They connect resting places and destination points which serve all activities in the park (Fig. 14). The historic geometry of agriculture is accentuated by the newly planted straight, tree-lined paths, which contrast with the biomorphic meander of the trails that move under the existing forest cover (see Fig. 15 and elevations

A–A through F–F in Fig. 16). At the heart of the Central Barn Complex is proposed a Central Green, the main gathering place. It is surrounded by the long barns that are recycled to serve as the interpretation center, park office, bicycle and cross-country ski rental, museum, equipment storage, and workshop. The Victorian farm house is to remain as the park manager's home (see Figs. 17 and 18 elevations G–G, H–H, and I–I and wide angle sketches in Fig. 19). Some long barns are proposed to be recycled as a picnic pavilion (Fig. 20).

MANAGING LANDSCAPE TO MAINTAIN THE HISTORIC PATTERN OF OPEN MEADOWS

For Northwest Park to be successful in satisfying its human goals in recreation, it must not only implement a good design but also develop a management organization. There is a need to establish a clearly defined decision-making structure; this would rest with a Northwest Park Management Committee. The day-to-day maintenance could be in the hands of a full-time Park Manager. Responsible to the committee who set policy, the Park Manager's role would change as the park is developed. A primary function would be to develop a plan and tasks to check plant succession in the meadows. This is considered as design maintenance since this activity would not only keep the field open but would determine which plant communities would define the floor of the meadow. By altering the mode, time, and frequency of cutting of the fields, the manager would determine whether grass, or early, middle, or late season wild flowers would occupy the fields. A plan would also consider the role of evergreen and deciduous shrubs and woodlot management to encourage the full complement of plant succession.

There is also the possiblity of leasing the fields to some of the few remaining local farmers and developing demonstration plots for educational and recreational purposes. Another area is the coordination and direction of volunteer workers to aid in the maintenance and interpretation. Above all, the park manager must have a sense of the dynamic between natural and cultural history. He must have an ongoing plan for the continuous job of managing for historic agricultural preservation.

CONCLUSION

Let us consider landscape preservation as a part of the whole planning, design, management, and maintenance of our environment. In design, history should not be feared or ignorantly denied, nor willfully destroyed; it should be part of the design process. History should, like site planning, regional-based climate control, community participation, and awareness of environ-

(Text cont. on p. 169)

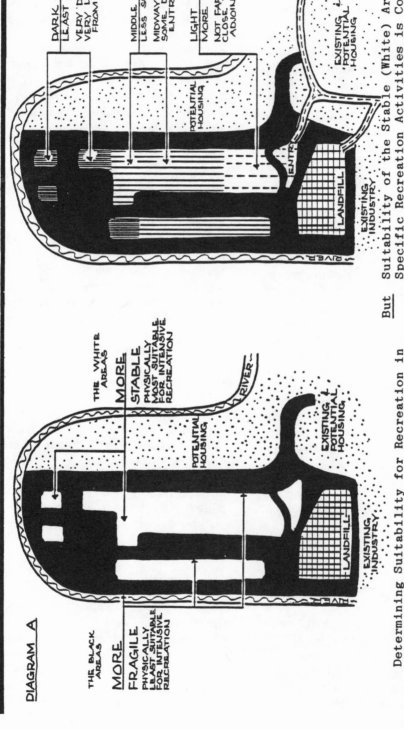

NORTHWEST PARK

INTERPRETATION OF INFORMATION -- DETERMINING SUITABILITY OF SITES FOR SUPPORTING RECREATION

INTERPRETIVE DIAGRAMS

DIAGRAM A

DIAGRAM B

THE BLACK AREAS

MORE FRAGILE

PHYSICALLY LEAST SUITABLE FOR INTENSIVE RECREATION

THE WHITE AREAS

MORE STABLE

PHYSICALLY MOST SUITABLE FOR INTENSIVE RECREATION

POTENTIAL HOUSING

RIVER

LANDFILL

EXISTING POTENTIAL HOUSING

EXISTING INDUSTRY

DARK GRAYS LEAST SUITABLE

VERY DEEP INTO PARK. VERY LONG DISTANCE FROM ENTRY.

MIDDLE GRAYS LESS SUITABLE

MIDWAY INTO PARK. SOME DISTANCE FROM ENTRY.

LIGHT GRAYS MORE SUITABLE

NOT FAR INTO PARK. CLOSE TO ENTRY TO ADJOINING HOUSING.

POTENTIAL HOUSING

STREET

RIVER

ENTRY

LANDFILL

EXISTING POTENTIAL HOUSING

EXISTING INDUSTRY

Determining Suitability for Recreation in Terms of Fragile Areas & Stable Areas is a "Black & White" Decision When Considering Only the Physical Characteristics of the Park ...

"BLACK AND WHITE" DECISIONS

But   Suitability of the Stable (White) Areas for Specific Recreation Activities is Considerably Modified by the Existing Uses of the Park (Loop Roads & Meadows) and by the Impending Development Around the Park. The Most Suitable Place to Put Intensive Recreation is the Area That Least Affects the Tranquility of the Park -- the Entry Area.

"SHADES OF GRAY" DECISIONS

JOSEPH S. R. VOLPE AND ASSOCIATES
EDWARD M. MAHONEY
LANDSCAPE ARCHITECTS AND PLANNERS

320 PINE STREET
AMHERST, MASSACHUSETTS 01002
(413) 549-5961

Fig. 8.

156

NORTHWEST PARK PROPOSAL -- CONCEPTUAL DIAGRAM

The Recreation Goals, the Intensity Levels of the Activities, and Their Purposeful Location in the Park

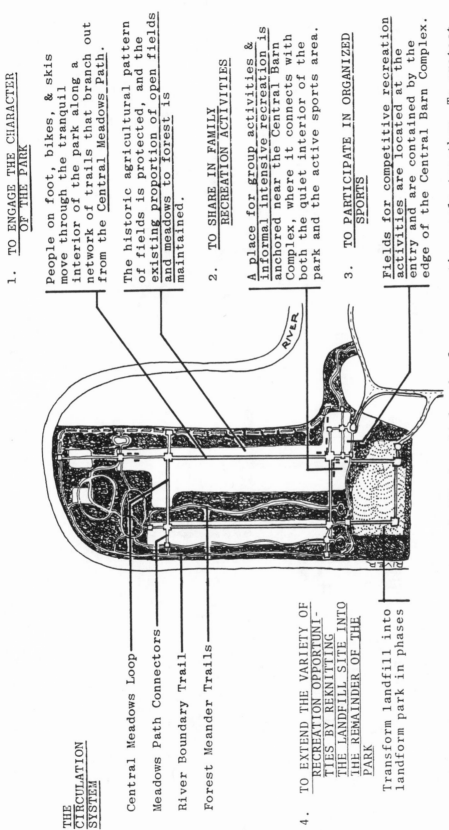

THE
CIRCULATION
SYSTEM

Central Meadows Loop

Meadows Path Connectors

River Boundary Trail

Forest Meander Trails

1. TO ENGAGE THE CHARACTER
   OF THE PARK

People on foot, bikes, & skis move through the tranquil interior of the park along a network of trails that branch out from the Central Meadows Path.

The historic agricultural pattern of fields is protected, and the existing proportion of open fields and meadows to forest is maintained.

2. TO SHARE IN FAMILY
   RECREATION ACTIVITIES

A place for group activities & informal intensive recreation is anchored near the Central Barn Complex, where it connects with both the quiet interior of the park and the active sports area.

3. TO PARTICIPATE IN ORGANIZED
   SPORTS

Fields for competitive recreation activities are located at the entry and are contained by the edge of the Central Barn Complex.

4. TO EXTEND THE VARIETY OF
   RECREATION OPPORTUNI-
   TIES BY REKNITTING
   THE LANDFILL SITE INTO
   THE REMAINDER OF THE
   PARK

Transform landfill into landform park in phases

Walking is the primary activity of NWP that links the four recreation goals together. To protect the tranquil nature of the park, as well as to eliminate the hazards and damage caused by motor vehicles, cars penetrate no farther than the parking lot at the entry points.

— WINDSOR, CONNECTICUT

NORTHWEST PARK

JOSEPH S. R. VOLPE AND ASSOCIATES
EDWARD M. MAHONEY
LANDSCAPE ARCHITECTS AND PLANNERS

320 PINE STREET
AMHERST, MASSACHUSETTS 01002
(413) 549-5961

Fig. 9.

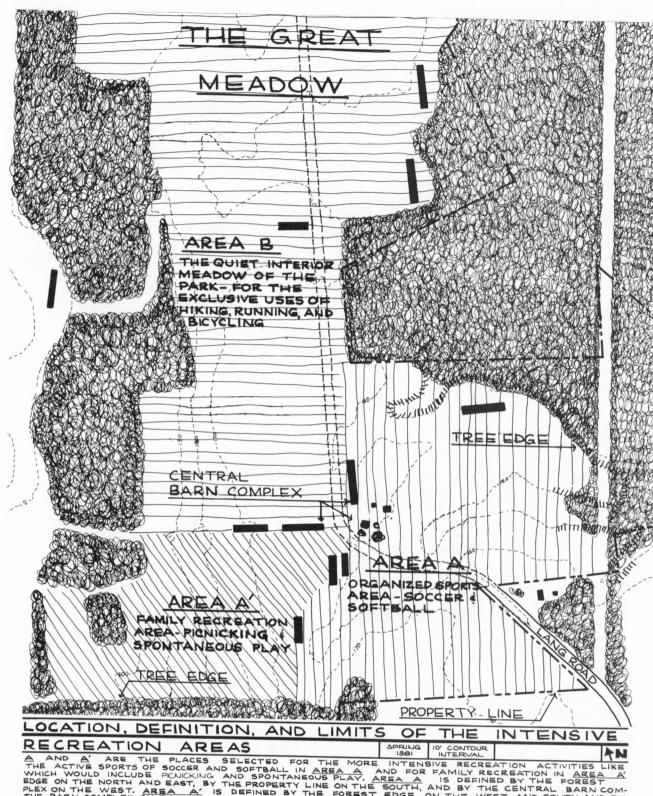

THE GREAT MEADOW

AREA B
THE QUIET INTERIOR MEADOW OF THE PARK - FOR THE EXCLUSIVE USES OF HIKING, RUNNING, AND BICYCLING

TREE EDGE

CENTRAL BARN COMPLEX

AREA A
ORGANIZED SPORTS AREA - SOCCER & SOFTBALL

AREA A'
FAMILY RECREATION AREA - PICNICKING & SPONTANEOUS PLAY

TREE EDGE

LANG ROAD

PROPERTY LINE

LOCATION, DEFINITION, AND LIMITS OF THE INTENSIVE RECREATION AREAS

| | SPRING 1981 | 10' CONTOUR INTERVAL | | ↑N |

A AND A' ARE THE PLACES SELECTED FOR THE MORE INTENSIVE RECREATION ACTIVITIES LIKE THE ACTIVE SPORTS OF SOCCER AND SOFTBALL IN AREA A, AND FOR FAMILY RECREATION IN AREA A' WHICH WOULD INCLUDE PICNICKING AND SPONTANEOUS PLAY. AREA A IS DEFINED BY THE FOREST EDGE ON THE NORTH AND EAST, BY THE PROPERTY LINE ON THE SOUTH, AND BY THE CENTRAL BARN COMPLEX ON THE WEST. AREA A' IS DEFINED BY THE FOREST EDGE ON THE WEST AND SOUTH AND BY THE BARN COMPLEX ON THE NORTH AND EAST. AREA B IS THE GREAT MEADOW, THE QUIET INTERIOR OF THE PARK, AND IS THE SINGLE GREAT SPACE OF NWP. THE GREAT MEADOW IS UNSUITABLE FOR INTENSIVE RECREATION ACTIVITIES AND IS FOR THE EXCLUSIVE USES OF LESS INTENSIVE ACTIVITIES LIKE WALKING, HIKING, AND BICYCLING.

NORTHWEST PARK — WINDSOR, CONNECTICUT

JOSEPH S. R. VOLPE AND ASSOCIATES
EDWARD M. MAHONEY
LANDSCAPE ARCHITECTS AND PLANNERS

320 PINE STREET
AMHERST, MASSACHUSETTS 01002
(413) 549-5961

Fig. 10.

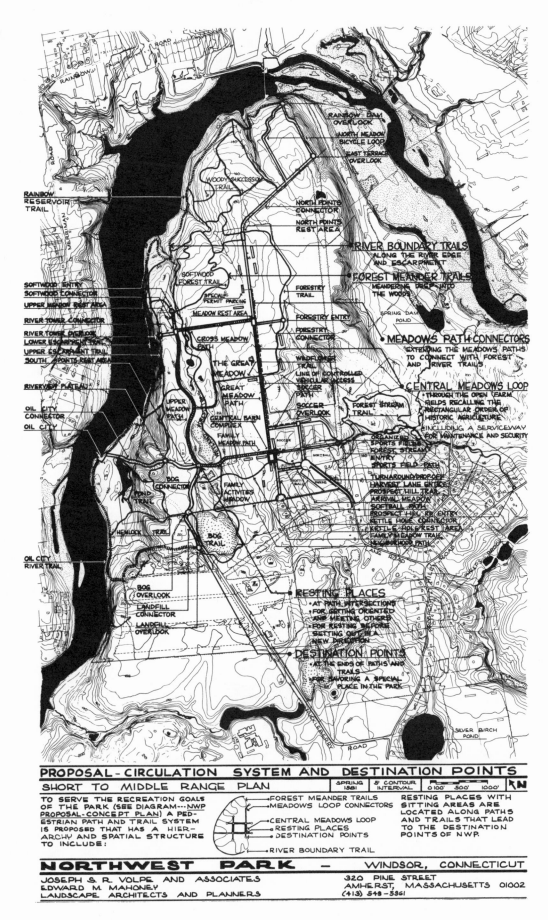

RAINBOW
RESERVOIR
TRAIL

SOFTWOOD ENTRY
SOFTWOOD CONNECTOR
UPPER MEADOW REST AREA
RIVER TOWER CONNECTOR
RIVER TOWER OVERLOOK
LOWER ESCARPMENT TRAIL
UPPER ESCARPMENT TRAIL
SOUTH POINTS REST AREA

RIVERVIEW PLATEAU

OIL CITY
CONNECTOR
OIL CITY

OIL CITY
RIVER TRAIL

RAINBOW DAM
OVERLOOK
NORTH MEADOW
BICYCLE LOOP
EAST TERRACE
OVERLOOK

WOODY SUCCESSION
TRAIL

NORTH POINTS
CONNECTOR
NORTH POINTS
REST AREA

SOFTWOOD
FOREST TRAIL

SPECIAL
PERMIT PARKING
MEADOW REST AREA

CROSS MEADOW
PATH

THE GREAT
MEADOW

GREAT
MEADOW
PATH

UPPER
MEADOW
PATH

CENTRAL BARN
COMPLEX
FAMILY
MEADOW PATH

BOG
CONNECTOR
POND
TRAIL

FAMILY
ACTIVITIES
MEADOW

HEMLOCK TRAIL

BOG
TRAIL

BOG
OVERLOOK
LANDFILL
CONNECTOR
LANDFILL
OVERLOOK

FORESTRY
TRAIL

FORESTRY ENTRY
FORESTRY
CONNECTOR

WILDFLOWER
TRAIL
LINE OF CONTROLLED
VEHICULAR ACCESS
SOCCER
PATH
SOCCER
OVERLOOK

FOREST STREAM
TRAIL

RIVER BOUNDARY TRAILS
ALONG THE RIVER EDGE
AND ESCARPMENT

FOREST MEANDER TRAILS
MEANDERING DEEP INTO
THE WOODS

SPRING DAM
POND

MEADOWS PATH CONNECTORS
EXTENDING THE MEADOWS PATHS
TO CONNECT WITH FOREST
AND RIVER TRAILS

CENTRAL MEADOWS LOOP
THROUGH THE OPEN FARM
FIELDS RECALLING THE
RECTANGULAR ORDER OF
HISTORIC AGRICULTURE
INCLUDING A SERVICEWAY
FOR MAINTENANCE AND SECURITY

ORGANIZED
SPORTS FIELDS
FOREST STREAM
ENTRY
SPORTS FIELD PATH

TURNAROUND/DROP-OFF
HARVEST LANE ENTRY
PROSPECT HILL TRAIL
ARRIVAL MEADOW
SOFTBALL PATH
PROSPECT HILL RD ENTRY
KETTLE HOLE CONNECTOR
KETTLE HOLE REST AREA
FAMILY MEADOW TRAIL
NEIGHBORHOOD PATH

RESTING PLACES
AT PATH INTERSECTIONS
FOR GETTING ORIENTED
AND MEETING OTHERS
FOR RESTING BEFORE
SETTING OUT IN A
NEW DIRECTION

DESTINATION POINTS
AT THE ENDS OF PATHS AND
TRAILS
FOR SAVORING A SPECIAL
PLACE IN THE PARK

SILVER BIRCH
POND

PROPOSAL-CIRCULATION SYSTEM AND DESTINATION POINTS

SHORT TO MIDDLE RANGE PLAN

| SPRING 1981 | 5' CONTOUR INTERVAL | 0 100' 500' 1000' | N |

TO SERVE THE RECREATION GOALS
OF THE PARK (SEE DIAGRAM---NWP
PROPOSAL-CONCEPT PLAN) A PED-
ESTRIAN PATH AND TRAIL SYSTEM
IS PROPOSED THAT HAS A HIER-
ARCHY AND SPATIAL STRUCTURE
TO INCLUDE:

FOREST MEANDER TRAILS
MEADOWS LOOP CONNECTORS
CENTRAL MEADOWS LOOP
RESTING PLACES
DESTINATION POINTS
RIVER BOUNDARY TRAIL

RESTING PLACES WITH
SITTING AREAS ARE
LOCATED ALONG PATHS
AND TRAILS THAT LEAD
TO THE DESTINATION
POINTS OF NWP.

NORTHWEST PARK — WINDSOR, CONNECTICUT

JOSEPH S. R. VOLPE AND ASSOCIATES
EDWARD M. MAHONEY
LANDSCAPE ARCHITECTS AND PLANNERS

320 PINE STREET
AMHERST, MASSACHUSETTS 01002
(413) 548-5361

Fig. 11.

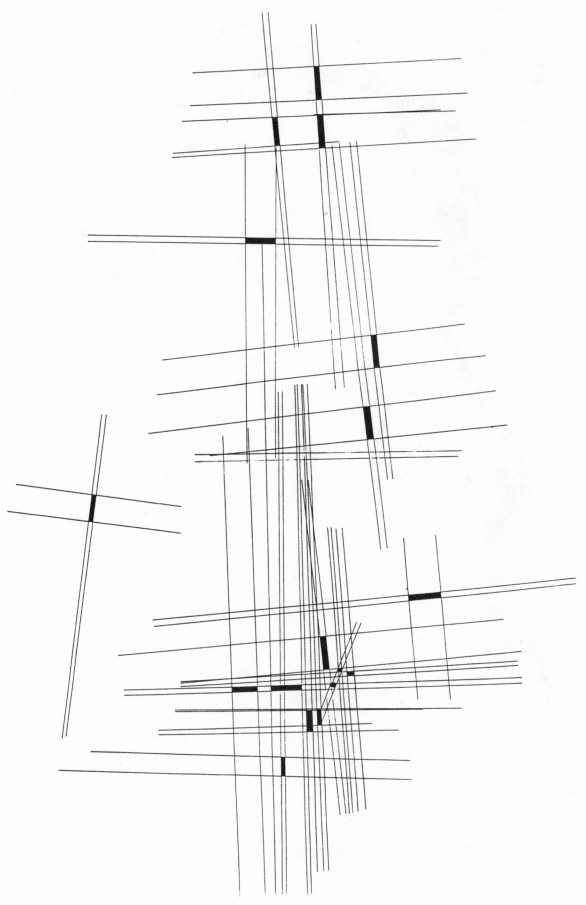

Fig. 12.

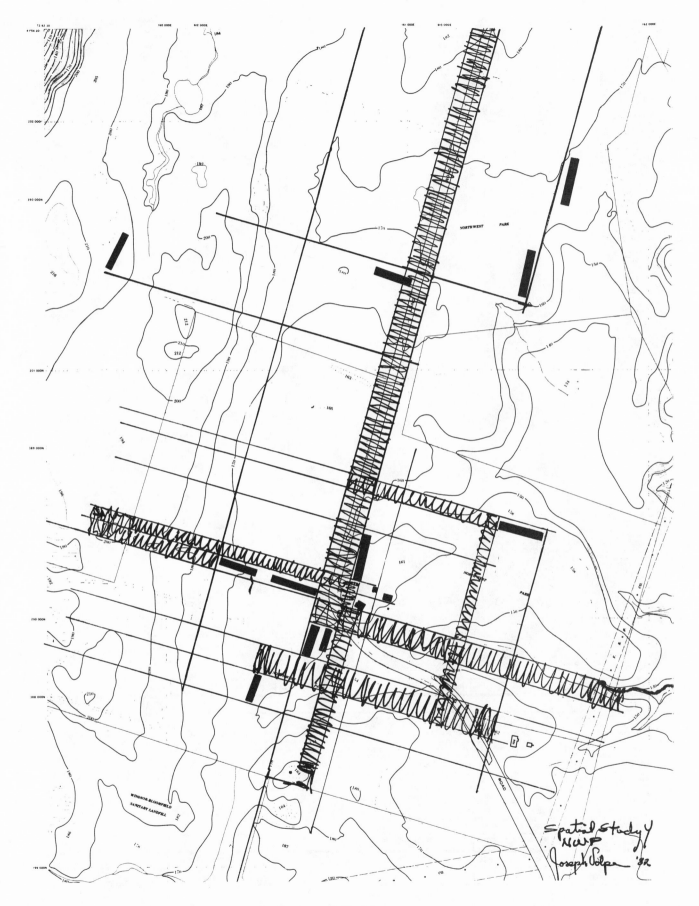

Fig. 13.

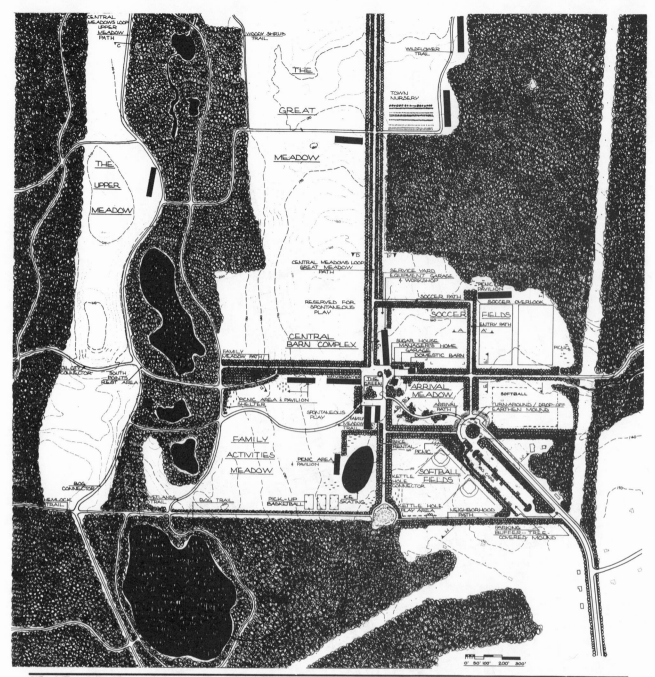

THE GREATER ENTRY AREA - A PROPOSAL

	SPRING 1981	2' CONTOUR INTERVAL	N

FROM THE DROP-OFF AND TURN-AROUND AT THE NEW TERMINUS OF LANG ROAD THERE IS A VIEW OF THE FARM HOUSE AND THE CENTRAL BARN COMPLEX WHICH SIT AT THE END OF THE PATH THROUGH THE ARRIVAL MEADOW. A PARKING LOT FOR 180 CARS IS LOCATED DUE WEST OF LANG ROAD. FROM THE LOT ONE CAN SEE THE SOFTBALL DIAMONDS. THE NWP ENTRY PATH, WHICH IS THE ONLY POINT WHERE SERVICE VEHICLES CAN ENTER THE PARK, LEADS TO THE SOCCER FIELDS NORTH OF THE DROP-OFF. THE PEDESTRIAN PATHS ARE LINED WITH SHADE TREES WHERE THEY MOVE THROUGH THE OPEN, SUNNY MEADOWS WHEREAS THE TRAILS TEND TO MEANDER UNDER THE COVER OF THE EXISTING FOREST. THE PATH SYSTEM, WHICH OCCUPIES FORMER FARM ROADS, HAS THE ORIENTATION OF THE LONG BARNS ALONG THE CARDINAL POINTS. THESE STRAIGHT, TREE-LINED PATHS CONTRAST WITH THE CURVING, GEOMORPHIC ALIGNMENT OF TRAILS THAT MOVE OVER THE CONTOURS OF THE LAND. SOUTHWEST OF THE CENTRAL BARN COMPLEX, ON A GENTLE INCLINE, IS THE FAMILY ACTIVITY MEADOW WHICH INCLUDES PLACES FOR PICNICKING AND SPONTANEOUS PLAY. TO THE NORTH AND WEST, BEYOND THE BOUNDARY OF THE INTENSIVE RECREATION AREAS, ARE THE GREAT MEADOW, THE WETLANDS, THE UPPER MEADOW AND THE FOREST. ONE ENGAGES IN THE LEISURE ACTIVITIES OF WALKING, HIKING, LOOKING, AND SEEING THIS GREAT LANDSCAPE. THIS SERVES THE HUMAN GOAL OF THE PARK, TO CONTEMPLATE THE QUIET WONDER OF NWP.

NORTHWEST PARK — WINDSOR, CONNECTICUT

JOSEPH S. R. VOLPE AND ASSOCIATES
EDWARD M. MAHONEY
LANDSCAPE ARCHITECTS AND PLANNERS

320 PINE STREET
AMHERST, MASSACHUSETTS 01002
(413) 549-5961

Fig. 14.

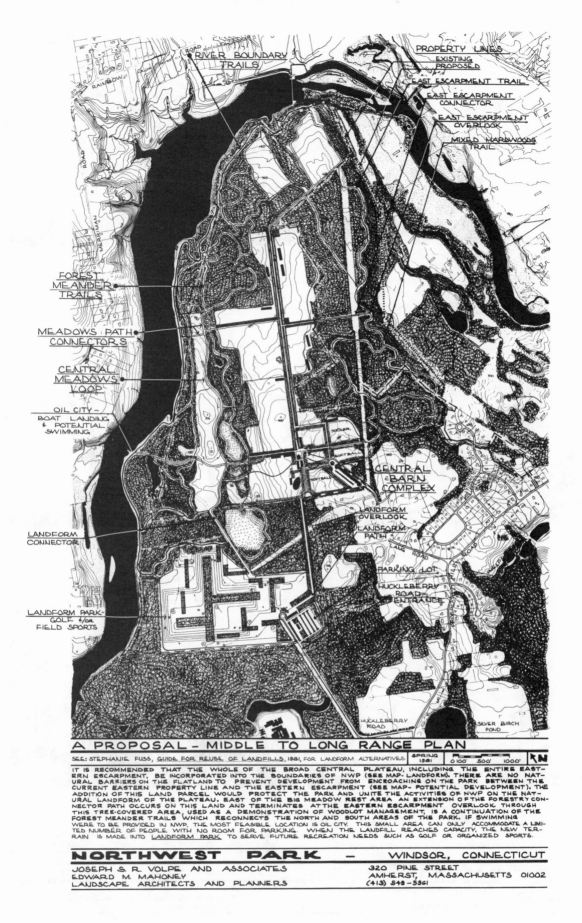

PROPERTY LINES
EXISTING
PROPOSED
EAST ESCARPMENT TRAIL
EAST ESCARPMENT CONNECTOR
EAST ESCARPMENT OVERLOOK
MIXED HARDWOODS TRAIL

RIVER BOUNDARY TRAILS

FOREST MEANDER TRAILS

MEADOWS PATH CONNECTORS

CENTRAL MEADOWS LOOP

OIL CITY – BOAT LANDING & POTENTIAL SWIMMING

LANDFORM CONNECTOR

LANDFORM PARK – GOLF &/OR FIELD SPORTS

CENTRAL BARN COMPLEX

LANDFORM OVERLOOK

LANDFORM PATH

PARKING LOT

HUCKLEBERRY ROAD ENTRANCE

HUCKLEBERRY ROAD

SILVER BIRCH POND

A PROPOSAL – MIDDLE TO LONG RANGE PLAN

SEE: STEPHANIE FUSS, GUIDE FOR REUSE OF LANDFILLS, 1981, FOR LANDFORM ALTERNATIVES   SPRING 1981   0 100' 500' 1000'

IT IS RECOMMENDED THAT THE WHOLE OF THE BROAD CENTRAL PLATEAU, INCLUDING THE ENTIRE EASTERN ESCARPMENT, BE INCORPORATED INTO THE BOUNDARIES OF NWP (SEE MAP- LANDFORM). THERE ARE NO NATURAL BARRIERS ON THE FLATLAND TO PREVENT DEVELOPMENT FROM ENCROACHING ON THE PARK BETWEEN THE CURRENT EASTERN PROPERTY LINE AND THE EASTERN ESCARPMENT (SEE MAP- POTENTIAL DEVELOPMENT). THE ADDITION OF THIS LAND PARCEL WOULD PROTECT THE PARK AND UNITE THE ACTIVITIES OF NWP ON THE NATURAL LANDFORM OF THE PLATEAU. EAST OF THE BIG MEADOW REST AREA AN EXTENSION OF THE FORESTRY CONNECTOR PATH OCCURS ON THIS LAND AND TERMINATES AT THE EASTERN ESCARPMENT OVERLOOK. THROUGH THIS TREE-COVERED AREA, USED AS A DEMONSTRATION OF WOODLOT MANAGEMENT, IS A CONTINUATION OF THE FOREST MEANDER TRAILS WHICH RECONNECTS THE NORTH AND SOUTH AREAS OF THE PARK. IF SWIMMING WERE TO BE PROVIDED IN NWP, THE MOST FEASIBLE LOCATION IS OIL CITY. THIS SMALL AREA CAN ONLY ACCOMMODATE A LIMITED NUMBER OF PEOPLE WITH NO ROOM FOR PARKING. WHEN THE LANDFILL REACHES CAPACITY, THE NEW TERRAIN IS MADE INTO LANDFORM PARK TO SERVE FUTURE RECREATION NEEDS SUCH AS GOLF OR ORGANIZED SPORTS.

NORTHWEST PARK — WINDSOR, CONNECTICUT

JOSEPH S. R. VOLPE AND ASSOCIATES
EDWARD M. MAHONEY
LANDSCAPE ARCHITECTS AND PLANNERS

320 PINE STREET
AMHERST, MASSACHUSETTS 01002
(413) 549-5861

Fig. 15.

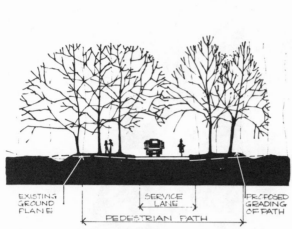

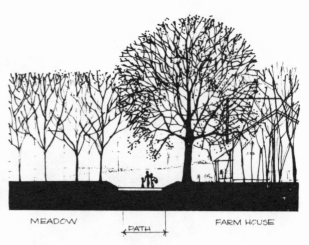

A·A' THE ENTRY PATH WITH CONTROLLED ACCESS FOR SERVICE VEHICLES

B·B' ARRIVAL PATH TO THE CENTRAL BARN COMPLEX. VIA THE ARRIVAL MEADOW

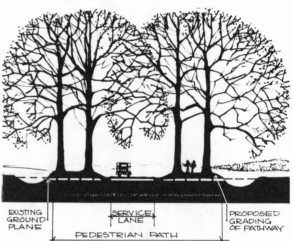

C·C' THE UPPER MEADOW PATH OF THE CENTRAL MEADOW'S LOOP

D·D' THE GREAT MEADOW PATH OF THE CENTRAL MEADOW'S LOOP

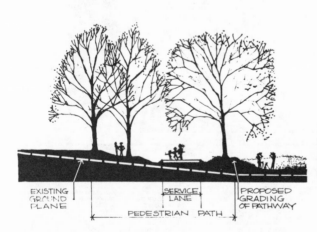

E·E' THE SPORTS FIELD PATH CONNECTOR

F·F' THE OLD 19TH CENTURY WAY USED AS A PART OF THE PATH SYSTEM

NORTHWEST PARK — WINDSOR, CONNECTICUT

JOSEPH S. R. VOLPE AND ASSOCIATES
EDWARD M. MAHONEY
LANDSCAPE ARCHITECTS AND PLANNERS

320 PINE STREET
AMHERST, MASSACHUSETTS 01002
(413) 549-5961

Fig. 16.

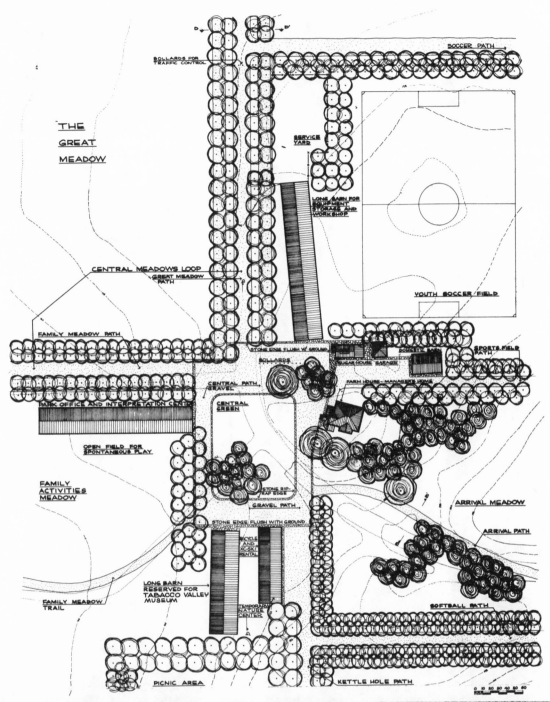

THE GREAT MEADOW

BOLLARDS FOR TRAFFIC CONTROL

SOCCER PATH

SERVICE YARD

LONG BARN FOR EQUIPMENT STORAGE AND WORKSHOP

CENTRAL MEADOWS LOOP
GREAT MEADOW PATH

FAMILY MEADOW PATH

YOUTH SOCCER FIELD

STONE EDGE FLUSH W/ GROUND
BOLLARDS
SUGAR HOUSE GARAGE
DOMESTIC BARN
SPORTS FIELD PATH

CENTRAL PATH GRAVEL
FARM HOUSE MANAGER'S HOME

CENTRAL GREEN

PARK OFFICE AND INTERPRETATION CENTER

OPEN FIELD FOR SPONTANEOUS PLAY

FAMILY ACTIVITIES MEADOW

STONE RIP-RAP EDGE

GRAVEL PATH

ARRIVAL MEADOW

STONE EDGE FLUSH WITH GROUND

ARRIVAL PATH

BICYCLE AND XC SKI RENTAL

LONG BARN RESERVED FOR TABACCO VALLEY MUSEUM

TEMPORARY NATURE CENTER

FAMILY MEADOW TRAIL

SOFTBALL PATH

PICNIC AREA

KETTLE HOLE PATH

0 10 20 30 40 50

THE CENTRAL GREEN AND CENTRAL BARN COMPLEX —
A PROPOSAL

| SPRING 1981 | 2' CONTOUR INTERVAL | N |

IN THE CHARACTER OF THE NEW ENGLAND COMMON, THE CENTRAL GREEN, DEFINED BY THE FARM HOUSE AND THE CENTRAL BARN COMPLEX, IS THE MAIN GATHERING PLACE IN THE PARK. THE GREEN IS SUNKEN 2 FEET BELOW THE SURROUNDING PATH AND IS EDGED IN A WIDE STONE RIP-RAP CURB. THE BROAD PATH IS SURFACED WITH COMPACTED GRAVEL AND IS CONTAINED BY A SURROUND OF FIELD STONES FLUSH WITH THE GROUND. PEOPLE MOVE FROM THE CENTRAL GREEN IN DIRECTIONS NORTH, SOUTH, EAST, AND WEST. ALL PATHS AND TRAILS IN THE PARK LEAD TO AND FROM THE CENTRAL GREEN. IN THIS VITAL AREA ARE THE PARK OFFICE, THE INTERPRETATION AREA, THE BICYCLE AND CROSS-COUNTRY SKI RENTAL SHOPS, THE SUGAR HOUSE, THE LONG BARN FOR LARGE EQUIPMENT STORAGE, THE PARK WORKSHOP, AND THE MANAGER'S HOME IN THE OLD FARM HOUSE. AROUND THIS HUB OCCUR ALL ACTIVITIES OF THE PARK.

NORTHWEST PARK — WINDSOR, CONNECTICUT

JOSEPH S. R. VOLPE AND ASSOCIATES
EDWARD M. MAHONEY
LANDSCAPE ARCHITECTS AND PLANNERS

320 PINE STREET
AMHERST, MASSACHUSETTS 01002
(413) 548-5961

Fig. 17.

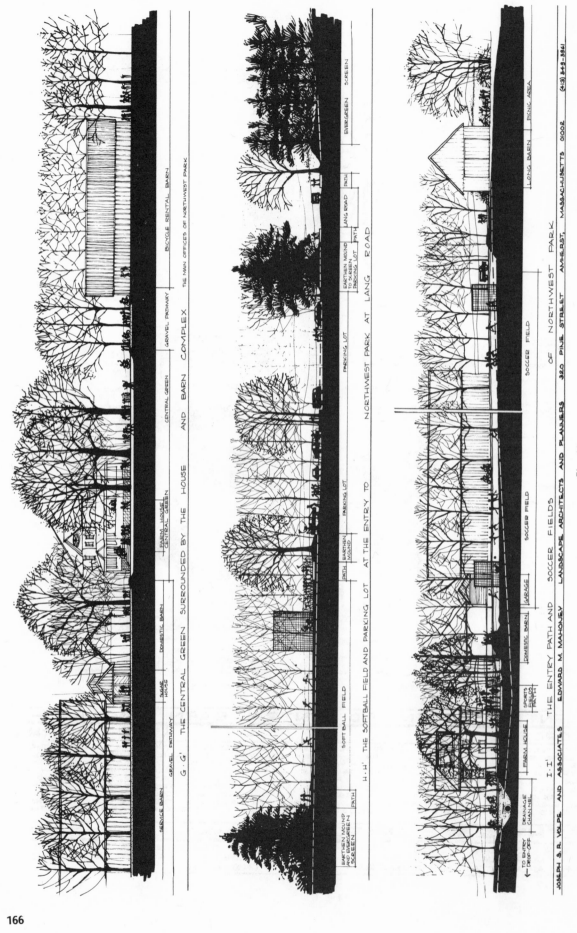

SERVICE BARN | GRAVEL PATHWAY | SUGAR HOUSE | DOMESTIC BARN | FARM HOUSE CENTRAL GREEN | CENTRAL GREEN | GRAVEL PATHWAY | BICYCLE RENTAL BARN

THE MAIN OFFICES OF NORTHWEST PARK

G · G' THE CENTRAL GREEN SURROUNDED BY THE HOUSE AND BARN COMPLEX

EARTHEN MOUND AND EVERGREEN SCREEN | PATH | SOFT BALL FIELD | PATH | EARTHEN MOUND | PARKING LOT | PATH | EARTHEN MOUND TO SCREEN PARKING LOT | PATH | LANG ROAD | PATH | EVERGREEN SCREEN

H · H' THE SOFTBALL FIELD AND PARKING LOT AT THE ENTRY TO NORTHWEST PARK AT LANG ROAD

← TO ENTRY DROP-OFF | DRAINAGE CHANNEL | FARM HOUSE | SPORTS FIELD PATH | DOMESTIC BARN | GARAGE | SOCCER FIELD | SOCCER FIELD | SOCCER FIELD | LONG BARN | PICNIC AREA

I · I' THE ENTRY PATH AND SOCCER FIELDS OF NORTHWEST PARK

JOSEPH S. R. VOLPE AND ASSOCIATES   EDWARD M. MAHONEY   LANDSCAPE ARCHITECTS AND PLANNERS   320 PINE STREET   AMHERST, MASSACHUSETTS   01002   (413) 843-5861

Fig. 18.

166

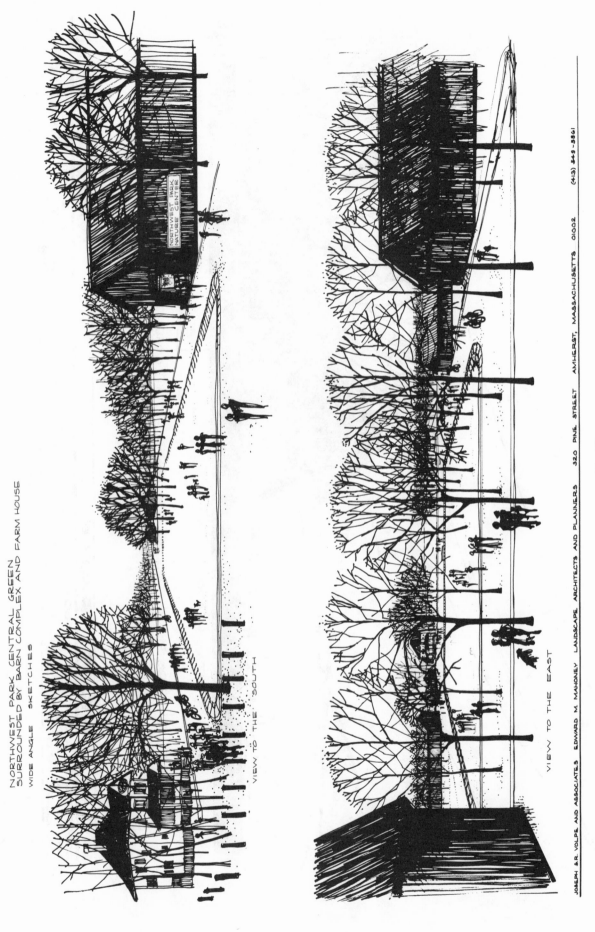

NORTHWEST PARK CENTRAL GREEN
SURROUNDED BY BARN COMPLEX AND FARM HOUSE

WIDE ANGLE SKETCHES

NORTHWEST PARK
NATURE CENTER

VIEW TO THE SOUTH

VIEW TO THE EAST

JOSEPH A.R. VOLPE AND ASSOCIATES   EDWARD M. MAHONEY   LANDSCAPE ARCHITECTS AND PLANNERS   320 PINE STREET   AMHERST, MASSACHUSETTS   01002   (413) 549-5561

Fig. 19.

167

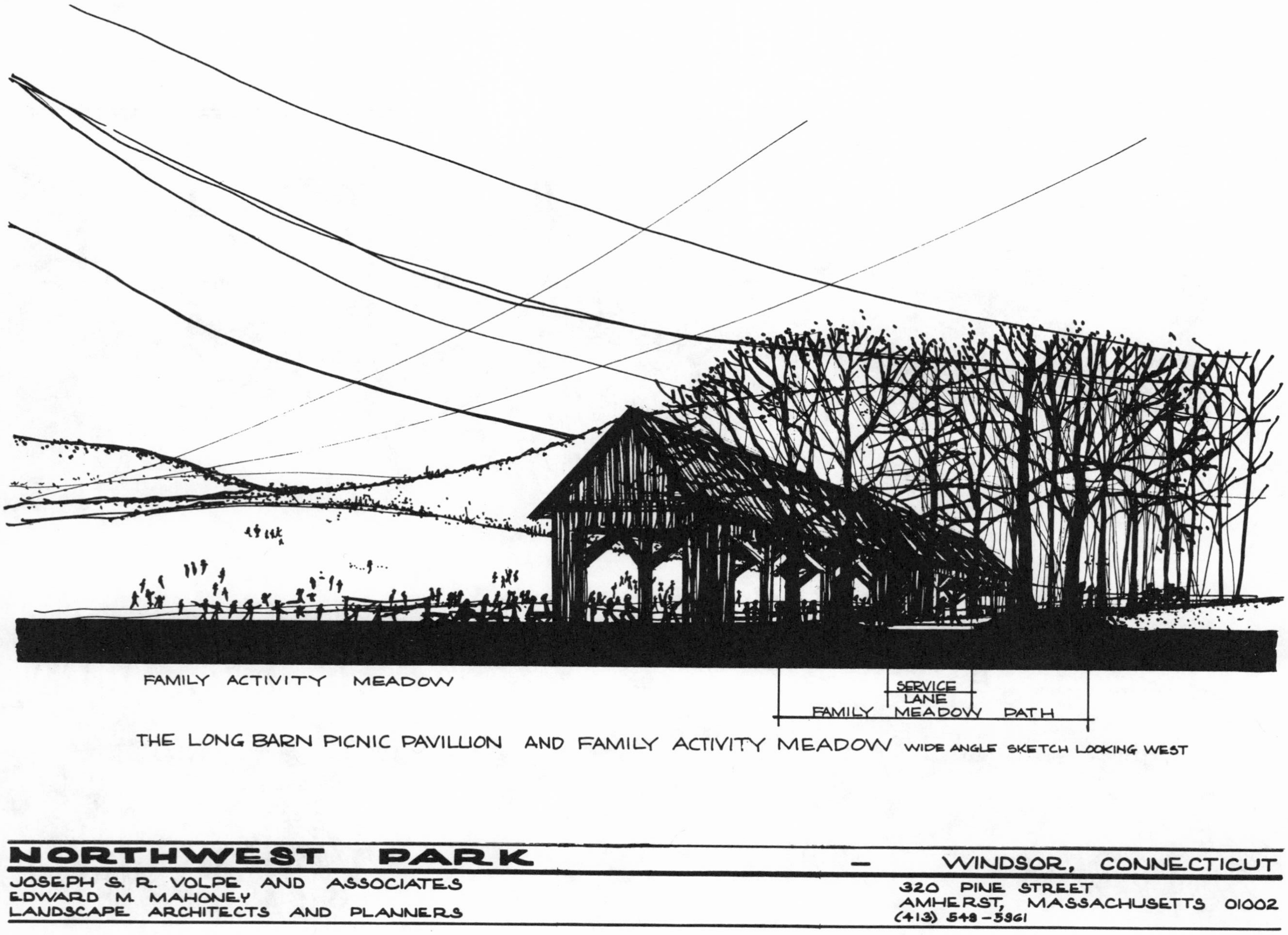

FAMILY ACTIVITY MEADOW

THE LONG BARN PICNIC PAVILION AND FAMILY ACTIVITY MEADOW WIDE ANGLE SKETCH LOOKING WEST

SERVICE
LANE
FAMILY MEADOW PATH

NORTHWEST PARK — WINDSOR, CONNECTICUT

JOSEPH & R. VOLPE AND ASSOCIATES
EDWARD M. MAHONEY
LANDSCAPE ARCHITECTS AND PLANNERS

320 PINE STREET
AMHERST, MASSACHUSETTS 01002
(413) 549-5961

Fig. 20.

mental impacts, be the means toward a fine work of landscape architecture. We may need expertise in environmental history for this or that particular problem, but it is proposed we include the role of our heritage as a creative force in our present experience and in our future plans.

BIBLIOGRAPHY

1. Dubois, Rene. *The Wooing of the Earth,* Charles Scribner's Sons.
2. Harvard Forest, "Harvard Forest Models," Monograph, Harvard University.
3. Jackson, J. B. *American Space,* Norton Press.
4. _____. *Changing Rural Landscapes,* University of Massachusetts Press.
5. _____. *Landscapes,* University of Massachusetts Press.
6. _____. *The Necessity for Ruins,* University of Massachusetts Press.
7. _____. "'Sterile Restoration' Cannot Replace a Sense of the Stream of Time", Landscape Architecture, V66 N3 1976.
8. Kelsey, Darwin, P. "Harvest of History," Historic Preservation V28 N3 1976.
9. Kunst, Lisa A. and O'Donnell, Patricia A., "Historic Landscape Preservation Deserves A Broader Meaning," Landscape Architecture V71 N1 1981.
10. Lowenthal, David. "Age and Artifact" in *The Interpretation of Ordinary Landscapes,* D. W. Meinig, Editor, Oxford University Press.
11. Lynch, Kevin. *What Time is this Place,* MIT Press.
12. _____. *A Theory of Good City Form,* MIT Press.
13. Metropolitan District Commission Maps, Hartford, Connecticut, 1961, 1973, 1977.
14. Raup, Hugh, "A View from John Sanderson's Farm," Monograph Harvard Forest, Harvard University.
15. Thomas, William L., Sauer, Carl O. and Mumford, Lewis, editors, *Man's Role in Changing the Face of the Earth,* The University of Chicago Press.
16. Tishler, William H., Townsend, F. E., "Tracing Patterns of the Past." Historic Preservation V29 N4 1977.
17. Utler, Robert M., "A Preservation Ideal," Historic Preservation, V28 N2 1976.
18. Windsor Planning Department, "Town of Windsor Historic Survey," 1981, Windsor, Connecticut.
19. Volpe, Joseph S. R., Mahoney, Edward M., Windsor Planning Department, *A Plan for Northwest Park* 1982, Windsor, Connecticut.

Back Bay Fens

Carol R. Johnson and Associates, Inc.

In 1877 Frederick Law Olmsted, Sr. was selected as landscape architect for a 100-acre park in Boston, Massachusetts. Coming twenty-one years after his Central Park design in New York City, the Back Bay Fens project was Olmsted's first public park in Boston. Working on the edge of an expanding city on a site replete with engineering problems back to the 1820s, Olmsted used this opportunity to design a park exemplifying the design concepts of the "Parks Movement," which traced its origin back to the English landscape school and early public parks of England. Like these first public parks, the Back Bay Fens came as a response to rapid and intense urbanization and worked to introduce a romantic return to natural, rustic settings into the city environment. Frederick Law Olmsted Jr. reiterated this design philosophy in 1911, when he wrote, "The landscape design of the Fens was to create a salt creek bordered by salt marshes, enclosed by high banks intended to be covered with wild flowers, low, compact shrubs, vines and creepers, and scattered trees—enough with the street trees to fairly well screen the future adjoining houses, but not enough to unduly shade out the ground cover. There are to be found many examples of this type of landscape where the little freshwater rivers of New England come to the sea level and mingle with keen delight by artists and lovers of natural scenery, but. . .probably never before. . .conceived of as a thing to be imitated in laying out a public park."*

The Fens, as designed by Olmsted, was primarily a park for passive recreation, although he provided paths for horseback riding and anticipated quiet cantering along the curving stretch of water and upstream tributaries. It was intended that waterfowl would be artificially introduced into the park, but the birds came to the area without stimulus, almost from the start of the project. This period of passive enjoyment, in the condition envisioned by Olmsted, was brief. Although many circumstances have altered the Fens during the past 70 years, the most significant change came as a result of the construction of the Charles River Dam in 1910. The dam broke down the mechanics of Olmsted's romantic vision by stopping tidal flooding of the stream and thickly vegetated marsh that had been introduced into the city and aggravated a recurrent pollution problem.

Subsequent plans by Arthur A. Shurtleff and Frederick Law Olmsted, Jr. modified the overall passive intent of the park, partially in response to these engineering dilemmas and partially in response to changes in park use. Starting in 1913 and for the next 20 years, Arthur A. Shurtleff, in conjunction with the Olmsted firm, studied the Fens and offered numerous schemes for circulation and new recreational pursuits. These plans added an athletic field, a formal Rose Garden, regraded the central lagoon, and added a new system of pathways with bridges. The marshland was filled and athletic fields, lawns, and a formal garden replaced the naturalized New England salt marshes. Finally, in the 1940s, both the Victory Gardens and the War Memorial were introduced to the park, and in 1970 two basketball courts were added. Despite the planned modifications and later uncoordinated "improvements," the Back Bay Fens remains one of Boston's finest historic parks and an important link in Olmsted's "Emerald Necklace" of interconnecting open space for city dwellers. Once on the outskirts of the city, this popular urban park is now two miles from downtown Boston, situated in a neighborhood known as the Fenway and surrounded by a number of Boston's most important educational and cultural institutions. The park is, therefore, in constant use by the young, by students, and by the elderly.

Throughout the 1960s and 1970s, as many city needs competed for limited operating funds, signs of inadequate maintenance at the park were clearly visible. Walkways and bridges had deteriorated under heavy use and lack of upkeep. One hundred years after Olmsted's original design, the City of Boston commissioned Carol R. Johnson & Associates, Inc. to prepare a Preservation Master Plan Report for the park. The purpose of the report was to set guidelines for park preservation and improvement and to coordinate construction materials and a design theme for the entire park area. The Preservation Master Plan was prepared with the assistance of both the City of Boston and the

---

* *36th Annual Report,* Board of Commissioners, Department of Parks, Boston, Massachusetts, 1911. Frederick Law Olmsted, Jr., author, p. 51.

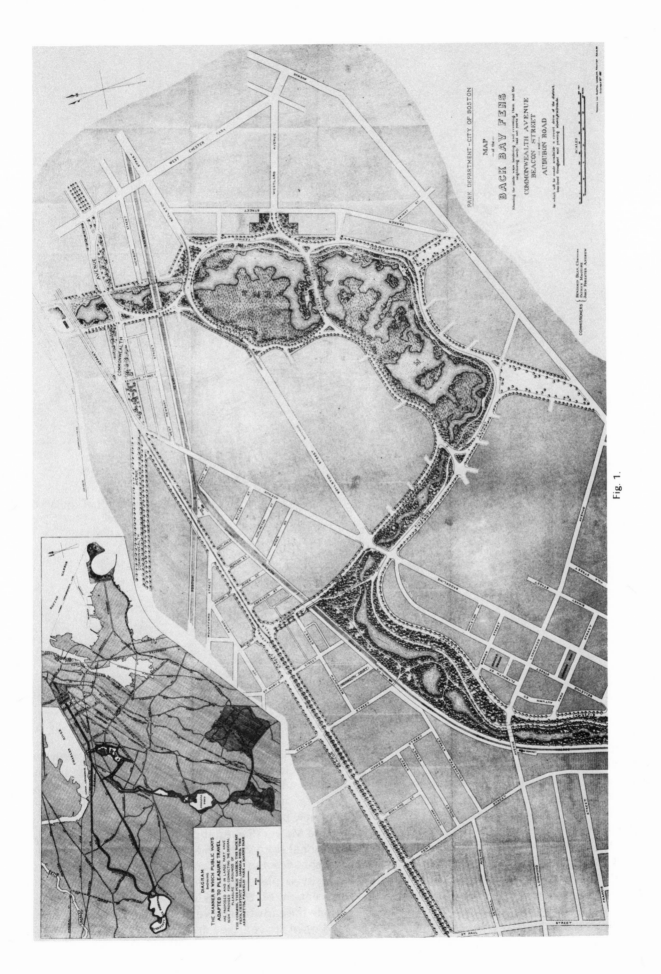

PARK DEPARTMENT—CITY OF BOSTON

MAP
—of the—
BACK BAY FENS

Showing the public ways bordering and crossing them, and the
neighboring newly laid out streets of

COMMONWEALTH AVENUE
BEACON STREET
—and—
AUBURN ROAD

by which will be made available a circuit drive of the district,
interlinked throughout and joining thoroughfares.

Fig. 1.

171

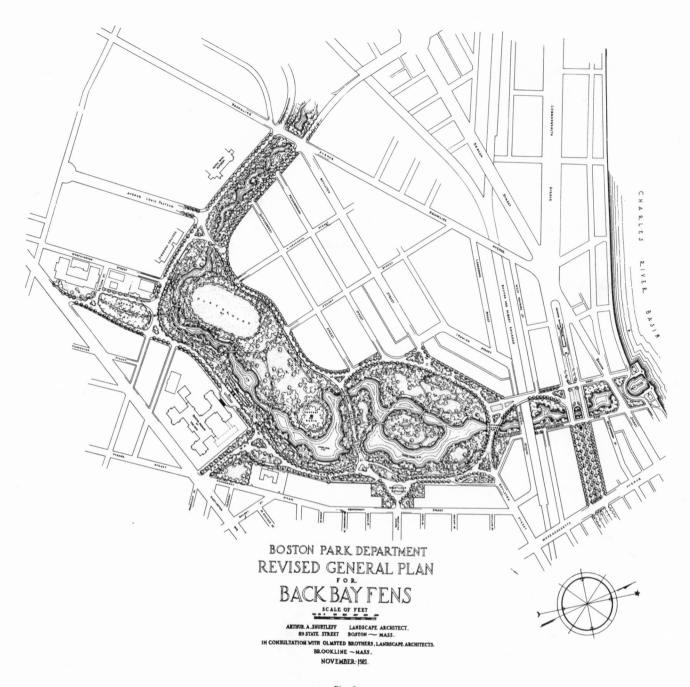

BOSTON PARK DEPARTMENT
REVISED GENERAL PLAN
FOR
BACK BAY FENS
SCALE OF FEET

ARTHUR A. SHURTLEFF   LANDSCAPE ARCHITECT.
89 STATE STREET   BOSTON — MASS.
IN CONSULTATION WITH OLMSTED BROTHERS, LANDSCAPE ARCHITECTS.
BROOKLINE — MASS.
NOVEMBER·1921.

Fig. 2.

Massachusetts Metropolitan District Commission. It advocated a renewed commitment toward restoration and maintenance, reinforcing the desirable features of the early park layout while suggesting contemporary improvements.

As the landscape architect studied the original concepts and design alongside today's existing conditions and current needs, it became clear that many desirable early park features could be restored and that improvements required to satisfy contemporary needs could be made to complement the Victorian heritage of the park: light-fixture design, stonework,

benches, and a meandering stonedust path system. In addition, new features were necessary to fill current needs: additional curbing, parking facilities, area lighting, increased children's recreational facilities, and new pathway routes for pedestrians.

The Master Plan exhibits the dual concern for both historical restoration and meeting contemporary use. To enhance the early concepts of Olmsted, a high priority is placed on the rejuvenation and selected placement of the park's perimeter tree plantings. While the early schemes emphasize passive recreation and open spaces, they do not provide for the recrea-

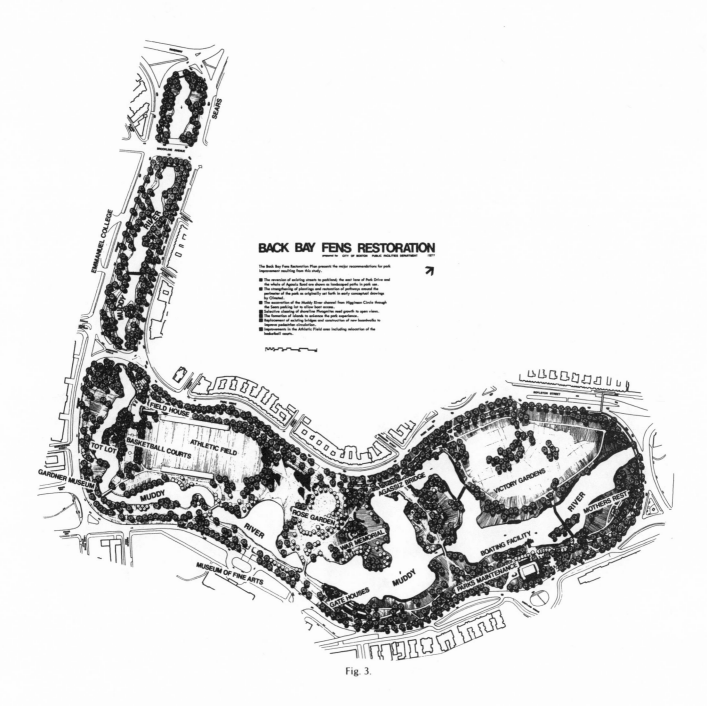

BACK BAY FENS RESTORATION

prepared for CITY OF BOSTON PUBLIC FACILITIES DEPARTMENT 1977

The Back Bay Fens Restoration Plan presents the major recommendations for park improvement resulting from this study.

■ The reversion of existing streets to parkland; the east lane of Park Drive and the whole of Agassiz Road are shown as landscaped paths in park use.
■ The strengthening of plantings and restoration of pathways around the perimeter of the park as originally set forth in early conceptual drawings by Olmsted.
■ The excavation of the Muddy River channel from Higginson Circle through the Sears parking lot to allow boat access.
■ Selective clearing of shoreline Phragmites reed growth to open views.
■ The formation of islands to enhance the park experience.
■ Replacement of existing bridges and construction of new boardwalks to improve pedestrian circulation.
■ Improvements in the Athletic Field area including relocation of the basketball courts.

Fig. 3.

tion needs of today's public. The clash between Olmsted's vision and current needs is exemplified in the basketball courts which, in their present location, detract from the view of the park and inhibit entrance into it. The resolution of this problem is to build new basketball courts, with adjacent parking, near the Field House.

Other recommendations that reinforce early concepts while considering present needs provide for: reconstruction of pathways and walkways; replacement of existing pedestrian bridges; use of original materials; construction of a boat facility; formation of islands, as envisioned by Olmsted; and restoration of usable space next to the water's edge. Of the above, certain priority items to improve park conditions were recommended:

1. new and reconstructed pathways, bridges and stairways
2. improved lighting
3. The creation of park features to highlight significant architecture that borders the park—the Boston Museum of Fine Arts, the Gardner museum, and Simmons College

Fig. 4. This footbridge represents phase I of the restoration project. The material is granite which matches the original stone used for bridges in the Back Bay Fens area. (Courtesy of Carol R. Johnson)

The Back Bay Fens Preservation Master Plan was submitted to the City of Boston in January, 1977. In the past five years, it is clear that the Master Plan is fulfilling its intended purpose as the key document for coordinating the phased construction of improvements. Unfortunately, due to Proposition 2½, a property tax limitation program, the improvements outlined have been suspended since Spring 1981, when local revenue to continue the project was lost. Since 1977, however, significant improvements have been made within the park:

1. clearing large areas of undergrowth for safety and better views

2. partial restoration of stonedust path system
3. reconstruction of two of Arthur A. Shurtleff's pedestrian bridges
4. partial restoration of plant massings
5. provision of new park benches

These improvements have made the area safer and more attractive. The Back Bay Fens, because of its central, urban location, will always play an important role for those who live around its borders. The Master Plan, in looking back to the origins of the park and at the same time focusing on present and future needs, provides for the coordination of all visions of the historic Back Bay Fens.

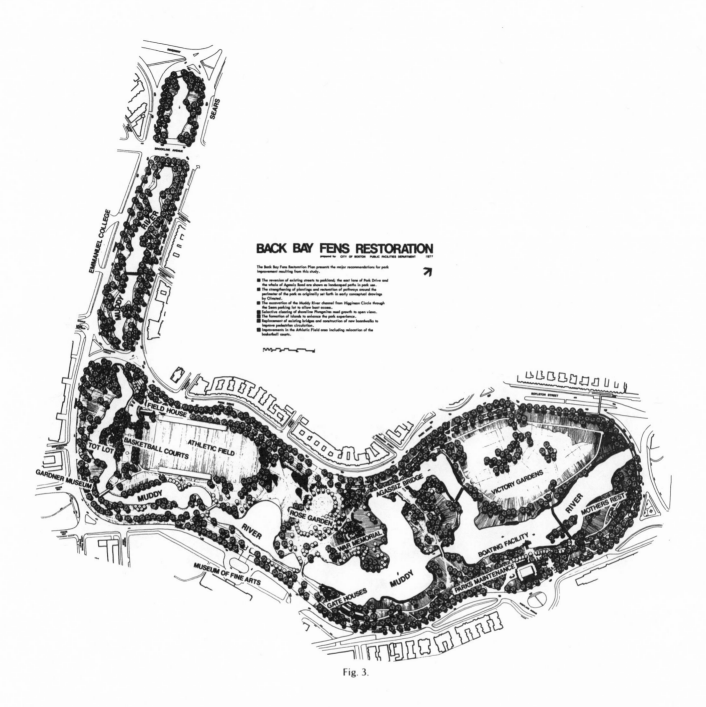

Fig. 3.

tion needs of today's public. The clash between Olmsted's vision and current needs is exemplified in the basketball courts which, in their present location, detract from the view of the park and inhibit entrance into it. The resolution of this problem is to build new basketball courts, with adjacent parking, near the Field House.

Other recommendations that reinforce early concepts while considering present needs provide for: reconstruction of pathways and walkways; replacement of existing pedestrian bridges; use of original materials; construction of a boat facility; formation of islands, as envisioned by Olmsted; and restoration of usable space next to the water's edge. Of the above, certain priority items to improve park conditions were recommended:

1. new and reconstructed pathways, bridges and stairways
2. improved lighting
3. The creation of park features to highlight significant architecture that borders the park—the Boston Museum of Fine Arts, the Gardner museum, and Simmons College

173

Fig. 4. This footbridge represents phase I of the restoration project. The material is granite which matches the original stone used for bridges in the Back Bay Fens area. (Courtesy of Carol R. Johnson)

The Back Bay Fens Preservation Master Plan was submitted to the City of Boston in January, 1977. In the past five years, it is clear that the Master Plan is fulfilling its intended purpose as the key document for coordinating the phased construction of improvements. Unfortunately, due to Proposition 2½, a property tax limitation program, the improvements outlined have been suspended since Spring 1981, when local revenue to continue the project was lost. Since 1977, however, significant improvements have been made within the park:

1. clearing large areas of undergrowth for safety and better views

2. partial restoration of stonedust path system
3. reconstruction of two of Arthur A. Shurtleff's pedestrian bridges
4. partial restoration of plant massings
5. provision of new park benches

These improvements have made the area safer and more attractive. The Back Bay Fens, because of its central, urban location, will always play an important role for those who live around its borders. The Master Plan, in looking back to the origins of the park and at the same time focusing on present and future needs, provides for the coordination of all visions of the historic Back Bay Fens.

Val-Kill: The Eleanor Roosevelt National Historic Site

Kane and Carruth, P.C.

In 1925, Eleanor Roosevelt along with two friends and associates, Marion Dickerman and Nancy Cook, constructed a stone cottage on the bank of the Fall Kill about two miles from Hyde Park, New York, on land given them by Franklin D. Roosevelt. Through the subsequent decades until her death in 1962, Val-Kill, as it was called, played a major role in the lives of the family, serving as a retreat and workplace for Mrs. Roosevelt and a place of entertainment for the leaders of this country and the world.

In 1926 the construction of a two-story stucco factory building was begun to house a craft enterprise, instituted to provide skills for the young men of the area. The last wing, added in 1929, was converted to a residence and in 1938 became Eleanor's home. The Fall Kill was bridged and dammed to create a pond. A swimming pool was built in 1925, primarily for Mr. Roosevelt. Gardens were created by Nancy Cook. Picnic areas were developed and a series of smaller outbuildings constructed. A new swimming pool was built in 1935. Extensive tree plantings were made to enhance the environment and to define compartments of the landscape.

In 1980 Kane and Carruth was engaged to prepare a comprehensive report on the historic and cultural landscape for the site. As far as it is known, this was the first time that such a report was requested by the National Park Service; therefore, while it may not prove to be the prototype, the report attempts to formulate a proper format for landscape considerations related to the National Park Service policy and guidelines for cultural resource management and preservation. In the future it is anticipated that a Historic Landscape Report will be required for all relevant cultural sites and will provide a function similar to the Historic Structures Report which has been required for a long time.

The basic requirements for such a report include research and documentation, a narrative description, recommendations, drawings and specifications, and cost estimates.

RESEARCH AND DOCUMENTATION

Many projects suffer from a lack of documentary evidence. However, this was not the case with Val-Kill. There was a wealth of information and much of it a delight for the investigator. The family albums, for example, were much like other family albums, with photographs of varying quality depicting family occasions and party antics. The difference was that the images were those of famous personages. There were additional stacks of photographs, 35-mm color slides, 16-mm color film, and aerial photographs taken in 1959 and 1970. There was a great deal of textual reference material, including accounts of items and expenditures for landscape projects. In addition, two gardeners, from two different periods, survive and were available for interviews.

Before this wealth of information could be properly evaluated, however, it was necessary to produce a plan that would accurately depict the existing conditions of the site, including the definition of plant material. In addition, a careful investigation of the site was required to locate surviving elements, such as stones, stumps, buried walks, etc. The field trips that were undertaken provided the opportunity to commence the photographic record of the site, both in black and white and in color slides (color documentation should include two seasons—with and without foliage).

Needless to say, possible recommendations inevitably evolve during the investigation phase. And, indeed, there are puzzles related to the construction of a sequential history, or narrative, that must be solved during the documentation period. Some puzzles have amusing answers. One related to photographs depicting a frog font at one end of the swimming pool. We struggled to determine the extent of the period during which this feature played its gushing role. One of the gardeners, Clifford Smith, solved the puzzle immediately by reporting that the device was rented for one day of photography. Certain shrubs and trees

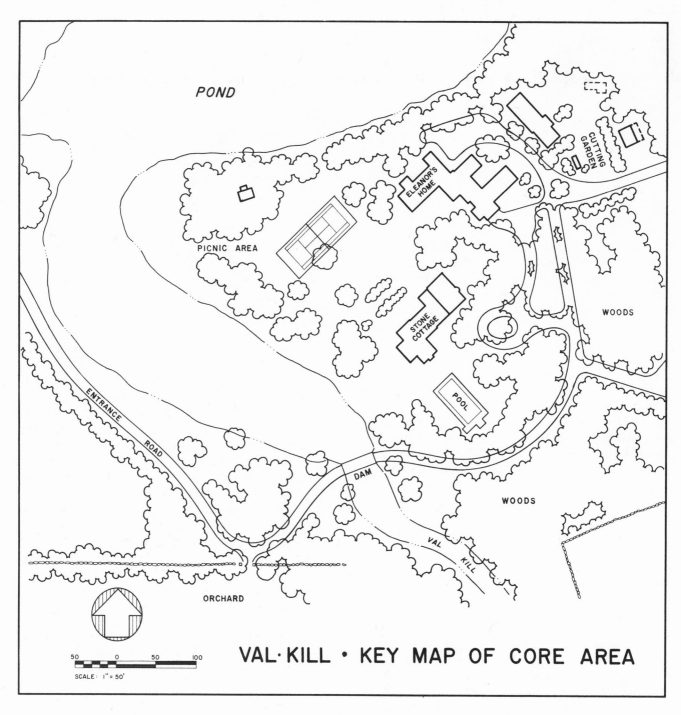

POND

ELEANOR'S HOME

CUTTING GARDEN

PICNIC AREA

WOODS

STONE COTTAGE

POOL

ENTRANCE ROAD

WOODS

DAM

VAL KILL

ORCHARD

VAL·KILL · KEY MAP OF CORE AREA

50 0 50 100

SCALE: 1" = 50'

Fig. 1.   Val-Kill Key Map of Peninsular Area.

seemed devilishly difficult to pin down until the same gardener complained that Nancy Cook would often have him move a plant several times in one day and would photograph it each time.

NARRATIVE DESCRIPTION

This is, of course, based on the preceding research and documentation and includes a chronological history of landscape characteristics and use throughout the time span impacted by the resource and, where pertinent, prior to its inception. In the case of the Eleanor Roosevelt National Historic Site, the story begins in 1925 when the site consisted of overgrown pastures in the process of ecological succession interspersed with wetland vegetation. The narrative continues through the development of water resources, gardens, structures, and the general environment to the period of disuse and decline. The two major periods of focus were devoted to the Stone cottage, while Eleanor

Fig. 2.   Val-Kill—A photograph used as a Christmas Card c. 1937 depicting the Pool and Stone Cottage. (Courtesy of National Park Service)

resided there, and to her home (in the factory wing), during the time of her active residency in later years.

The text of the narrative is supported by the graphics in the plan depicting existing conditions; including the location of features no longer extent and dates for the installation of definable structures and features. The role of individuals and social events are woven into the narrative as they affect conditions and developments in the landscape.

LANDSCAPE RECOMMENDATIONS

These deal with the recommended steps for preservation, stabilization, restoration, or reconstruction and are shaped by an evaluation of the information gained through research and documentation and through insights derived from the production of the narrative history and the concomitant familiarity with the site. The recommendations are also influenced by any administrative decisions relating to treatment and interpretation that must be addressed in the report.

The textual recommendations must include justification for suggested treatment. In the case of this project, the recommendations were divided into sections relating to several scopes which define the site by scale and by the intensity of treatment. Each section was supplemented by a plan drawing that delineated recommendations and, in fact, included directions right on the plan (detailed textual recommendations can be intolerably cumbersome, while notes on the plan can be more explicit and work in the field can be accomplished in large measure directly from the plan).

At Val-Kill the site was addressed at three levels. First, the peninsular area of about six acres, which includes the developed portion of the site, was accomplished by plans at a scale of 1" = 20'. Second, within the peninsular area, more detailed plans were developed for the stone cottage, Eleanor's home, and the cutting garden at a scale of 1/8" = 1'. The third level, the core area, includes that portion of the total acreage of the property that relates directly and visually to the peninsular area. Recommendations in this surrounding area concerned general treatment relating to views toward and from the central area in

177

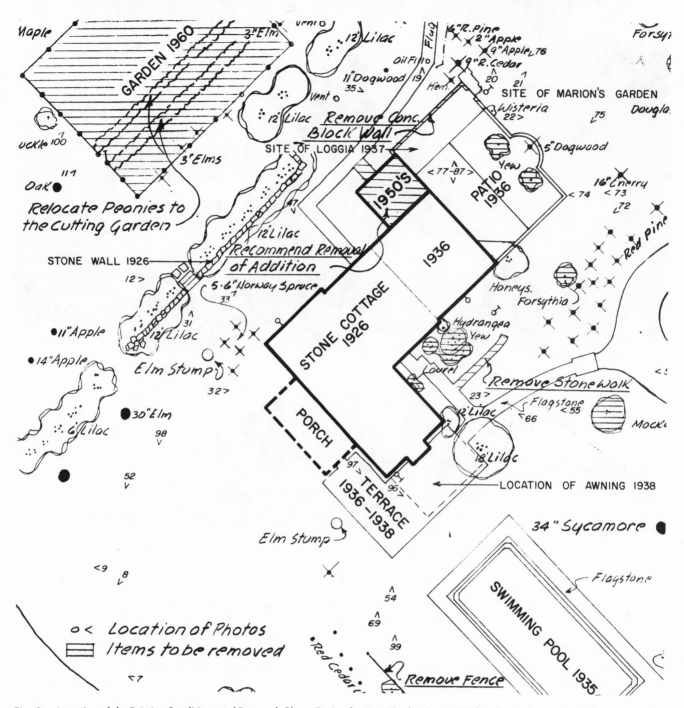

Fig. 3. A portion of the Existing Conditions and Removals Plan—Peninsular Area (Scale 1" = 20'). This plan is also used to indicate dates for significant elements and the locations of photographs documenting the site at the time of the report.

regard to both historic conditions and protective requirements. A scale of 1" = 50' was selected to illustrate these recommendations.

The recommendations for the peninsular area included the removal of recent intrusions and the general preservation and restoration of the picnic area, the screen plantings, and the background woodlands. In addition, recommendations were made for: the restoration of the gardens around the stone cottage, including the reconstruction of the loggia (which faced the patio) to their condition in the late 1930s; the reconstruction of the cutting garden to its

peak in the late 1930s and early 1940s; and the restoration of the landscape and plantings around the factory and Eleanor's apartment to their condition in the late 1950s.

Sources of all information appearing in the narrative and influencing the recommendations must be included in the report.

The terms "restoration" and "reconstruction" require some interpretation when applied to the landscape. If one knows exactly where a certain species of tree or shrub existed and recommends the planting of an exact species replacement in the same location, this would be called restoration rather than reconstruction because of the organic realities concerned. In the case of the patio, the basic structures remain and the location of plants are known; therefore, it can be restored. The loggia, on the other hand, is not extant and can only be reconstructed. The remainder of the gardens around the stone cottage can be restored to the extent that some fabric and plants remain and the location of the beds and plant species is known; the fencing and brick edging are gone, however, and must be reconstructed. At the factory, the walks, drives, and much of the plant material remain; with some cleanup and the infill of missing plants, based on good documentation, the landscape can be restored. On the other hand, while good documentation is available for the cutting garden and portions of the perimeter hedge remain, the garden itself must be reconstructed. Often a project is called restoration or reconstruction when, in fact, it creates a studied environment, as it might have been, and should be called a period setting.

Another important consideration in landscape recommendations is their relationship to structures that are to be addressed in a parallel Historic Structures Report, as was the case at Val-Kill. When structures seriously impact the landscape, and vise versa, there will be overlapping recommendations and a need to resolve them. For example, it was recommended in the landscape report that a laundry room added to the stone cottage by John Roosevelt in the 1950s be removed in order to reconstruct the loggia and complete the restoration of the patio garden. In addition, it was recommended that the glass-enclosed porch be restored to a screened porch and metal awnings be put back so that the climbing vines, which contributed so much to the scene in the 1930s, could be allowed to do so once again.

DRAWINGS AND SPECIFICATIONS

These define the landscape recommendations. The following are the requirements for the drawings and the techniques used in this report.

An accurate survey of existing conditions, at a scale reflecting the detailed requirements of the site, is the first step. It should include the location of all physical features, underground utilities, topography, and the location and identification of all plant material. The inclusion of tree canopy can be helpful in creating a picture, but the essential information is the location and caliper of trees and the location and height of shrubs. We have found it useful and efficient to combine the information on the survey with the recommended removals, presenting them as Existing Condition and Recommended Removals. This was the case with one of the 20-scale plans for the peninsular area. Additional information included on the plan was the location and view angle of the black-and-white

photographs recording existing conditions, the dating of major elements, and the location of elements no longer extant.

The second plan for the peninsular area was the Landscape Restoration Plan which, with the use of graphics and notes, explains the recommendations.

Because of the detail required for three locations within the peninsular area, two Landscape Restoration Plans were prepared at 1/8" scale for the stone cottage and for Eleanor's home and cutting garden. In addition to dimensioned layouts and planting plans, these drawings included details for the restoration of the patio wall and the reconstruction of brick edgings, fences, and stone steps at the pond.

A general area plan is usually required to address the environment of the resource. In this case, because of the large acreage involved, the general area plan was identified as the General Landscape Restoration Plan—Core Area and drawn at 50 scale. The essential recommendations were for the restoration of the view across the pond from the developed area on the peninsula and the screening of recent housing development in two locations, one 800 feet away and the other 2000 feet away.

Finally, to complete the recommendations, Outline Specifications are required. They can be placed on the drawing sheets or, as was the case in this report, included with the text. Six pages covered the site-work restoration and construction as well as site planting and site seeding. The plant lists were incorporated in the drawings, including identification keys, quantities, botanical and common names, sizes, and comments.

PRELIMINARY COST ESTIMATES AND PRELIMINARY PLANS

For this project these were grouped into definitive projects, which included General Removals, General Additions, Stone Cottage and Pool Area, Cutting Garden Area, and Eleanor's Home.

In preparing a Cultural and Historic Landscape Report, it cannot be assume that all or any of the recommendations will be followed. Therefore, it is necessary that these recommendations (including the plans) be presented in such a way that they allow for future development and, if possible, serve as a record of historic conditions at a defined period or periods.

Too often guidelines recommend plants *similar* to those existing in a historic period. Professional landscape architects and horticulturists need not have such a laissez-faire attitude when sources for the *exact* replacement of historic plants, requiring no more than serious investigation, exist.

Many elements of the landscape are inert and can be treated as structural elements. The land itself can be addressed as structural when considering grading

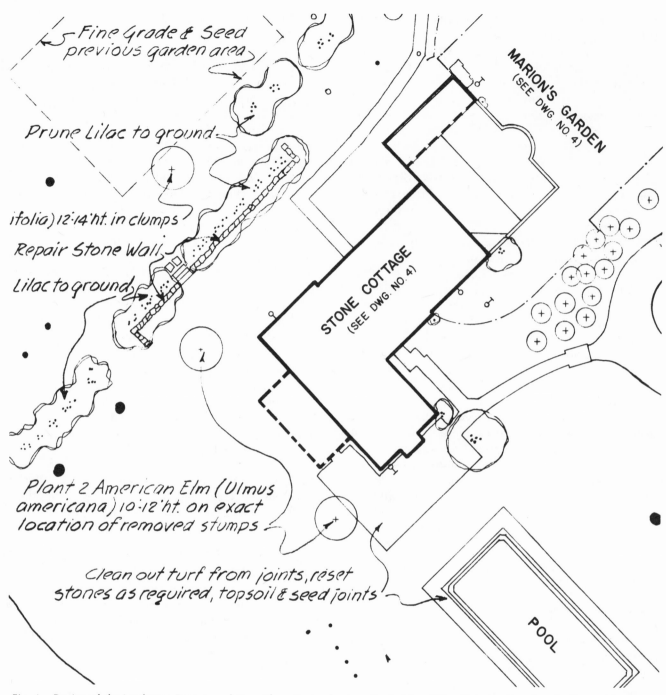

Fine Grade & Seed previous garden area

Prune Lilac to ground

ifolia) 12·14' ht. in clumps

Repair Stone Wall

Lilac to ground

Plant 2 American Elm (Ulmus americana) 10·12' ht. on exact location of removed stumps

Clean out turf from joints, reset stones as required, topsoil & seed joints

MARION'S GARDEN (SEE DWG. NO. 4)

STONE COTTAGE (SEE DWG. NO. 4)

POOL

Fig. 4.   Portion of the Landscape Recommendations Plan—Peninsular Area (Scale 1" = 20') with instructions for planting and landscape treatment.

or earth forms and can be restored in form even though the soil particles are new. Ponds and streams can be said to be restored even though the water moves on or evaporates. Plants distinguish landscape preservation from architectural preservation. Plants are organic—they germinate, grow, and die. There are no static plants, though some can be kept in size for decades and some can live for centuries. Therefore, judgment is required in addressing plants within the historic context. This does not justify loose interpretation, however. It may or may not be justifiable, for ex-

ample, to remove a majestic oak because it was a modest tree when "X" inhabited the place. It may or may not be justifiable to clear out a jumble of plant accretions to leave only those determined to represent the period. It will usually help to first establish why the resource is to be preserved. Is a specific date the controlling influence? Is a lifetime the controlling influence? Is the period style the important consideration? Or is continuum the story to be told? This will help in decisions. In the final analysis there is no substitute for rational and experienced judgment that

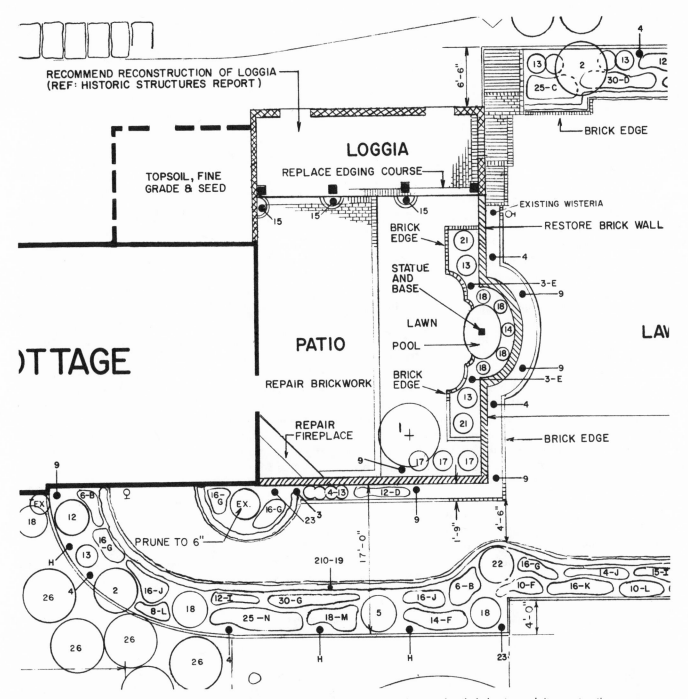

Fig. 5. Portion of Landscape Restoration Plan—Stone Cottage (Scale 1/8″ = 1′) indicating detailed planting and site construction recommendations.

credits the public with an intuitive understanding of time and natural processes.

Because of the organic factor, landscape recommendations must include long-range preservation, maintenance, and replacement guidelines. In some areas a 100-year cycle may suffice, but if the fabric includes oaks or pears, etc., the cycle will escalate to 200 years or more. The landscape is ephemeral but it is also ageless.

Black Settlements In America

Entourage, Inc.

The Black Settlements in America study, which began in 1976, was undertaken in order to document the roles of Blacks in the development of the American built landscape from 1865 to the present. The investigation was based upon the hypotheses that Blacks *had* contributed to the built environment and that this participation was, in some cases, subtle, yet identifiable.

In 1979, the National Endowment for the Arts, Design Arts Program granted a fellowship to advance the initial investigation. This one-year study addressed the origin, evolution, and destiny of communities in order to expose Black settlements as a significant national phenomenon and to demonstrate their importance as historic and cultural resources. The initial assumption was that "the built landscape is an evolving process, and the Black settlement should be studied as an integral component of this development, and not necessarily as an end product in itself." Therefore, placing the Black community in a historical and cultural context for professionals, academicians, and the general public was a primary task; one that had not been previously achieved. A data inventory

was compiled for more than 800 communities in 40 states. In order to give exposure to significant concepts and case studies, a ten-piece educational exhibit was published in 1980 by Entourage, Inc., and funded by the National Endowment for the Arts.

The pioneering nature of the study posed a number of challenges, yet it forged innovative and fresh products. Lack of significant work on the topic produced voids in existing documentation sources and methodologies, interpretive guidelines, analytical models, and application strategies; the volume and nature of data uncovered in the first three areas demanded discipline and creativity, and pressing needs of currernt Black communities mandated implementation of the final component. Several settlement patterns were identified from highly fragmented information furnished by oral informants, family records, legal documents, newspapers, magazines, archives/libraries, museums, and field investigation. This resulted in the definition of a community typology, which was then applied to an evolutionary time line. Case studies were undertaken to validate or invalidate

A TOWN OWNED BY NEGROES

Fig. 1. Photograph accompanying article on Mound Bayou, Bolivar County, Mississippi, in *Century Illustrated* magazine, c. 1910. (Courtesy Weidner Library, Harvard University)

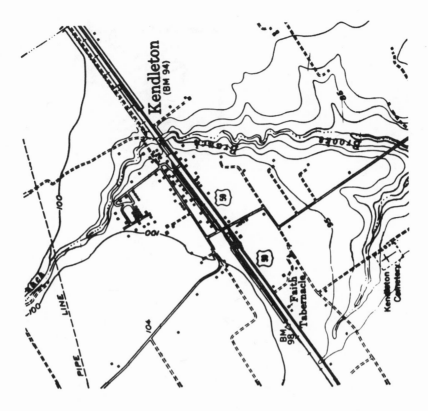

Fig. 2. Black Town case study showing the railroad community of Kendleton, Ft. Bend County, Texas, c. 1976. (Map courtesy U.S. Geological Survey)

each type. In the process of analyzing individual cases, specific information was gleaned regarding community planning rationale; social and functional impacts of physical order of the landscape; and evolution of detailed design practices. Thirteen case studies were analyzed and interpreted for the final exhibit under the following typologies: Slave Village, Freedmans Village, Rural Village, Black Town, Rural Resettlement, Urban Enclave, and Alley Dwelling. The time line was refined into a written and graphic format for contextural representation of settlement types. The final typologies and time line have sustained testing through several field studies since their definition. In fact, various subtypes have emerged and proven significant.

The typology identification indicates a more sophisticated rationale than Black community builders are historically given credit for by landscape historians. Each new investigation reinforces the notion that all Black communities were not meant to serve the same purpose. Situations have been encountered in which several settlements were clustered in close proximity, with each village providing a unique service to its neighbors. Because most of the settlements did not grow into large communities, their major function usually remained singular. In comparative analysis, it becomes evident that the physical

arrangement of the village landscape was meant to serve the primary purpose of the community. There were no super blocks or radial plans because these were not appropriate formats to meet community needs and philosophies. The independent settlements (Rural Village, Black Town) show less adherence to regimented and geometric organization and more dependence on intuitive planning; as a result, these were often classified as "disorderly" by outside visitors. The monofunctional perspective carries over to the parcel of land under individual ownership. Relatively few Black landowners in separate settlements used their property for more than one or two activities. Historically, there has been little "adaptive use" of land when one operation declined in prosperity or when heirs decided to discontinue agricultural pursuits. Thus, we find tracts being abandoned or allowed to lie underutilized. Those living in urban areas were more likely to assign multiple functions to property, but the majority tended to employ a parcel for one activity as long as possible.

As the evolution of Black settlements is studied, questions related to the process, relative to social and physical development, arise. From a physical standpoint, it becomes apparent that the communities that endured over time must have formed theories regarding the environment and environmental components

183

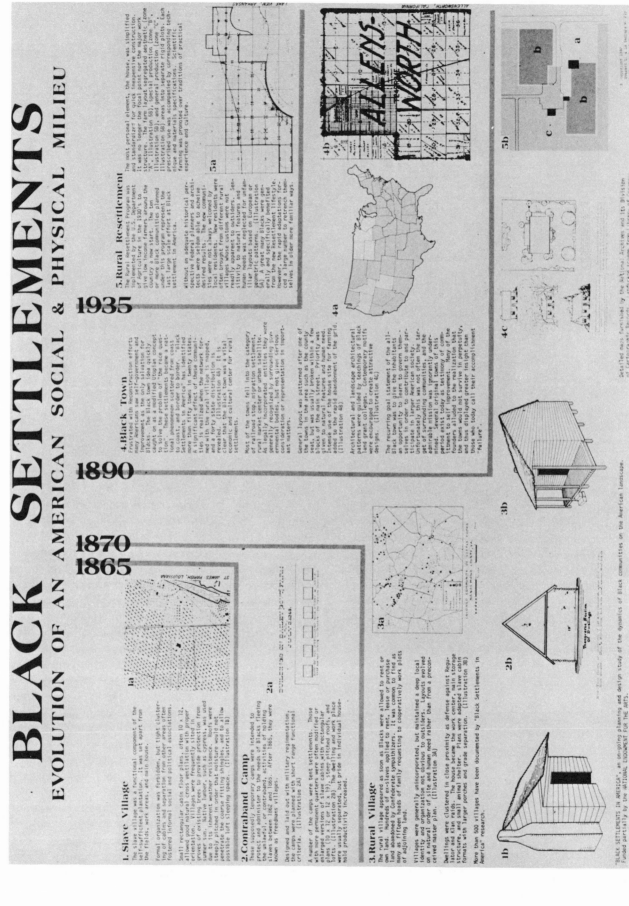

Fig. 3.   Evolutionary time line panel from "Black Settlements in America" exhibit. (Courtesy Entourage, Inc.; photograph by Everett L. Fly.)

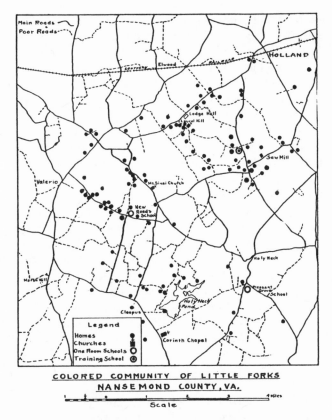

Fig. 4. Rural Village case study showing schematic arrangement of physical elements in a rural Virginia settlement, c. 1920. (Map courtesy Howard University Library, Spingarn Collection, Washington, D.C.)

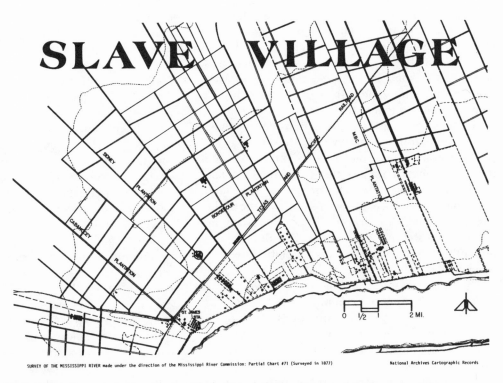

Fig. 5. Slave Village case study showing typical clusters of slave cabins on plantations along the Mississippi River, c. 1877. (Map courtesy Cartographic Division, National Archives, Washington, D.C.)

185

around them. Once the environmental concept was developed, it had to be passed along to succeeding inhabitants. In most cases researched in the Black Settlements study, community inhabitants perceived themselves as subordinate to the contextual setting. In fact, many rural southern settlers saw nature as a matriarch. Exploitation of natural resources that sustained life was not considered or practiced. Landscape features were thought of and used in basic functional roles as they existed in their natural forms. Black pioneers and planners seemed to go well out of their way to integrate their communities into the existing scheme of the native landscape. Thus, until the First World War, there was little or no drastic modification of naturally evolving landscapes of Black American settlements.

In some current settlements, there is renewed interest in maintaining vernacular community patterns regarded as status symbols. Analysis of these and similar properties in the investigation reveals that the functional/indigenous theory was carried down to relationships of individual elements such as open space, visual order, plant material, earthforms, architecture, and construction materials. Observations make it clear that open space has historically been maintained in settlements for functional and security reasons and for health purposes (through ventilation and solar exposure). Recreational or romantically aesthetic uses of open space have not held high priorities until very recently. However, when assuming these roles, the "Country Park" motif seems to have been the preference. Visual order was determined again by function, security, and social custom rather than by abstract or geometric patterns. Plant material was chosen for medicinal, nutritional, functional, and superstitious reasons first. If space and time allowed for ornamental cultivation, then that was included. Documentation indicates that during the period of slavery Blacks participated in activities that involved major manipulation of earthwork. However, as independent community builders, they rarely initiated earthwork projects in their settlements. The Black layplanners preferred to search for an existing land feature that met their requirements, or to adapt to the topography they were forced to use. Because individual ownership of structures was so desirable in nineteenth-century Black society, architecture was held in higher esteem than landscape composition. Thus, in most cases, the landscape serves as a backdrop to the house, commercial structure, or public building. Economic conditions and trade discrimination made it necessary for early community builders to use indigenous materials frequently. In many cases it was discovered that these were more durable than manufactured imports, while producing a distinctively harmonious design composition. As time advanced, these enduring vernacular works

gained respect and frequently became the quality and character benchmark for the community.

Eventually, the pragmatic concepts of everyday community evolution and management became formalized in Black educational institutions such as Tuskegee Institute, Alabama, and Hampton Institute, Virginia. These and other industrial training schools promoted self-help through trade-skills development and agricultural enterprise. The principles of what is now known as landscape architecture were taught under such headings as "Nature Study" and "Landscape Gardening." Examination of specific curricula reveals an emphasis on practical application and experience. No formal design courses were offered. Aesthetic understanding and theory were addressed through observance of nature. These teachings were distributed to the general public in the form of educational pamphlets. They contained conceptual text and illustrations of desirable and undesirable landscape techniques and compositions. Because these schools were so influential and the printed materials so widely distributed, the pragmatic approach to planning and design became the accepted rule in Black communities around the United States.

Since 1980, Entourage, Inc. has shown the Black Settlements In America research to various audiences around the United States. The fundamental concepts of the work have been readily applied to art, tourism, architecture, landscape architecture, planning/public administration, research methodology, historic preservation, and neighborhood revitalization. The national orientation offers a framework for regional and local planning/design recommendations. Black Settlements interpretive guidelines were used in 1979 to establish historic architectural significance for Winks Panorama Lodge, Pinecliff, Colorado, which was placed on the National Register of Historic Places. Documentation methodologies, interpretive guidelines, and analytical models were applied to historical research and recording of 15 rural Black communities in northeastern Montgomery County, Maryland, in 1981. Later in the year, the interpretive guidelines were again employed to determine the national significance of 14 Black urban enclaves in Miami-Dade County, including the Liberty City riot district.

Entourage, Inc. has accepted Black Settlements In America as a perennial project. New issues and implications promise to be revealed as the investigation is extended to fill data voids. Additional applications are discovered as more Americans are exposed to the study. Models and methodologies will continue to be tested against these new inputs. The ultimate goal calls for the work to be developed to an advanced state of comprehension which would expand our understanding of the total cultural, social, and physical landscape.

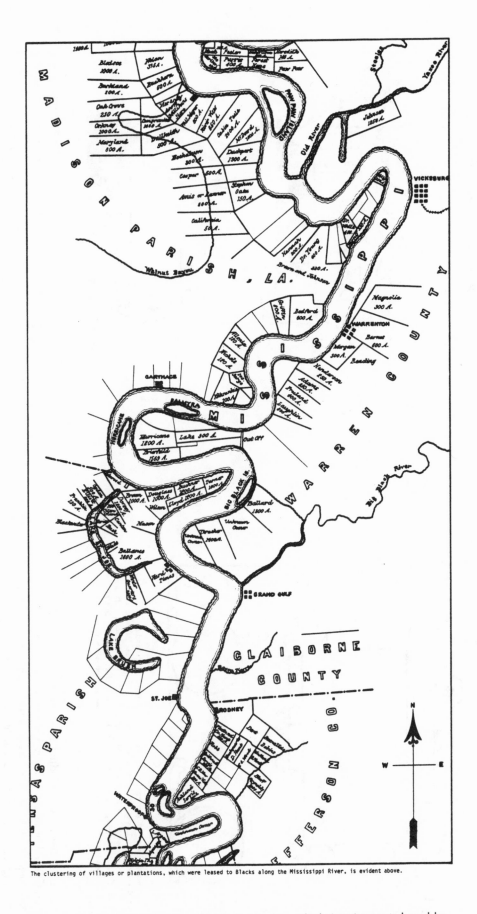

The clustering of villages or plantations, which were leased to Blacks along the Mississippi River, is evident above.

Fig. 6. Rural Village case study with labeled land parcels designating tracts leased by Blacks, c. 1865. (Map courtesy Cartographic Division, National Archives, Washington, D.C.)

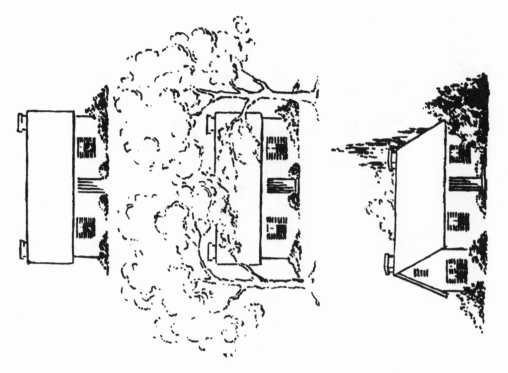

1 Foundation planting serves to relate the building to the landscape.

2 Trees planted on either side of a house front act as a picture frame as one approaches.

3 By the intelligent use of plant forms the outline of the building is partially concealed, thus securing the charm of mystery.

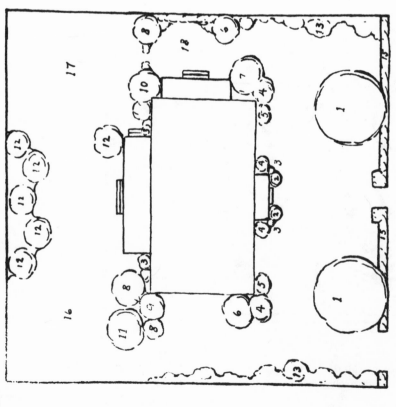

1 Pecan trees 2 Box bushes or red cedars cut low, or lavender 3 Climbing rose 4 Rosemary 5 Lavender 6 Pink crepe myrtle 7 Red cedar allowed to grow tall 8 American holly 9 Dogwood 10 Cherokee rose 11 Magnolia 12 Figs 13 Climbing roses, flowering shrubs and hollyhocks 15 Privet hedge 16 Chicken yard 17 Clothes yard and vegetable garden 18 Rose garden with rose hedge, and climbing roses on the fence.

The garden itself, including the rose garden, should be so related to the house as to seem a part of it, located usually at the sides or back of the house, with high plants or vines connecting and relating the garden to the building.

Fig. 7.   Landscape planting guidelines distributed by Hampton Institute, c. 1900. (Courtesy Library of Congress, Washington, D.C.)

188

About the Authors

RICHARD L. AUSTIN—Mr. Austin is Associate Professor at the University of Nebraska-Lincoln, College of Architecture/Horticulture. He serves as the coordinating editor for the Yearbooks of Landscape Architecture and as the editor of the Landscape Architecture Series published by Van Nostrand Reinhold Company.

KENNETH I. HELPHAND—Mr. Helphand is Associate Professor and Head of the Department of Landscape Architecture, University of Oregon with degrees from Brandeis University and the Harvard Graduate School of Design. He has taught at Ball State University and was a Visiting Professor at the Technion, Israel Institute of Technology, 1980–81. Helphand teaches landscape history and has written and lectured widely on gardens, landscape photography and film, McDonald's environmental autobiography, and landscape perception.

CATHERINE M. HOWETT—Ms. Howett is a landscape architect, historian, and critic of the American landscape currently teaching in the School of Environmental Design at the University of Georgia. Her recent research interests have centered around the evolution of regional landscape forms in the Southeast, and on broader issues of the relationship between landscape and myth.

THOMAS J. KANE—Mr. Kane is a landscape architect in the firm of Kane and Carruth, P.C., Pleasantville, New York. He is a Fellow in the ASLA, a member of AICP, and president of the Alliance of Historic Landscape Preservation. He has been active in planning and restoring historic landscapes for twenty years.

ANN LEIGHTON—Mrs. Leighton is a historic garden consultant in Ipswich, Massachusetts. She has authored numerous materials on the plants for historic areas and is a collector of eighteenth and nineteenth century garden books.

RICHARD MACIAS—Mr. Macias has focused on Urban Landscape Architecture since receiving his MLA from the University of Michigan. He brings a greater awareness of site design to the traditionally architectural field of preservation. He is currently the Chairman of the ASLA Historic Preservation Commission.

ANN LESLIE MARSTON—Ms. Marston is an assistant professor in the Department of Landscape Architecture and Regional Planning at the University of Massachusetts in Amherst. Current research is investigating the effectiveness of exhibit design in two interpretation centers, one in Rock Creek Park, Washington, D.C., and the other in the Great Smokies National Park, Tennessee, both for the National Park Service.

E. STEVE McNIEL—Mr. McNiel is an Assistant Professor in the Department of Landscape Architecture, School of Natural Resources, College of Ag and Life Sciences at the University of Wisconsin, Madison. He has directed the planning and architectural portion of the Community Development Project in Dane County for four years.

ROBERT Z. MELNICK—Mr. Melnick has long had an interest in formal and vernacular American landscapes. He recently joined the Department of Landscape Architecture at the University of Oregon after eight years at Kansas State University. He is currently working on a study of cultural and historic landscapes for the National Park Service.

DARREL MORRISON—Mr. Morrison is John Bascom Professor of Landscape Architecture at the University of Wisconsin-Madison, where he has taught for fourteen years. His teaching and research focus on planting design, native vegetation restoration and management. He earned his B.S. in Landscape Architecture from Iowa State University, and M.S.L.A. from the University of Wisconsin.

PATRICIA M. O'DONNELL—Mrs. O'Donnell is a landscape architect and urban planner. She specializes in behavioral research and historic landscape preservation, attempting to integrate the often conflicting issues of current use and historic integrity. She serves on the ASLA Historic Preservation Committee and the National Association for Olmsted Parks Steering Committee.

THOMAS PAINE—Mr. Paine is a consultant to preservation organizations, communities, and individuals on a wide spectrum of landscape preservation issues. His most recent contribution to landscape preservation methodology is the Charles River (Mass.) Corridor Plan, which culminated in the designation of the Charles as a local scenic river.

REUBEN M. RAINEY—Mr. Rainey is Chairman of the Division of Landscape Architecture at the University of Virginia School of Architecture. Before entering the field of Landscape Architecture, he taught Philosophy of Religion at Columbia University and Middlebury College. His major area of interest is History of Landscape Architecture.

SUZANNE TURNER—Ms. Turner is Assistant Professor of Landscape Architecture at Louisiana State University. Her research efforts involve the documentation of early nineteenth century horticultural and landscape practices in South Louisiana as a vehicle for interpreting the land ethic.

Index